Cooking from the Farm to the City

The Very Best
Recipes

of

Rich & Sandy Allison
and Their
Family and Friends

1st Printing - December, 2003
Revised 2nd Printing - September 2009

1ˢᵗ Place Winner - National Honey Board - 2006
"Honey of a BBQ Tailgating Contest"

SMOKED PULLED PORK SANDWICHES WITH HONEY BBQ SAUCE
— By Rich & Sandy Allison

4 lb. pork butt (bone-in pork shoulder)

Pork Rub Ingredients:

Make a rub using any or all of the following ingredients that you like:

¼ C. white sugar
1 tbsp. chili powder
1½ tsp. onion powder
2 tsp. paprika
1 tsp. cumin
1 tsp. salt
1 tsp. black pepper
1½ tsp. garlic powder
¼ tsp. cayenne pepper
1½ tsp. Lawry's seasoning salt

Honey BBQ Sauce:

1½ C. prepared barbeque sauce
1½ C. honey
1 C. ketchup

Combine all rub ingredients together and whisk well with a wire whisk.

Have pork butt at room temperature. Put some of rub all over pork butt and rub into meat. Save remaining pork rub for other meats later storing in a Ziploc plastic bag. Let set for ½ hour. Soak 2 C. hickory chips in water for 15 minutes and drain. Wrap in foil. Punch holes in the foil and place chips on top of gas grill burners on high. Eventually the hickory will begin smoking.

Sear the pork butt on all sides and leave in the gas grill with lid covered for approximately ½-¾ hour. Do not let it burn. However, some black or "bark" on the meat is needed.

Remove from grill and place pork butt in a plastic roasting bag (turkey size) with one C. of water. Seal bag. Place roast and bag in roasting pan, but punch a few holes in the bag with a knife for steam to escape.

Bake in the oven at 300° for 3 to 3½ hours until meat is tender and pork butt bone can be pulled out easily.

Remove from oven, remove bones, let cool until you can shred or pull pork apart with your hands into small pieces removing any fat. Add the juices from the cooking bag removing any excess fat. Also, chop larger pieces into bite size pieces for sandwiches.

Combine the remaining three ingredients for the Honey BBQ Sauce: 1½ C. barbeque sauce, 1½ C. honey and 1 C.ketchup in a sauce pan and cook until all ingredients are mixed well and honey is dissolved.

Combine most of this sauce with your 4 lb. of shredded pork butt, continue adding sauce until meat looks moist. Mix well and serve in rolls with extra sauce on the side. Also, serve jalapeno peppers, onions and pickles with the sandwiches for those who desire them.

This is our recipe that we have served at Penn State tailgate parties for years for very large crowds. They love our Honey BBQ Sauce on everything - chicken, pork, sausages, beef, etc.

Makes approximately 20 sandwiches.

— Rich & Sandy Allison

This is the recipe for our claim to fame as winners of the National Honey Board. This is the recipe that we make quite often for tailgating for Penn State and Pittsburgh Steeler games.

Cooking from the Farm to the City

All of our lives revolve around food. It always has. We eat to live and live to eat!! No matter what the occasion – a birthday, a celebration of a life, a wedding, a holiday or a family get together, we celebrate that event by eating. And what a wonderful way to share with others than by giving of your best skills – cooking and sharing recipes.

Ever since we were little children, we can remember the smells of the farmhouse kitchen and the summerhouse cookstove turning out that vast array of foods on the farm.

Cooking from the Farm to the City covers recipes from the past ten years as well as many of our great recipes from the cookbook we published back in September, 1993.

The original intent back in 1993 was to preserve many family recipes that had been passed down from generation to generation. Many had not previously been written down.

Since that time in 1993 we have developed many new recipes and many new techniques in cooking. Things like roasting red peppers, caramelizing onions, roasting garlic and using many fresh herbs are what we do now. However, we still cook many of those old favorite dishes from our Pennsylvania Dutch heritage.

We grew up in the Claysburg and Queen, PA area in south central Pennsylvania nestled in a valley in the Appalachian Mountains with the Allegheny Mountain on one side and Dunnings Mountain on the other. This is where the Pennsylvania Dutch German style of cooking is prominent. This is where we learned firsthand how to cook. However, we think that many of our new techniques will work well with some old dishes.

Two hours and twenty minutes does not sound like much, but in that amount of time, we are transformed from one culture of cooking to a totally different one. That is the amount of time or 135 miles from our Claysburg, PA hometown to where we lived in McMurray, PA. It doesn't sound far, but the cooking styles, recipes and techniques are really different.

In that two hours and twenty minutes we are transformed back to our childhood memories. We go back to a quieter and a slower life. We go back to and re-live the memories of food, the aromas that wafted in the air and the memories of get togethers.

We believe that we have included some of the best of all these ideas from the farm and from the city that we have as well as our family and friend's ideas. Many of the recipes have been passed down through the generations either verbally or on paper. Some of these recipes may have started in a magazine or newspaper or handwritten on the back of a napkin, but generally they have been changed along the way. They have been adapted to someone's own flavor and style of cooking.

We encourage you to try these recipes and alter them in any way you want. Chances are that you will come up with a better recipe or a totally different version.

Growing up in the Claysburg and Queen, PA areas and coming from family farms, we always had the best and freshest ingredients.

Fresh milk daily from the cows and fresh cream separated from the fresh milk was stored in the water troughs of the milkhouse where cool spring well water was pumped. It was a way of life. The pigs on the farm got the "old milk" which was one day old!!!

Freshly churned butter from the cream gave us butter where only some salt was added for flavor. The bright yellow color of the butter and the rich creamy flavor still remains in our minds when we think of those cold winter mornings and drinking hot chocolate and eating homemade bread toasted and then slathered with butter and dipped into the cocoa cup. The flavor is unexplainable!

Eggs were gathered daily. Some were so fresh that in the winter months, the steam was still coming off of them as they lay in the nests before gathering them.

Fresh ingredients in the ice cream freezer churned away with the fresh milk, cream and eggs from the farm. The twelve quart freezer turned out chocolate, vanilla, strawberry or teaberry ice cream on a regular basis.

Fresh vegetables to us were picked in the garden immediately before cooking. Things like fresh sugar peas and new red skin potatoes were an absolute necessity to have on the table by the Fourth of July each year. That dish was cooked to perfection and then fresh heavy cream and a cornstarch/flour thickening was added with salt and pepper and fresh parsley from the garden garnished this dish. Now that is fresh!

Tomatoes that were lovingly ripened by the sun were picked at the last minute, sliced and served still warm from the sun. Only salt and pepper was needed with them. A dish of green onions was freshly pulled and cleaned before each meal. They were served at the table with each of us having a small salt dish to dip our green onions in the salt.

In the spring our family eagerly awaited the first fresh greens of the year. Dandelions would start appearing in the yards and fields around the farm in late April or early May. They would be gathered, washed. chopped and cooked with a sweet and sour vinegar cream bacon dressing and served with slices of homecured ham or sausage along with fried potatoes.

By early June the first lettuce in the garden made way for the same type of meal, but with lettuce you did not have the bitter taste of dandelion.

Our meals on the farm consisted of eating three times a day – breakfast, dinner (lunch) and supper with the dinner or lunch meal being the heartiest. Normally the hired hands and family filled the table at dinner or lunch and the table was absolutely filled with dishes of excellent quality.

Our Sunday dinner immediately after church normally consisted of a roasted chicken, mashed potatoes, stuffing, gravy, noodles, several vegetables, salad and desserts as well as homemade bread. Homemade noodles were made from the fresh farm eggs and flour bought at the local milling company. About once every two months as we left the church, we would ask the minister and his wife if they had any plans for dinner after church, and if not, they would be at our house. The chicken was so fresh that the day before, the poor rooster was still living a great life in the hen house not realizing that tomorrow he was going to be the Sunday dinner. We still do not have the ability to cut the head off that rooster like my mother did on Saturday, dip the chicken in scalding water, remove the feathers and the internal organs and still be able to eat that same animal the next day!

Pots of rival soup, pot pie and soups were always abundant. The soups were loaded with the extra vegetables from the garden and had generous portions of meat or poultry in them.

Growing up on the farm certainly gave you a perspective on how life began, how it evolved and how it ended. In the spring new life bloomed and blossomed on the farm. Baby calves or "hommys" as the Pennsylvania Dutch called them were born. The spring shipment of 100 new Rhode Island Red chicks or "peepies" arrived around Easter. Newly born pigs, dogs, cats, rabbits, banny chickens and ducks were born and hatched. In the fall many of the farm animals were butchered before the winter months.

The same happened with the garden with the plantings in the spring, eating all summer and fall from the garden and the canning, freezing and drying of vegetables and fruits from the trees. For the winter the fruit cellar was filled with jars of all types of canned goods. Baskets of potatoes and apples lined the floor. A crock of sauerkraut was fermenting in one corner.

Fresh strawberries, fresh raspberries, elderberries, cherries from the tree, peaches from the peach orchard, pears from the Bartlett pear tree and apples of all kinds were picked, preserved and stored for the winter months. We had English walnuts from a tree in the front yard and black walnuts and chestnuts from trees in the backyard, and hickory nuts from the neighbor's yard.

Cider was made from the apple tree's abundant harvest. Most was used to make the annual kettle of applebutter normally yielding about 25 gallons per kettle some of which was sold. One barrel of cider was used to replenish the vinegar barrel that had the "mother" in it to make new vinegar.

Corn was cooked on the cob with much of it frozen, some canned and some dried on the cookstove.

When butchering time came in November, the neighbors came to help. The hogs were butchered and sausage was made as well as scrapple, pudding and lard. The treat was to eat the cracklins which were the fried pork rinds that were left after the fat was pressed or rendered into lard.

The old washhouse was a busy place with the curing of hams and bacon. Most were done in a barrel of salt brine where enough salt was added to "float an egg" and where the meat stayed in the barrel for six weeks. Sometimes some of the meat was cured on a table with a mixture of brown sugar and salt doing the job.

The smokehouse would then omit aromas of fired hickory wood while the hams, bacon and sausage would take on their great flavors. Additionally once in a while a whole pork loin was put in the salt brine and then smoked to have smoked pork chops. Also, once in a while the bladder of the hog was stuffed with sausage and smoked for another delicacy.

Once the sausage was smoked, the first cooking of it was done in a large iron skillet. The grease that was left from cooking the sausage was then diluted with water, and the resulting mixture was called "soppy". Homemade bread was then dipped in this "soppy" and eaten. Slices of hams were fried and milk gravy was made from the ham drippings with the rich, thick, creamy milk. The milk gravy was served over bread.

The pork tenderloin at the time was called "preacher's meat" and was only used when the preacher came. It was the most tender and choice cut found in the hog.

Back then, butchering the beef cows yielded a lot of beef roasts, hamburg and steaks. However, most of the steaks were turned into roasts or hamburg since we did not know what grilling was in the 1950's.

In addition to all the domestic food, we also had fresh trout from the stream in the front yard and deer or venison from the backyard.

Baking was a tradition at the farm. As a small child, our babysitter, Aunt Wilmie would walk to our house to babysit and always baked cookies in the cookstove in the summerhouse. When we were done, there would be a bushel of cookies, most of them her famous sugar cookies. Normally that was enough for a week.

Different flavors of fudge were routinely made and placed to cool on the front porch on top of the fuse box. A month before Easter the kitchen was filled with relatives while they made the annual tradition – the famous peanut butter Easter eggs. Normally 50 plus pounds were made with only a few kept at the farm. The rest were decorated with icing with names and given away.

Bread was baked weekly on Friday so it was fresh for the weekend. Homemade cinnamon rolls and pies were always in abundance – apple, cherry and always coconut cream.

We always seemed to have some type of cake setting around for visitors.

The table was always filled with food at every meal, and there was always room for one or two more people who might show up. On holidays it seemed that we asked everyone who did not have a place to go for the holidays and those who were less fortunate.

We have also been spoiled with our association with the friends we have at the Chesapeake Bay where crabs, oysters and fish are so fresh. If they would be any fresher, they would be back in the Bay!

Even bringing fresh crab and oysters back home directly from the Bay does not taste quite as good as they do at the Bay. Quality changes quickly on food.

However, today we are blessed with better transportation, better methods of keeping produce and meat and seafood fresh on its way to market. While it may not be as fresh as the "old days on the farm," it certainly has improved a lot over the last 30 years.

We encourage you to visit farmer's markets, farm produce stands, specialty meat markets, specialty cheese stores to find the best and freshest products and usually at reasonable prices.

The old farmhouse did sit empty part of the time for 15 years, but now it springs to life for many occasions. The house comes alive with the aromas of food just as it has done for over 125 years. The memories become more vivid as we sit and talk and reminisce.

The creaky floorboards in the house are sighing in relief that the house is again full of people having a good time, who are eating well and enjoying each other's company.

Today our tables are like our parents' – overflowing with abundance and always ready to feed another person or two. We do not know how to cook in small quantities, never have and never will.

Our lives are filled with memories. Most of those memories are associated with an event and with great food. We believe we have captured many of those memorable moments in this book.

Take a look at some of these old recipes. You can imagine years of passing down from generation to generation either verbally or on a scrap piece of paper.

As you try some of these recipes, you are actually enjoying a piece of history while you eat the food.

We hope you enjoy these recipes and suggestions.

Eat well and enjoy life!

— Rich & Sandy Allison

COOKING FROM THE FARM TO THE CITY

The Very Best Recipes

of

Rich & Sandy Allison

and Their

Family and Friends

165 Allison Drive
Claysburg, PA 16625
Phone: 814-239-2901

email: rich@allisonfarm.com
or sandy@allisonfarm.com
Website: www.allisonfarm.com

SIMPLIFIED THINGS
TO KNOW ABOUT COOKING

Roasting Peppers

Take a whole red, yellow or orange pepper (not green) and place over a gas burner, gas grill or under an oven broiler. Let the pepper char and continue turning until all sides are charred.

Take the whole pepper and place it in a paper or plastic bag and seal the bag. Let the pepper steam in the bag for about 15 minutes. Remove from the bag, and remove the charred skin. Do not run water over the pepper, because it will dilute the flavor. Remove the seeds from the inside of the pepper and cut the pepper into julienne strips. These can be frozen if not all used. When ready to serve, sprinkle with some Kosher salt and drizzle with extra virgin olive oil. Use on salads, antipasto platters or in pastas.

Caramelizing Onions

Take 2-3 large Vidalia or sweet onions, sliced and add 1 stick margarine and ½ C. of brown sugar and add salt and pepper.

Place all the above in a large skillet and cook on medium high heat about 20 minutes until onions are soft and liquid has become syrupy or caramelized. The onions will be very sweet.

Serve on mashed potatoes, salads or on a vegetable platter.

Roasting Garlic

Take one bulb of garlic and remove papery skin and place cloves in a baking dish with ½ stick of margarine. Cover with aluminum foil and bake at 350° for 30 minutes until the pieces of garlic are soft.

You can use the garlic in salads, potatoes, vegetables, casseroles, etc. The baked garlic has a milder flavor and is not as harsh as raw garlic.

Sun Dried Tomatoes

Take Italian plum tomatoes and thinly slice. Place in a dehydrator if available and dry until all moisture is removed for about 24 hours. Change the positions of the trays every 6 hours moving the top tray to the bottom.

If a dehydrator is not available, you can dry in a warm oven.

Place cooled tomatoes in a Ziploc bag. If any moisture appears in the bag after they have been sealed for a while, the tomatoes are not totally dried and will spoil. Re-dry them for a longer period.

The sun dried tomatoes can be reconstituted by putting them in a C. of water and microwaving for 2 minutes.

They can be used in pastas, salads, pizzas and antipasta platters, etc.

Grilled Tomatoes for Salads

Slice thick pieces of tomatoes and season heavily with kosher salt and freshly ground pepper on both sides. Drizzle with olive oil.

Place tomato slices on a hot grill preferably in a vegetable pan. Cook about 1 minute on each side to give the tomato a charred appearance and flavor and also the tomato will be warm.

Serve warm on top of salads or with mozzarella cheese or as a side dish.

Grilled Vegetables

Take your favorite vegetables such as peppers, onions, squash, zucchini, mushrooms, etc. Cut into large pieces. Season with Kosher salt and fresh ground black pepper. Drizzle with olive oil. Toss to coat. Place in grill basket. Grill over medium high heat for about 7 minutes stirring regularly. Remove while the vegetables are still slightly crunchy.

SIMPLIFIED THINGS
TO KNOW ABOUT COOKING

Herbs

When using herbs in cooking, keep a portion of the herbs until the final two minutes of cooking your recipe. Cooking fresh herbs for a long period causes them to lose their flavor and pungency. Putting the herbs in during the last two minutes of cooking will give intensity of flavor to your dish.

If a recipe calls for 1 teaspoon of a dried herb, it will take approximately 3 times that amount of fresh herbs for the same flavor, because the dried herbs have become concentrated. However, there is no comparison in flavor in the dried herbs to the fresh herbs. If you have fresh herbs, use them!

Bouquet di Garni

Bouquet di Garnis are a combination of your favorite herbs tied together with a piece of string and placed in a broth or stew or hot liquid to give additional flavoring. After the cooking is done, the bouquet is removed and thrown away.

Herbs in Olive Oil

Fresh herbs steeped in olive oil give great flavoring to the oil. Take your favorite combination of herbs or any one herb, add some olive oil and simmer in a saucepan for approximately 15 minutes. Use different combinations of herbs and try garlic cloves, peppercorns, hot peppers, etc.with them. Let the mixture cool and use on salads with your favorite vinegar, etc. The mixture can also be used for a dipping sauce with bread or on pizza dough, etc.

Because of the moisture in the herbs, this mixture can be safely stored in a refrigerator for no more than one week. After that the moisture can cause botulism to form.

After refrigerating, the olive oil will congeal or turn white. Simply take out of the refrigerator and let set for about 10 minutes and then vigorously shake or stir and the olive oil will become reconstituted.

Herbs with Vinegar

Herbs can also be steeped with white distilled vinegar and kept in bottles and used on salads. Heat the vinegar to its boiling point and remove just before boiling. Add herbs and let steep in a covered container preferably a jar. However, please make certain that the jar does not have a metal lid. If it does, it will have a reaction with the vinegar. Cover the jar with plastic wrap or wax paper before putting the lid on the jar. Let steep 3 weeks. Taste it and if strong enough, strain the herbs and run the vinegar through a coffee filter to get rid of any sediment. You can put fresh herbs in after the straining process for appearance, but it is not necessary. These vinegars do not need to be stored in the refrigerator, because of the acidity in the vinegar. Try different combinations of herbs along with garlic, peppercorns or hot peppers for different flavors. The vinegar will keep for a long, long time. Use on salads, etc.

Herb Garden

Whether you live on a farm, a house or an apartment, you should have some fresh herbs. You can grow them in a flower pot, in a flower bed or in a garden. Start out with one plant each of the following or some of these that you prefer: Basil, Rosemary, Oregano, Sweet Marjoram, Summer Savory, Parsley, Dill, Chives, Sage, Mint, Tarragon and Thyme. Basil, Marjoram and Savory are annuals and need planted each year. All the others are perennials and should grow the next year depending on your cold climate. Close to a frost, make an herb box for in your house and enjoy fresh herbs for the next several months.

Olive Oil with Seasoning for Dipping

For a simple bread dipping sauce, take olive oil, add some Italian Seasoning, grated Romano cheese and freshly ground black pepper. Stir well, place in a small bowl and dip Italian bread in it. Simple and flavorful.

SIMPLIFIED THINGS
TO KNOW ABOUT COOKING

Honey Pecan Butter

1 lb. butter
¼ C. + 2½ tbsp. light brown sugar
2 tsp. vanilla extract
½ C. + 4 tbsp. roasted pecans
5½ tbsp. honey

Whip butter until softened, add remaining ingredients one at a time and continue to mix. Refrigerate to store. Let sit out at room temperature. Serve on bread.

Melting Chocolate

To melt chocolate smoothly, do not overheat. Overheating will cause it to seize, to turn hard and grainy.

Break up the chocolate into small pieces.

It will melt smoothly at around 100° F. Place in a covered pan in the oven and stir frequently until smooth.

Chocolate can also be melted in the microwave. Break into pieces and place on Power 3. Stir every 30 seconds until smooth. This is the easiest way of melting chocolate.

If you have overheated your chocolate and it has stiffened, you can smooth it out by beating in a little water, setting the pan in hot water, and stirring it about. It will usually not smooth out enough to become a frosting, but it will often be suitable for use in cakes or puddings.

Meringue

Make sure egg whites are at room temperature – chilled whites do not mount well, and tend to fleck.

A speck of yolk prevents the whites from mounting into a mass of tiny bubbles. Make sure not even a speck of yolk is present.

Using a large whisk, handheld mixer or a mixer on a stand, start beating the egg whites at a moderately slow speed until they are foaming throughout – two minutes or so.

Add a pinch of salt and for four egg whites, add ¼ tsp. of cream of tartar – a stabilizer.

Gradually increase the speed to fast (moderately fast, if you have a heavy duty mixer) and continue until stiff shining peaks are formed.

In most desserts and cake recipes, a tablespoon or more of sugar is beaten in at the point where the egg whites form soft peaks; they are then beaten to stiff peaks. Sugar stiffens and stabilizes the whites.

If egg whites are over beaten, they lose their smooth sheen and begin to look grainy. You can reconstitute them by adding another egg white and beating briefly until they are smoothly reconstituted.

Gravy

Take the broth of the meat you are cooking and strain the broth. Use 2 C. of broth and if necessary, add bouillon for more flavor.

Mix ¼ C. of cornstarch or cornstarch and flour combined with 1 C. cold water. Mix well with a wire whisk until there are no lumps. Stir into the broth before it is boiling, then place on heat and bring to a boil for approximately 10 minutes, stirring constantly to prevent sticking. Season with seasoning salt and pepper.

If it is a chicken stock, use white pepper and seasoning salt and add yellow food coloring to give the gravy a rich yellow appearance.

If a beef or pork gravy, add a small amount of Gravymaster to give a dark caramel color to the gravy and add seasoning salt and black pepper to taste.

SIMPLIFIED THINGS
TO KNOW ABOUT COOKING

Simple Syrup

Take 1 C. sugar and 1 C. water and place in a saucepan. Bring to a boil and let mixture boil until it becomes clear and loses its cloudy appearance. Let cool and use in icings, drinks, etc. Always use equal amounts of sugar and water regardless of the size of batch that you need.

White Icing Glaze

Use 1 C. simple syrup from above and add confectioner's sugar stirring well. Continue adding sugar until the desired consistency. Normally a slightly runny consistency is used on cinnamon rolls, breads, donuts, etc.

Whipping Cream

Chill your empty mixing bowl and beaters before mixing. Also, place your container of whipping cream in the freezer for several minutes prior to mixing. The chilled cream and utensils will speed the whipping process.

Beat cream until stiff peaks are formed. One C. of whipping cream should yield two C. of whipped cream.

Smoker and Grill Hints

The smoker is an excellent way of cooking beef, ham, pork and poultry. Outside temperatures must be above 60° for the smoker to maintain ideal cooking temperatures.

For a moister finished meat or poultry, use the drip basin supplied with the cooker and keep filled with water. Also, as you baste your food, those drippings and the grease will fall into the pan and help to flavor the food during cooking.

Always use a meat thermometer to make certain that the meat is properly cooked. It also ensures that you do not overcook and dry out the meat or poultry.

Use mesquite chips for poultry or beef. Hickory chips should be used for poultry and pork. Chips should be soaked in water according to package directions.

Lay the wood chips on top of hot coals or lava rock wrapped in aluminum foil and jabbed with holes with a fork in order for them to catch on fire.

Temperatures vary according to the size of the meat and the type of meat. However, a guide would be as follows:

Boneless pork loin: approx. 5 hours
Medium turkey: approx. 6 hours
Pre-cooked medium ham: 5 hours
Beef brisket: 3-4 hours
Chicken: 2-3 hours

Again use your meat thermometer for the best accuracy.

Use various basting sauces listed in the sauce section, bought at the stores or create your own.

Cooking on the smoker is a good ½ day event or longer and can be a lot of fun.

Basic Seasonings for Meat and Poultry

Make a seasoning or rub mixture of:
4 parts garlic powder
2 part seasoning salt
1 part fresh ground pepper

Mix well and use this on beef, pork or chicken. Generously sprinkle and rub mixture into meats on both sides.

If desired, also pour Kraft Zesty Italian dressing over meat and let marinate for 15-30 minutes. However, if you do not have time to let it marinate, pour the dressing over and grill immediately.

SIMPLIFIED THINGS
TO KNOW ABOUT COOKING

Roux

A roux is a thickening agent and can be either a white roux or a dark roux. However, the beginning rule is that equal amounts of flour and fat (normally butter, but it can be oil) are mixed together in a skillet and cooked until you get the desired color. This can take from five minutes to 30 minutes depending upon the color you want to achieve.

Once the flour is cooked with the oil, an addition of broth, cream or milk is added depending upon what you are cooking.

If you are cooking soups, you can add the roux to the cooked broth to thicken the soup. If it is a cream based soup, you can also add the roux to thicken.

If making a gravy or sauce, you can cook the roux until the desired darkness color and add to broth or cream.

Depending upon what is added to the roux, you could have:

Veloute – a sauce made of roux and broths of chicken, veal or fish. The sauce is normally a light colored white sauce.

Bechamel – a sauce made of roux and milk or cream to create a white cream sauce.

Brown Sauce or Espagnole – a sauce made of dark roux and a dark broth or reduction of normally veal or beef stock.

All of these sauces can have a combination of herbs, spices, and for additional flavor a mirepoix of carrots, celery and onions added and then strained or mashed and added to the sauce for a thickening agent.

The brown sauce can be further reduced to half of its size and then it becomes a demi-glaze sauce with additional flavors from the reduction.

Breaking the Band

While cooking the various sauces especially cream sauces, it is important to keep the sauces at a lower temperature while simmering and reducing them in quantity. Cooking at high temperatures will cause the sauce to separate or "break the band". This gives a curdled appearance and can usually be corrected by cooling the sauce by placing ice cubes in the broken band and wire whisking and reconstituting the sauce.

Trinity Vegetables

The combination of celery, onions and peppers are called "the trinity vegetables" and are used regularly for cooking in Cajun and Creole cooking by the French and New Orleans style cooking.

Mirepoix Vegetables

The mirepoix vegetables are the combination of carrots, celery and onions and are used regularly in most cooking. While the name is French in origin, the mirepoix vegetables are widely used by the Germans, Italians and others of European descent. With our Pennsylvania Dutch style of cooking, you will find the mirepoix vegetables in many dishes.

Pink Pasta Sauce

For a quick pink pasta sauce, take your favorite 8 oz. spaghetti sauce, simmer and then remove from heat. Add an equal amount (8 oz.) heavy cream, add to sauce and return to heat. Simmer on low for another 5-10 minutes to reduce the cream. For an enhanced flavor, add one shot of vodka.

10 TIPS FOR KITCHEN SUCCESS

Tips – every cook has them. They make preparing meals a little easier: They add depth of flavor to even the most ordinary dishes. And they place you in the realm where your friends will ask, "How do you do that?"

Here are 10 favorites:

1. If you are using a recipe, read it in its entirety before you start. Don't just grab the first few ingredients and start cooking up a storm, thinking it will all come together in a matter of minutes. Sometimes you discover too late that dough must be refrigerated for several hours – and not one minute shorter – before you can proceed on to the next step. Once you have finished reading the recipe, then gather all of your ingredients, making sure you have enough time to let the butter come up to room temperature or the turkey to thaw.

2. When making a tomato-based pasta sauce, use vodka to take the sauce to a new level. Simply sauté a chopped onion and a couple cloves of minced garlic in olive oil, then add some good canned tomatoes that you break up by hand as you squeeze them into the pot. Season with salt and pepper. Then add the piece de resistance – a splash of vodka. Mysteriously, the addition of vodka to tomato sauce gives the tomatoes a flavor jolt, even after the alcohol in the vodka is cooked off. Add cream for an amazing tomato cream sauce.

3. There are several secrets to making great pasta. Cook it in plenty of salted water and don't add oil, which keeps the sauce from adhering properly. (If you use enough water and bring it to a good boil before adding the pasta, it won't stick). Cook pasta just until al dente, or barely tender: (Check by removing a strand and tasting it or cutting it in half.

There should be a pinhead-sized dot of white left in the center). Don't drain the pasta into a colander and rinse it with water, rather, use tongs to lift the pasta from the water and put it into the pan where you have part of the pasta sauce. Gently fold the pasta into the sauce using an upward, forward movement with your tongs. You probably will need to add a bit of the pasta cooking water to the sauce as you're blending it together; you want the mixture to be slightly loose and flowing, not dry.

4. Making perfect pie crust is a matter of practice, to be sure, but there are also some techniques that help ensure you have a tender, flaky crust. Using all butter makes a crust that isn't as tender and flaky as you want; instead, combine butter with shortening for best results. When cutting the fat into the salted flour; don't go overboard. You want to end up with pieces that are pea-sized or ¼ to ½" in diameter. When you add water, it should be ice cold. Before rolling out, refrigerate the ball of dough for 30-60 minutes to firm up the fat, which makes the pastry flakier. Don't overwork the dough when you roll it out.

5. Rather than using a mallet with teeth, use the flat side of a meat pounder. Instead of pounding up and down on the meat, use the pounder (or a saucer) to push the meat outward and flatten it. Don't spend much time in the center of the meat – one or two pushes should do it, then work outward until you have a thin scaloppini of equal thickness.

6. To get enough salt in your potato salad, it is easier and more thorough to lay the diced, cooled potatoes out on a cookie sheet and salt them this way. You'll be sure each bite is salty enough (or as salty as you wish) without having to do a lot of mixing when you add the mayonnaise and the rest of the vegetables to the potatoes.

7. Scrambled egg devotees take heed: If you love creamy eggs, you might think adding milk is the best way to make them even creamier. Actually, a teaspoon of water with two or three scrambled eggs will yield a moister product. The answer is in chemistry. Water slows down the coagulation of the egg yolk, making a creamier product. Milk products work the opposite way, tending to harden the yolk. We've tried it both ways and we lean toward the water-added method. Remember, for really tender curds of scrambled eggs, cook very slowly.

8. So many of us grew up putting fried things, from bacon to batter fried chicken, on paper towels to blot the fat. This works, but a wire rack is even better. Paper absorbs not just fat, but other moisture from the food and the steam. This is absorbed back into the breading, making for soggy bottoms. Put a wire cookie rack over a cookie sheet and set it in a warm oven. This is a good way to hold batter fried food for a few minutes before serving.

9. That crack in the top of a cheesecake bothers some cooks more than others. If you're putting a topping on it, the sour cream or fruit spread can usually disguise it. If you really don't want a crack, take the cake out a little sooner. If a small circle in the center (about the size of a silver dollar) is still a little wobbly, that's OK. The cake will continue to cook after it's been removed from the stove. (Don't refrigerate it right away).

10. If you are using fresh herbs in a cooked dish, save a few to toss in at the last minute. The taste will be more vibrant.

OLD HOUSEHOLD HINTS FROM GRACE ALLISON'S HANDWRITTEN COOKBOOK

- Use white vinegar to clean your iron. Do this twice.
- Use stain remover to remove chewing gum.
- To clean toilet bowl put in 1 C. vinegar and let stand over night.
- Take juice from left over pickles and slice 1 cucumber, 1 onion and salt. Let stand 3 hours. Pour off juice and heat juice and then put back on pickles.
- Pickle juice is good to season potato or macaroni salad.
- Spread margarine on chicken, salt and pepper and put in oven to bake.
- Grease grater when grating cheese. It won't stick.
- When baking cherry pies, roll a piece of aluminum foil or wax paper and stick in pie like a straw and the pie won't boil over.
- Cook dry beans in ½ tsp. soda water until about half soft. It will take the gas out of them.
- Use vanilla to take odors out.
- For meringue for pies, use 3 level teaspoons of powdered sugar for one egg white and vanilla. Beat it stiff. Use three egg whites per pie. Bake at 350°.
- When putting adhesive paper in cupboards, spray the shelf first with window cleaner. You can wipe the wrinkles out easier.
- Use baby oil to take the tar off children's feet.

ABBREVIATIONS

Cup	C.
Dozen	dz.
Gallon	gal.
Hour	hr.
Hours	hrs.
Large	lg.
Medium	med.
Minute	mi.
Minutes	mis.
Ounce	oz.
Package	pkg.
Pieces	pcs.
Pint	pt.
Pound	lb.
Quart	qt.
Small	sm.
Square	sq.
Tablespoon	tbsp.
Teaspoon	tsp.

ACKNOWLEDGEMENTS

Our sincere thanks to all of you whom have given of your time and your recipes to add to this great collection of material.

We have been blessed with good relatives, friends and neighbors who have always given us their very best recipes. Giving your recipes is giving a piece of yourself and your heritage to others.

Thank you to Patty Holland who did so much to assist in typing and assembling information for us. Her help was invaluable. Also, thank you to Karen Gardner and to Vicki Shipley of American Printing & Mailing for editing and critiquing layouts of our work.

Thank you everyone.

— Rich & Sandy Allison

EMERGENCY SUBSTITUTIONS

1 C. Cake flour = 1 C. minus 2 tbsp. all purpose flour.

1 C. Self-rising flour = 1 C. all-purpose flour, ½ tsp. salt, and 1 tsp. baking powder.

1 tbsp. Cornstarch (for thickening) = 2 tbsp. flour or 2 tsp. quick cooking Tapioca.

1 tsp. Baking powder = ¼ tsp. baking soda plus ½ C. buttermilk or sour milk (to replace ½ C. liquid in recipe).

1 C. Powdered sugar = 1 C. granulated sugar plus 1 tsp. cornstarch. Whirl in blender or processor until powdered.

½ C. Brown sugar = 2 tbsp. molasses in ½ C. granulated sugar.

1 C. Whole milk = ½ C. evaporated milk plus ½ C. water or 1 C. reconstituted non-fat dry milk plus tbsp. butter.

¾ C. Cracker crumbs = 1 C. bread crumbs.

1 Square chocolate (1 oz.) = 3 or 4 tbsp. cocoa plus 1 tbsp. butter or margarine.

1 tbsp. Fresh herbs = 1 tsp. dried herbs.

1 Small fresh onion = 1 tbsp. instant minced onion rehydrated.

1 tsp. Dry mustard = 1 tbsp. prepared mustard.

1 C. Tomato juice = ½ C. Tomato sauce plus ½ C. water.

1 C. Catsup or chili sauce = 1 C. tomato sauce plus ½ C. sugar and 2 tbsp. vinegar. (for use in cooking)

1 lb. Dates = 1½ C. dates pitted and cut.

10 Miniature marshmallows = 1 large marshmallow.

APPETIZERS

Cooking from the Farm to the City

The Very Best
Recipes
of

Rich & Sandy Allison

and Their
Family and Friends

BLEU CHEESE CRACKER SPREAD

1 (8 oz.) Cream cheese softened
⅛ C. onions, diced (green)
4 splashes Worcestershire sauce
⅛ tsp. white pepper

Beat with mixer.

Add: 3 oz. of a 4 oz. block of Bleu Cheese - crumble.

Beat with mixer.

Chill and serve with crackers.

— Rich & Sandy Allison

This is probably our most used recipe for appetizers.

There is a great restaurant in Pittsburgh that has been famous for its Bleu Cheese spread for many, many years. They serve it at their bar.

For many, many years we have tried to duplicate this recipe. We have tried coercing the bartenders for the recipe.

Finally one night years ago, we told the bartender that we were close to copying the recipe but not exactly there. He said, "Try white pepper. That's the secret ingredient." And it was!

We developed this recipe from another great Italian restaurant in Pittsburgh. If you like artichokes, you will love this!

Try this buffalo chicken dip on crackers, but for a variation, spread the bleu cheese spread on the cracker before putting the buffalo chicken dip.

BUFFALO CHICKEN DIP

6 C. or 3 lb. Chicken, cooked and shredded
10 oz. Red Hot Sauce
2 (8 oz.) cream cheese, softened
1 C. ranch dressing
1 C. chopped celery
1½ C. cheddar jack cheese, shredded

Preheat oven to 350°. Let chicken cool enough to put in food processor (or shred it). Combine cream cheese and red hot in a saucepan, heat until melted. Add chicken and remaining ingredients. Put in 13"x9" pan. Bake 30 minutes.

Serve with crackers or nacho chips.
Serves 20.

— Pat Holland

ARTICHOKE HEARTS

1 can (13-15 oz.) artichoke hearts packed in water. Drain.

Place in a pie pan.

Melt ½ stick margarine and add ¾ tbsp. granulated garlic powder. Mix well and pour over artichokes.

Squeeze juice of ½ lemon over artichokes.

Sprinkle heavily with Romano cheese.

Cover artichokes with Italian bread crumbs.

Place under the broiler until it starts browning.

— Rich & Sandy Allison

GOOP

Place the following in a quart jar:

Take one head of garlic, peel all cloves and smash with flat side of meat cleaver and coarsely chop.

Roast a sweet red pepper and green pepper over an open flame until the skin is black and blistered. Place in a paper bag and allow it to steam for approximately 20 minutes. Remove from the bag and peel the charred skin. Remove seeds. Slice julienne strips and place in jar.

Add ¾ C. of pitted assorted olives to jar.

Get sprigs of fresh oregano, basil, marjoram, thyme, chives and parsley. Place some whole springs in the jar but finely chop the remainder and place in the jar.

Chop one bunch of green onions with tops and place in the jar. Add 6-8 sun dried tomatoes if available.

Add Gorgonzola cheese sliced into ¼" thick pieces. Also, feta cheese can be added.

Fill jar with cheese, peppers and olives - alternating layers,

Fill jar to top with extra virgin olive oil.

Let set at room temperature up to six hours prior to serving.

Serve with crusty Italian bread cut into small pieces. Place mixture on bread and eat as an appetizer or place Goop on half slices of Italian bread and place under the broiler and serve Bruschetta style.

You will need two loaves of bread for one quart of mixture.

Refrigerate, oil will congeal. Set back out at room temperature for one hour prior to serving and oil will liquefy. Keep for maximum five days.

— Rich Allison

We called this GOOP, because we couldn't think of a better name for it. We had our first taste of something like GOOP when we were on the big island of Hawaii at a small deli that had feta cheese in oil with fresh herbs served on bread.

Later at another deli in South Carolina, we had olives in olive oil with fresh herbs. From these different ideas, we made a combination of our own GOOP. It is great served as a Bruschetta.

BEAN DIP

1 (15 oz.) can cannelli beans, lightly drained
2 cloves garlic
1 handful fresh parley without stems
¼ C. olive oil
¼ tsp. salt
¼ tsp. pepper
1 tbsp. Balsamic vinegar
¼ C. Romano cheese

Blend in processor and serve with Italian bread or pitas.

— Rich Allison

Again this mixture was concocted from visiting another Italian restaurant in Pittsburgh.

APPETIZERS

DRUNKEN MUSHROOMS

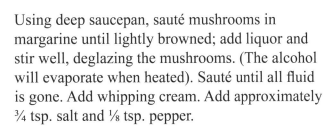

8 oz. mushrooms, thinly sliced
3 tbsp. margarine
2 tbsp. Brandy or Apple Schnapps
2 pts. Heavy whipping cream
Toast Points

Using deep saucepan, sauté mushrooms in margarine until lightly browned; add liquor and stir well, deglazing the mushrooms. (The alcohol will evaporate when heated). Sauté until all fluid is gone. Add whipping cream. Add approximately ¾ tsp. salt and ⅛ tsp. pepper.

Boil on high, stirring constantly. Cook until mixture has consistency of gravy and color darkens slightly. (It will take approximately 15 minutes of boiling, so don't get discouraged; it's worth the wait). Serve over toast points.

— Roger Knisely
— Rich Allison

FIRE ROASTED SALSA

5 garlic cloves, peeled and chopped
8 Italian plum tomatoes, quartered
1 large onion, quartered
1 Jalapeno pepper seeded and cut in two
½ red pepper, quartered
½ green bell pepper, quartered
1 (28 oz.) can crushed tomatoes
1 bunch green onions, chopped
2½ tsp. salt
1½ tsp. black pepper
2 tsp. cumin
¼ C. lime juice
8 oz. tomato juice
1 bunch cilantro, finely chopped
1 small can diced green chilies

Take a metal pan or cookie sheet that can be placed under the broiler and place the first six ingredients in it - skin side up. Drizzle with 2 tablespoons olive oil. Place under the broiler and let the skins start to char, but not totally black. They should have a blistered appearance. This will take about 10 minutes.

Remove from the broiler and put through the food processor and coarsely chop. Meanwhile, while the mixture is in the oven, take a large bowl and add the remaining ingredients. To this mixture, add the items that were put through the food processor.

Chill and serve with white corn tortilla chips.

— Rich & Sandy Allison

CRAB STUFFED MUSHROOMS

24 mushrooms (about 1¼ lbs.)
5 tbsp. butter or margarine
2 tbsp. minced green onion (use part of tops)
1 tsp. lemon juice
1 C. (8 oz.) crab meat
½ C. bread crumbs
1 egg, beaten
¾ C. shredded jack cheese
1¼ C. or more white wine

Remove stems from mushrooms and finely chop. Melt 2 tbsp. butter over medium heat. Add mushroom stems, onion and cook stirring until onion is limp. Remove from heat and stir in lemon juice, crab, bread crumbs, egg,¼ C. wine and ⅓ C. of the cheese.

Melt remaining 3 tbsp. butter in 9"x13" pan. Turn mushroom caps in butter to coat. Place mushrooms in pan, cavity side up. Evenly mound filling in each mushroom cap. (At this point you may cover and refrigerate until next day).

To bake, sprinkle mushrooms with remaining cheese and pour 1 C. of white wine into pan.

Bake uncovered at 400° for 15-20 minutes or until hot throughout.

— Teri Ellenberger Coffman

GARLIC BREAD SPREAD

⅛ C. butter, room temperature
1 tsp. garlic salt

Mix above together. Slice Italian bread and spread all surfaces with butter. Wrap in aluminum foil and bake at 350° for 15-20 minutes.

— Bonnie Schultz

CRAB CHEESE MELT

1 lb. crab meat
1 stick butter, softened
1½ tsp. mayonnaise
5 oz. jar Cheese Whiz
1 tsp. pepper
Mix above altogether.

6 English muffins (split in half)

Top with crab mixture

Put under broiler:

Fresh: 5-7 minutes
Frozen: 10-20 minutes

— Minnie Ridgeway

This crab cheese melt makes a great appetizer. Just cut up the muffins into bite size pieces before serving.

SPINACH & ARTICHOKE DIP

1 can artichokes, in water, diced
½ (10 oz.) package chopped spinach

Cook in water for 10 minutes and drain.

Mix:

1 (8 oz). cream cheese
½ C. Romano cheese
3 drops red hot sauce
¼ tsp. salt
⅛ tsp. white pepper
6 oz. heavy cream

Mix well, add artichokes and spinach.
Heat over medium heat and wire whisk.
Bake at 300° for 15 minutes. Serve in round bread with tortilla chips.

— Rich Allison

APPETIZERS

PEPPERONI ROLLS

1 loaf frozen bread dough
Let thaw (about 4 hours)
Divide into 2 pieces

1. Roll 1 piece into circle to about ¼" thick, like a pizza.
2. Cover with spaghetti sauce.
3. Sprinkle heavily with garlic powder and Italian seasoning.
4. Cover with grated mozzarella cheese.
5. Totally cover with pepperoni slices.

Begin rolling up like a jelly roll and folding the edges in so sauce does not ooze out. When rolled up, crimp edge well or it will open up.

Bake at 375° for approximately 18 minutes, until golden brown. Can be frozen.

— Rich Allison

> *Try the pepperoni roll recipe or the bread sticks recipe and do variations of seasonings and cheeses for a different taste.*

BREAD STICKS

Pizza Dough, rolled flat like bread sticks.
Spread liquid margarine over dough.

Sprinkle black pepper, oregano and garlic over dough.

Bake at 425° for 15 minutes (until brown).

— Rich Allison

MINI CHICKEN PASTRIES

1 lb. boned chicken breast
3 tbsp. lemon juice
2 tbsp. olive oil
1 tsp. finely chopped or crushed garlic
1 tsp. oregano
½ tsp. salt
½ C. butter
½ lb. phyllo pastry

Cut chicken into 1" cubes. Combine lemon juice, oil, garlic, oregano and salt into a small bowl, mix well. Add chicken and stir to coat with marinade. Cover and refrigerate overnight. Melt butter. Cut sheets of pastry in half lengthwise. Use only 1 or 2 at a time and keep the rest covered to prevent drying out. Fold 1 strip of phyllo in half crosswise and brush with butter. Place 2 pieces of chicken at one end and roll up in pastry about half way. Fold sides toward center and continue rolling to end. Brush all over with butter and place seam-side down on a baking sheet. Repeat with remaining chicken and phyllo.

Bake at 400° for 15 minutes or until golden brown. Serve hot. Unbaked rolls may be frozen. If frozen, when ready to use, brush with more butter and bake for about 20 minutes.

Yield: About 2 dozen

> *This recipe came from a restaurant where we live in Peters Township. Although it takes some time to make, it makes a great appetizer.*
>
> *The lemon juice and seasonings give it a great flavor.*

MEXICAN SPOON BREAD

1 lg. pkg. Pillsbury Grand Buttermilk style biscuits (8 count)
1 sm. Pillsbury Grand Buttermilk style biscuits (5 count)
1 (16 oz.) jar chunky salsa (Pace)
1 bell pepper, small
½ C. chopped green onions
1 (2¼ oz.) can black olives, sliced and drained
2 C. Monterey Jack cheese, shredded

Separate biscuits and cut each into eighths. Toss with salsa in mixing bowl to coat. Add bell pepper, onions and olives, then blend. Pour mixture into a lightly greased 9"x13"x2" baking dish, sprinkle cheese over top.

Bake 30 minutes at 350°. Make sure the middle of the casserole sets. Let stand 15 minutes before cutting and serving. Makes 24 squares.

In memory of
— Louise Hidlebaugh

MUSHROOM SPREAD

1 lb. mushrooms, sliced
2 tbsp. butter
1 small onion, chopped

Sauté above together for 3 to 5 minutes. Drain some of liquid caused by mushrooms when cooked.

In separate bowl combine:

1½ C. Hellmann's Mayonnaise
10 strips of bacon, fried and crumbled
⅓ tsp. Lowry's Season salt

Mix everything together.
Bake at 350° for 20-25 minutes.
Serve with Pepperidge Farm butterfly crackers.

— Teri Ellenberger Coffman

JALAPENO CRAB DIP

1 lb. Crabmeat (picked over for shells)
Salt & pepper to taste
3-4 splashes hot sauce
3-4 splashes Lea & Perrins
¾ C. mayonnaise
1-2 jalapenos, chopped
15 garlic cloves, chopped

Mix and place in baking dish.
Cover with jack cheese.
Bake at 325° for 20 minutes.
Serve with crackers or crusty bread

— Rich Allison

CRABMEAT STUFFED MUSHROOMS

½ lb. mushrooms (8 oz.) clean and set aside.
Remove stems and chop finely.
¼ lb. crabmeat
¼ C. Tomato-Basil bread crumbs
1 small onion, diced

Sauté onion and stems in margarine, add to above.

Add:

3 tbsp. mayonnaise
2 tbsp. Old Bay
Dash Tabasco sauce
Dash Worcestershire sauce
Lemon pepper
1 tsp. garlic, chopped
⅛ C. sharp cheddar cheese

Garnish with paprika.

Broil under broiler until brown.

— Rich Allison

BAKED BRIE WITH CARAMELIZED ONIONS

Use Large Skillet:

2 tbsp. sweet butter, melted
8 C. onions, sliced
Start to cook over high heat

Add:

1 tbsp. fresh thyme, minced
Salt & pepper

Lower heat and cook uncovered for 25 minutes.

Add:

4 cloves garlic, minced
½ C. dry white wine
1 tbsp. white sugar

Put on medium heat for 10 minutes

2½ lb. Brie, unwrap (put remainder back in box)

Put in baking dish and let stand until reaches room temperature, add caramelized onions on top.
Bake at 350° for about 10 minutes or until softened.

Serve with French bread.

— Rich Allison

With a little practice, you can make this easily, and it will taste as good as the commercially prepared Onion Blossoms. Try different sauces for dipping.

ONION BLOSSOM

1 lg. Vidalia or other sweet onion
2 tbsp. all-purpose flour
1 lg. egg, lightly beaten
1 C. saltine crackers, crushed
Vegetable oil
½ tsp. salt (optional)
Commercial dark honey-mustard or ranch-style salad dressing.

Peel onion, leaving root end intact. Cut onion vertically into quarters, cutting within ½" of root end. Cut each quarter vertically into thirds.

Place onion in boiling water for 1 minute; remove and place in ice water for 5 minutes. Loosen "petals" if necessary. Drain onion, cut side down.

Place flour in a heavy-duty, zip-top plastic bag; add onion, shaking to coat. Dip onion in egg.

Place crushed crackers in plastic bag; add onion, tossing to coat. Chill onion 1 hour.

Pour oil to depth of 3" into an electric fryer or heavy saucepan, and heat to 375°.

Fry onion 5 to 7 minutes or until golden brown; drain on paper towels. Sprinkle with salt, if desired. Serve with honey-mustard or salad dressing.

Yield: 2 appetizer servings.

— Sandy Allison

FRIED PICKLES

Seasoned Flour:

1 lb. flour
2 tbsp. white pepper
4 tbsp. Old Bay seasoning

Combine all ingredients until well blended.

Fried Pickles:

Seasoned flour (all)
1 qt. buttermilk
¼" cut crinkle dill pickles

Place pickles into flour and toss until all pickles are well coated, remove pickles and place into buttermilk. Stir pickles gently, remove pickles and place back into flour. (A little at a time, letting excess buttermilk drip off). Gently toss pickles with flour until well coated. Immediately place pickles into a 350° fryer/pot with frying oil.

Fry for approximately 7 minutes until golden.

Serve with sour cream.

> *These pickles have a great taste. We found this recipe down in Tennessee and also near Wellsburg, WV where we go for wings.*

MEXICAN CORN DIP

2 sm. cans Mexican corn
1 (8 oz.) jar Hellmann's mustard
1 (8 oz.) sour cream
1 can diced green chilies
1 jalapeno, seeded and chopped
12 oz. shredded Cheddar or Colby Jack cheese
1 diced onion

Mix all above together and serve with tostados.

In memory of
— Louise Hidlebaugh

MUSHROOM SANDWICH

3 tbsp. softened butter
½ lb. chopped, fresh mushrooms
4 shallots or small onions
6 tbsp. white wine
3 tbsp. sour cream
¼ C. grated Jarlsberg cheese
Loaf of sliced white bread

Melt butter in a skillet over medium heat. Add mushrooms and shallots and sauté until soft, not browned. Add wine and cook until alcohol evaporates.

Stir in sour cream. Salt and pepper to taste. Remove from heat and cool completely. Add cheese to the mixture.

Lightly butter both sides of bread. Spread mushroom mixture on one side. Put other piece of bread on top to make sandwich. Grill sandwiches in skillet until golden brown. Trim the crust and cut into bite size pieces.

— Sandy Allison

"BRAVO" OLIVE OIL

Use all or any of the below items with olive oil for a dipping oil for bread.

Mix:

Olive oil
Sun dried tomatoes, chopped
Salt
Rosemary
Thyme
Garlic
Basil

— Rich Allison

BAKED ARTICHOKE DIP

5 tbsp. grated Romano cheese (packed, about 1 ounce)
3 tbsp. light mayonnaise
3 tbsp. light sour cream
½ tsp. dried marjoram
¼ tsp. ground black pepper
¼ tsp. onion salt
⅛ tsp. garlic powder
1 (14 oz. can artichoke hearts, packed in water, well drained, chopped into ¼" pieces.
¼ tsp. paprika
French-bread baguette slices, toasted

Whisk 4 tbsp. grated Romano cheese, light mayonnaise, light sour cream, dried marjoram, black pepper, onion salt, and garlic powder in medium bowl to blend. Stir in chopped artichoke hearts. Transfer mixture to 1½ C. ramekin. (Can be prepared 1 day ahead. Cover mixture and refrigerate.)

Preheat oven to 375°. Bake dip until heated through, about 20 minutes. (About 30 minutes if chilled).

Preheat broiler. Sprinkle dip with remaining 1 tbsp. grated Romano cheese and paprika. Broil until cheese melts, about 2 minutes. Serve warm with toasted baguette slices.

Makes about 1⅓ C.

NACHO DIP

2 lb. Velveeta Cheese, cubed
1 lb. Mexican mild cheese, cubed

Add:

1 lb. ground meat, fried
1 pkg. taco seasoning
16 oz. salsa

Put in crock pot on low for at least one hour and stir occasionally

— Rich Allison

MUSHROOM PUFFS

1 can refrigerated crescent rolls (8 count)
3 oz. cream cheese
1 tbsp. milk
4 oz. can mushroom pieces and stems, drained and chopped
½ tsp. horseradish
1 egg, beaten
2 tbsp. poppy seeds

Preheat oven to 400°.

Unroll dough, separate into 4 rectangles, seal perforation. Combine cream cheese and milk in a medium mixing bowl. Beat at high speed until smooth. Stir in mushrooms and horseradish. Roll as for jelly roll enclosing the filling. Cut each roll into 6 equal slices. Dip each slice into the egg mixture. Arrange cut side down on un-greased 11"x17" baking sheet. Sprinkle with poppy seeds.

Bake 10-12 minutes, or until puffed and golden brown.

CRAB DIP

Mix Together:

1 lb. back fin crab
2 C. mayonnaise
2 C. milk
8 hard cooked eggs, diced
10 slices bread, cubed

Sprinkle top with cheddar cheese.
Bake at 325° for 45 minutes.

Serve with Pepperidge Farm crackers.

— Dolly Simms

GRILLED CHICKEN PIZZA

Take 1 pizza crust. Cover with olive oil. Splash balsamic vinegar over oil. Blend together with a vegetable brush. Season heavily with oregano and garlic powder. Cover with mozzarella cheese.

Grill chicken and cut into bite size pieces. Put on top of cheese. Add seasoning salt. Add additional cheese. Slice Italian tomatoes thinly and put on pizza. Take sun dried tomatoes and soak in hot water for 30 seconds. Add to pizza.

Bake at 375° for 16 minutes.

— Rich Allison

PORTABELLAS WITH SAUSAGE AND BOURSIN CHEESE

Sauté 4 Portabellas without stems in margarine. Drain.

Fry 6 oz. sausage, crumbled. Seasoned with garlic powder.

Drain and place in top of Portabella's bottom side up.

Crumble a small amount of Boursin cheese with garlic and herbs. About 1 oz. on top of 4 mushrooms.

Place under the broiler until bubbly.

— Rich Allison

This is a great appetizer with portabellas and sausage and boursin cheese. This can be made with just the sausage or the boursin cheese with the mushrooms.

This grilled chicken pizza is good as an appetizer or as a main dish. The combination of tomatoes, chicken and olive oil give it great flavor.

GEORGETOWN APPETIZER
ITALIAN ANTIPASTA ON A SHELL

Take a pizza shell and brush with olive oil infused with Rosemary. Sprinkle with Romano cheese. Bake until lightly brown. Remove from oven.

Place the following on the pizza shell:

3 slices ham, cut into ¼" strips
3 slices turkey, cut into ¼" strips
3 slices salami, cut into ¼" strips
3 slices Muenster cheese, cut into ¼" strips
3-4 pieces romaine lettuce, chopped
Assortment of pitted olives, coarsely chopped
Roasted red pepper, cut into ¼" strips
Caramelized onions
½ can artichoke hearts, drained and chopped
Crumble Asiago cheese on top.

Drizzle with olive oil infused with rosemary. Season with salt and pepper.

— Rich Allison

There is a great restaurant in Georgetown, Washington, DC on Wisconsin Street that caters to the celebrities and politicians. It is an Italian restaurant. On one occasion the chef who was a friend of Brian's made a special appetizer for us. It was great. It was something like the above recipe.

APPETIZERS

DRIED BEEF CHEESE BALL

2 (8 oz.) cream cheese
1 tbsp. mayonnaise
2 tbsp. parsley
1 tsp. Worcestershire sauce
1 tbsp. onion, diced
5 oz. Hormel dried beef (finely chopped)

Mix, form into ball and refrigerate. Wrap in Saran Wrap. (This can be frozen).

DILL DIP

⅔ C. sour cream
⅔ C. Hellmann's mayonnaise (do not substitute)
1 tbsp. grated onion flakes
1 tbsp. parsley, chopped
1 tsp. dill weed
½ tsp. Accent
2 or 3 drops Tabasco sauce
1 tsp. Lowry's Seasoning salt
½ tsp. Worcestershire sauce

Mix altogether and refrigerate. Serve with cut vegetables or chips.

Double recipe for a good supply.

— Sandy Allison

BLEU CHEESE DIP
OR SALAD DRESSING

1 pt. Hellmann's Mayonnaise (no substitute)
6 oz. can evaporated milk
3 tbsp. lemon juice
½ tsp. garlic powder
Pinch salt and pepper

Mix by hand and add ½ lb. Bleu Cheese wedge, crumbled. Mix well.
— Mary Muffley

HAM DIP

2 (10 oz.) cans Hormel Tender Chunk Ham — chopped into small pieces.
12 oz. sour cream
3 tbsp. spicy brown mustard
2½ tbsp. parsley flakes

Mix well and refrigerate for several hours before serving. Serve with assorted crackers.

— Sandy Allison

JALAPENO & CHEESE APPETIZER

8 oz. Cheddar cheese, grated
8 oz. Monterrey cheese, grated
8 oz. jalapeno peppers, sliced

Put in Blender:

1 can evaporated milk
¼ C. flour
2 eggs

Put ½ of the jalapeno peppers on the bottom of a casserole dish. Then layer on the cheese. Pour on the blender ingredients. Put the rest of the jalapenos on the top.

Bake at 325° for 1 hour.

— Rich Allison

DRIED BEEF DIP

2 (8 oz.) pkgs. cream cheese, softened
4 tbsp. milk
4 tbsp. instant onions
5 oz. dried Beef, chopped fine
1 tsp. pepper
1 C. sour cream
4 tbsp. green pepper, chopped fine

Mix above ingredients with mixer. Put in a baking dish. Sprinkle with one C. chopped nuts. Bake at 350° for 15 to 25 minutes.

Keep warm while serving. Serve with crackers.

— Joan Leach

APPETIZERS

SPINACH DIP

1 pkg. (10 oz.) frozen, chopped spinach, drained
1 C. sour cream
½ C. mayonnaise
½ C. minced parsley
1 tsp. salt
½ tsp. celery salt
¼ tsp. pepper
⅛ tsp. nutmeg

Thaw spinach and place in a sieve. With the back of a spoon, remove excess water.

Mix the remaining ingredients and fold in the spinach. Refrigerate at least 24 hours.

May be prepared up to 3 days in advance. Makes about 3 C. About 35 calories per tablespoon. Serve with fresh vegetables.

— Sandy Allison

MINI-HAM PUFFS

1 pkg. (2.5 oz.) processed ham, chopped
1 sm. onion, chopped (about ¼ C.)
½ C. (2 oz.) Swiss cheese, shredded
1 egg
1½ tsp. Dijon mustard
⅛ tsp. ground black pepper
1 pkg. (8 oz.) refrigerated crescent rolls

Preheat oven to 350°.

Use food processor or finely chop ham, cheese and onion. Place in bowl. Add egg, mustard and pepper to mix.

Lightly spray mini-muffin pan with oil. Unroll crescent rolls and press dough into one large rectangle. Cut rectangle into 24 pieces using a pizza cutter. Press dough pieces into muffin cup and add filling.

Bake at 350° for 13-15 minutes, or until lightly browned.

— Beccie Weyant

MEXICAN DIP CASSEROLE

Layer in a small glass baking casserole (7"x11") the following ingredients:

2 cans Bean Dip or refried beans

Mix Together:

1 C. mayonnaise
1 C. sour cream
¾ pkg. taco seasoning

Spread over beans

Layer the following on top:

Diced tomatoes and green onions
1 can chopped black olives
10 oz. shredded cheddar cheese

Bake at 350° until bubbly, approximately 10-15 minutes. Serve hot with tortilla chips.

—Pam Bowser Knisely

COCKTAIL MEATBALLS IN STROGANOFF DILL SAUCE

Mix 2 lb. hamburger into cocktail size meatballs and lightly brown.

For the sauce:
Take:

2 tbsp. butter
2 tbsp. flour
Mix together in a skillet to form a roux. Slightly brown.

Add:

1 C. water
1 C. sour cream
1 tsp. dill weed
1 tbsp. ketchup

Mix well and add meatballs and let simmer for at least 30 minutes or longer. Makes about 60 meatballs.

MUSHROOMS STUFFED WITH SAUSAGE

Remove stems from mushrooms. Stuff caps with sausage. Sprinkle heavily with garlic powder.

Place under a broiler until brown and sausage is done.

— Rich Allison

GARLIC PRETZELS

2 (16 oz.) bags large broken pretzels
1 bottle Orville Redenbacher Gourmet popcorn oil
1 pkg. Hidden Valley Dry Salad Dressing
1 tsp. garlic powder
1 tsp. dill weed

Put pretzels in roaster.

Mix everything together and pour over pretzels.

Bake at 200° for one hour. Stir every 10 minutes.

— Pam Bowser Knisely

CHEESE SPREAD

1 lb. extra sharp cheddar cheese
1 lb. Velveeta Cheese
8-9 hard boiled eggs
1 med. onion

Put above ingredients through food grinder.

Melt ¾ lb. butter. Pour over above mixture. Mix well. Add 3-4 tbsp. cider vinegar.

Beat well when you pour on hot butter. Use a wooden spoon.

Use three loaves of rye – Country Hearth, if available.

Spread on bread and cut sandwiches in half.

In memory of
— Louise Hidlebaugh

FRUIT DIP

1 can Coco Lopez coconut mix
1 (12 oz.) container cool whip
1 (8 oz.) pkg. cream cheese

Mix Coco Lopez and cream cheese together and fold into cool whip.

Cut out ½ of a pineapple and fill with dip.

Serve with grapes, pineapple bits, cantaloupe, watermelon, bananas, etc. Sprinkle with Fruit Fresh.

— Joyce Yingling

CHIPPED BEEF HORS D'OEUVRES

16 oz. cream cheese
4 tbsp. milk
4 oz. chipped beef, shredded
½ C. green or yellow pepper, chopped
4 tbsp. onion, minced
½ tbsp. garlic salt
1 C. sour cream

Have cream cheese at room temperature. Blend with milk and sour cream. Add all other ingredients. Put in shallow casserole. Top with chopped pecans.

Bake at 350° for 20 minutes.

— Thelma Absher

The Cheese Spread makes good sandwiches that can be served as an appetizer or taken for a football tailgate. They have a good flavor and the cheese mixture keeps well in the refrigerator.

PARTY MIX

2 (15.6 oz.) boxes Rice Chex
2 (1 lb.) boxes Wheat Chex
2 (1 lb.) boxes Corn Chex
4 (15.25 oz). boxes Honey Nut Chex
4 (16 oz. or 1 lb.) containers cashews, salted
3 (16 oz. or 1 lb.) containers mixed nuts, salted
4 (14 oz.) pkgs. Snyder's Pretzel Sticks

Stir together in turkey roasters (4) that have been sprayed with Pam.

Blend & Heat in Microwave:

4 C. margarine
2 tbsp. seasoning salt
2 tbsp. garlic salt
4 tbsp. Worcestershire sauce
2 tbsp. granulated garlic powder

Pour over dry ingredients.
Mix well.

Heat oven to 200°. Heat in oven for 2 hours stirring every 15 minutes. If not flavorful enough, sprinkle more granulated garlic powder over mixture and blend well.

Cool in pans before Ziploc bagging.

— Sandy Allison

In memory of
— Donna Burket

The Party Mix is a variation from Sandy's mother's recipe. This recipe is made for the Christmas holidays and also is made during football season for tailgating. This is a good recipe to send off to college with your kids. It keeps well, but usually doesn't last too long with a bunch of kids!!!

BURGUNDY WINE HOT DOGS

Melt over medium heat:

2 (10 oz.) jars apple jelly
2 (10 oz.) jars red currant jelly

After jelly is melted add:

¾ C. Gulden's prepared mustard
1 C. Burgundy Wine

Cut raw hot dogs in bite size pieces.
Simmer about 20 minutes in jelly mixture. Use 5 lb. hot dogs.

Serve hot. Leftover sauce can be refrigerated and re-used.

Cocktail sausages are not good for this dish.

— Anne Kimble

CRABMEAT-MUSHROOM APPETIZER

¾ lb. mushrooms, rinsed and dried
8 tbsp. margarine, melted
1 (7½ oz.) can crabmeat
2 eggs, lightly beaten
6 tbsp. soft bread crumbs
2 tbsp. mayonnaise
2 tbsp. chopped chives or onions
1 tsp. lemon juice
⅛ tsp. white pepper

Brush mushroom caps with 7 tbsp. margarine.
Arrange on a lightly greased baking dish.

In a small bowl mix remaining ingredients except 1 tbsp. margarine and 2 tbsp. bread crumbs.

Fill each cap. Combine remaining margarine and bread crumbs and sprinkle over mushrooms.

Bake at 375° for 15 minutes.

— Connie Burket

DEVILED EGGS

4 hard cooked eggs
½ tsp. salt
1½ tsp. cider vinegar
1 tbsp. mayonnaise
⅛ tsp. pepper
¼ tsp. spicy brown mustard
1 tbsp. cream or milk

Cut eggs lengthwise in half. Remove yolks and mash until smooth. Add other ingredients except cream and mix well. Add part or all cream if needed. Refill the whites and garnish with paprika and parsley.

Serves 4.

— Sandy Allison

HOT SAUSAGE AND CHEESE PUFFS

1 lb. hot Italian sausage
1 lb. sharp cheddar cheese, shredded
3 C. biscuit baking mix
¾ C. water

Remove sausage from casings. Cook in large skillet, breaking up the meat with a fork until no longer pink – about 8-10 minutes. Drain off fat.

Spoon sausage into large bowl and cool completely. Add cheese, biscuit mix and water, Mix with a fork until just blended.

Roll into 1" balls. Place on a large cookie sheet about 2" apart. Bake at 400° for 12-15 minutes or until puffed and brown. Serve warm.

Makes about 50 servings – 120 puffs. Can be frozen and reheated at 375° for 10 minutes.

In memory of
— Louise Hidlebaugh

CRAB DIP

½ C. sour cream
2 tbsp. mayonnaise
1 (8 oz.) pkg. cream cheese, softened
1 tsp. prepared horseradish
½ tsp. dry mustard
½ tsp. Worcestershire sauce
½ tsp. Tabasco sauce

Mix well and add:

1 C. sharp cheddar cheese, grated
½ lb. crab meat
2 tsp. Lipton Onion Soup Mix

Mix well and sprinkle with paprika.
Serve with crackers.

Serve cold or heat in microwave and serve hot.

— Min Ridgeway

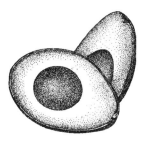

GUACAMOLE DIP

15 med. avocados
24 oz. hot picante salsa (Pace brand)
6 serrano peppers, finely diced
1 sm. white onion, finely diced
1 lime, juiced
1 tsp. salt
2 bunches cilantro leaves, finely chopped
6 Roma tomatoes, diced
Black pepper

Combine avocados, salsa, serranos, onion, lime juice, and salt. Add cilantro, tomatoes and black pepper. Stir gently.

SAUERKRAUT BALLS

½ lb. bulk pork sausage
¼ C. onion, chopped
1-16 oz. can sauerkraut
2 tbsp. fine dry bread crumbs
4 oz. cream cheese, softened
2½ tbsp. fresh parsley, finely snipped
1 tbsp. sweet hot mustard
Dash garlic salt
Dash pepper
⅓ to ½ C. all purpose flour
2 eggs
2 tbsp. water
⅓ to ½ C. fine dry bread crumbs
cooking oil for deep-fat frying

In a large skillet cook sausage and onion until sausage is brown, breaking sausage into small pieces. Drain.

Drain sauerkraut, pressing out as much liquid as possible. In a large mixing bowl, combine sauerkraut, sausage mixture, 2 tbsp. bread crumbs, cream cheese, parsley, mustard, garlic salt and pepper. Mix well. Cover and chill for at least 3 to 4 hours.

Put flour in a shallow container. In another shallow container, beat eggs and water until combined. Put ⅓ to ½ C. fine bread crumbs in a third shallow container.

Using about 2 tablespoons for each, shape sauerkraut mixture into balls. Roll balls in flour, then egg mixture, then in bread crumbs. Fry a few at a time in deep hot fat for about 2 minutes, or until brown. Remove from fat and drain. They are now ready to serve.

Enjoy!

— Charmayne Holland

CLAM DIP

2 cans mixed clams
1 tsp. onion juice
6 oz. cream cheese with chives-softened
6 oz. cream cheese-softened
1 tbsp. mayonnaise or enough to mix together in a mixer.
1 tbsp. lemon juice
1 tbsp. Worcestershire sauce.

Mix all together. Makes enough for 8. Serve with chips and pretzels.

— Shirley Knisely

VEGETABLE PIZZA

Take 2 (8 oz.) Pillsbury Crescent Rolls and pat out flat in a 15"x10" jelly roll pan. Bake according to directions for rolls.

Blend Together:

2 (8 oz.) cream cheese-softened
¾ C. mayonnaise
1 pkg. Dry Hidden Valley Ranch Dressing.

Spread on cooled crust.

Top with ¾ C. or less of each.

Celery, carrots, onion, broccoli, cauliflower, green pepper, tomato.

Sprinkle with grated cheddar cheese.

Top with crabmeat or diced shrimp.

— Jan Brisky

CORNED BEEF DIP IN A ROUND RYE BOWL

1⅓ C. sour cream
1⅓ C. mayonnaise
½ C. corned beef, diced (¼ lb.)
2 tsp. dill seed
2 tbsp. onion flakes
2 tbsp. chopped parsley

1 loaf round seedless rye bread.

Mix all ingredients. Refrigerate. Right before serving, scoop out center of bread and fill with mixture.

Keep bread pieces which were scooped out and place around bread loaf for dipping into the mixture.

— Sandy Kardos

MINI BAGELS

1 jar Hormel Real Bacon Bits
1 lb. grated sharp cheddar cheese
1 C. mayonnaise
1 pkgs. Lender's Mini Bagels

Mix all ingredients and spread 1 tsp. on each ½ Bagel.

Broil until bubbly – approximately 2 minutes.

Makes 40 bagels.

— Sandy Kardos

CHEESE BELL

1 (8 oz.) pkg. Cracker Barrel Brand sharp cheddar
  cold pack cheese food
1 (8 oz.) cream cheese, softened
2 tsp. pimiento, chopped
2 tsp. green pepper, chopped
2 tsp. onion, chopped
1 tsp. Worcestershire Sauce
½ tsp. lemon juice.

Combine Cracker Barrel cheese and cream cheese, mixing until well blended. Add remaining ingredients and mix well.

Mold into bell shapes using Cracker Barrel plastic containers lined with plastic wrap.

Chill until firm. Unmold. Garnish with parsley and pimiento strips.

Serve with Triscuits.

— Joy Dodson

PEPPERONI LOAF

1 (23 oz.) loaf day old bread grated in blender.

Add:

Salt, pepper, oregano, garlic powder, chopped parsley, and grated parmesan cheese to taste and 1 green pepper, diced.

Slice and quarter one stick pepperoni and fry until grease comes out of it. Spoon it into bread mixture.

Add 6-7 eggs and more if needed. Mix together and form a long loaf.

Use a large piece of foil. Put spaghetti sauce and parmesan cheese on foil. Place loaf on foil and add extra sauce over loaf along with parmesan cheese.

Close foil and bake 1 hour at 350°. Heat extra sauce and pour over it when done baking.

In memory of
— Louise Hidlebaugh

COCKTAIL MEATBALLS

3 lb. ground beef
½ C. seasoned bread crumbs
2 onions, minced
4 tbsp. prepared horseradish
2-4 garlic cloves, crushed
1½ C. tomato juice
4 tsp. salt
Dash of pepper

Combine above ingredients and form into 1" balls. Place meatballs in a cake pan. Brown in oven at 450° for 10 minutes. Remove and drain off grease.

Meatball Sauce:

¼ C. margarine
2 onions, chopped
¼ C. flour
3 C. Campbell's Beef Broth
1 C. Reunite Red Wine
¼ C. brown sugar
¼ C. ketchup
2 tbsp. lemon juice
2 tsp. salt
Dash of pepper

Melt butter and sauté onions. Blend in flour. Add beef broth and stir until smooth. Stir in remaining ingredients and heat 15 minutes at low heat. Add meatballs. Simmer 5 minutes more. Serve hot in a crock pot.

Makes 85 meatballs.

—Kathy Chabala

NACHOS

Brown 1 lb. hamburger, drain off grease. Add 1 package taco seasoning and cook as per directions on taco seasoning package.

Arrange taco chips on aluminum foil on a cookie sheet. Spread out chips.

Top with hamburger, salsa and any of the following:

Sliced black olives
Diced tomatoes
Sliced Jalapenos
Diced onions
Chopped green chilies

Pour salsa and then toppings over chips.
Top with grated cheddar or Monterray Jack cheese.

Place under broiler until chips start to brown on the edges. Serve with salsa.

— Rich Allison

OYSTER CRACKER SNACK

2 lg. boxes oyster crackers
1 C. oil
1 tsp. dill weed
½ tsp. garlic salt
½ tsp. garlic powder
1 pkg. Dry Ranch House Dressing

Mix crackers in oil. Mix dry ingredients. Mix both together. Serve as a snack.

— Shirley Knisely

ITALIAN BREAD SANDWICH

Take 1 loaf of Italian bread and slice in have lengthwise creating a top and bottom piece.

For the bottom piece, make a mixture of relish, mayonnaise and ketchup. Mix well and slather on the bottom piece. Layer the following on the bread building a sandwich:

Ham
Hard salami
Munster cheese
Turkey breast
Sandwich pepperoni
Colby or Longhorn cheese

Top this with sliced tomatoes, grilled caramelized onions, roasted red peppers. Drizzle with small amount of olive oil and season with salt and pepper.

Put mayonnaise on top piece of bread. Place top piece of bread on sandwich. Press it down very tightly. Slice and serve.

This sandwich is very messy, but very tasty. Serves 8 people.

— Rich Allison

SHRIMP CANAPES

1 (4½ oz.) can small shrimp, drained
⅓ C. mayonnaise
¼ C. onion, chopped
Dash pepper
Dash paprika

Chop shrimp. Add mayonnaise, onions and seasonings. Mix well.

Take 16 club crackers and 6-8 slices of American cheese. Cut cheese to fit crackers. Place cheese on crackers. Top each cracker with 1 tbsp. of shrimp mixture.

Sprinkle ¼ C. parmesan cheese over crackers and mixture.

Broil 8-10 minutes at 350° until lightly brown.

— Rich Allison

CHEESE-A-BUTTER

Beat ½ C. butter with:

¾ tsp. Italian seasoning
⅛ tsp. garlic powder
⅛ tsp. black pepper

Blend in 1 C. shredded cheddar cheese and 1 tsp. lemon juice.

Form into a log shape and place on waxed paper and refrigerate. Serve melted on your favorite meats and vegetables.

— Bonnie Schultz

SAUCES & DRESSINGS

Cooking from the Farm to the City

The Very Best

Recipes

of

Rich & Sandy Allison

and Their

Family and Friends

SAUCES & DRESSINGS

HONEY BARBEQUE SAUCE

¾ C. barbeque sauce
½ C. honey
½ C. ketchup
6 tbsp. brown sugar

Heat until mixture comes to a boil and sugar is dissolved.

— Rich & Sandy Allison

This honey barbeque sauce was developed after visiting a restaurant near Wellsburg, WV where it was actually a wing sauce. It works well on wings, chicken, pork and other meats.

COUSIN HERMIE'S CRAB DIPPING SAUCE

Use a pint jar:

Fill ½ full with white vinegar

Add:

½ C. Old Bay or Crab Seasoning

Fill jar to top with water.
Shake well because sauce separates.
Use as a dipping sauce for the crabmeat.

— Cousin Hermie Harrison

Cousin Hermie Harrison lives on the Eastern Shore of Maryland on the Chesapeake Bay where he is a waterman who harvests crabs, oysters and fish. He is actually a cousin of our friends, Jim and Min Ridgeway. We rely on Herman for fresh seafood when we visit the bay. This is his sauce for dipping crabs. We have promised Herman royalties, but he has not seen any to date and probably never will.

TEXAS HOT DOG SAUCE

1 C. diced onions
1 C. water
2 tbsp. chili powder
1 tbsp. sugar
1 C. ketchup

Boil above ingredients until onions get soft.

Brown 1 lb. ground meat seasoned with salt. Drain off grease.

Add ground meat to above mixture.

Cook hot dogs and place in buns and put above sauce over them.

— Sandy Allison

This is a recipe from a Hot Dog shop in central PA. We used this at the festivals and street fairs held in Claysburg, PA

HOEZEL DRESSING

¼ C. olive oil
¾ C. light vegetable oil
¼ C. tarragon vinegar
¾ C. cider vinegar
2 tsp. salt
3 tsp. crushed black peppercorns

Makes 2 C. of dressing.

Serve over salads or over fresh crabmeat.

— Rich Allison

This is a recipe from a Pittsburgh business club that is a tradition. It is great over crabmeat or salads!

BARBEQUE SAUCE FOR RIBS

1 C. brown sugar
1 C. molasses
1 C. cider vinegar
1 C. ketchup
1 C. Heinz Grandma's Old Fashioned BBQ Sauce or any BBQ sauce
1 C. honey
3 tbsp. dark mustard
3 tbsp. garlic, minced
1 tbsp. whole peppercorns
½ tbsp. kosher salt
½ tsp. ground ginger
½ tsp. anise seed
¼ C. soy sauce
3 splashes Tabasco sauce

Cook until mixture comes to a boil and wire whisk the entire time.

Remove from heat and let sauce cool. Cover pork ribs with sauce in a plastic container over night.

Next day remove ribs from sauce and bake at 350° for 2 hours in the oven.

15 minutes before ready to eat, grill over medium heat basting with sauce until ribs are glazed. Discard remaining sauce that was used for marinade.

— Rich Allison

This sauce for ribs is a take-off on a local restaurant in Pittsburgh famous for their ribs. The anise seed gives it a different flavor.

CHICKEN BASTING SAUCE

1 pt. white vinegar
1 C. Crisco Oil
3 tbsp. poultry seasoning
3 tbsp. salt
1 tsp. pepper
1 tbsp. garlic powder
1 tbsp. Worcestershire Sauce
2 eggs

Place all ingredients in blender and mix well.

Marinate chicken in a pan with basting sauce up to several hours before placing chicken on the grill.

Continue basting with the sauce while chicken is cooking. Chicken will become a golden brown and will not burn as quickly as with other sauces.

— Rich Allison

We have been using this chicken basting sauce for 30 years. It rarely will burn unless you are absolutely using too hot of a fire. The sauce has good flavor.

SAUCES & DRESSINGS

OLD BILL'S BARBECUE SAUCES

Take Chicken Basting Sauce recipe and use the mixture as follows:

To each C. of basting sauce, add 4 heaping tsp. of yellow mustard.

Use as a base on pork chops, chicken or beef. Grill over mesquite chips and continue to baste until the meat is done.

When meat is done, serve the following red barbecue sauce over the barbecued meat after it is taken off the grill.

Take 1 C. of Open Pit Barbecue Sauce and add 4 heaping tsp. of Heinz Dark Brown Spicy Mustard and add ½ C. water. Mix well. Place in a squeeze ketchup bottle and squirt all over the meat prior to serving.

— Rich Allison & Aimee Schultz

Old Bill lived near Finleyville, PA and used to live in the Hill District of Pittsburgh. He apparently made barbeque for many years. Rumors are that Old Bill would make sauce and ship it to Joe Montana when he was in California. Old Bill set up shop in Finleyville in the early 1990's. While his shop did not meet the Department of Health standards, he served a lot of food. He was shut down several times. He usually cooked his food on a wire rack over a kettle filled with charcoal, but it was his sauce that really set off the flavor. It took a lot of trips for us to finally come up with a recipe close to Old Bill's and about 20 different variations on a Labor Day till Aimee Schultz and Rich finally came close to Old Bill's. He has been closed for years and since then has died, but his barbeque memories live on.

EASY MARINADE AND BARBECUE SAUCE

For use on steaks, pork chops or seafood:

Season meat or seafood well with the following:

Garlic powder
Seasoning salt
Fresh ground pepper

Pour Kraft Zesty Italian Dressing over meat or seafood and let marinate for approximately one hour before grilling.

Grill as you normally would and continue basting until meat or seafood is done.

— Rich Allison

ALABAMA BARBEQUE SAUCE

2 tbsp. oil
1 onion, minced
1 lg. garlic clove, minced
½ C. ketchup
½ C. cider vinegar
⅓ C. honey
¼ C. Worcestershire Sauce
2 tsp. dry mustard
1 tsp. ground ginger
1 tsp. salt
Juice of one lemon

Heat oil in saucepan over low heat. Add onion and garlic and sauté until soft. Add all remaining ingredients and simmer for 15 minutes.

Remove from heat and set aside. Sauce will keep refrigerated for up to two weeks.

Use on pork or chicken.

— Rich Allison

ALL PURPOSE BARBECUE BASTING SAUCE

½ C. Crisco Oil
½ C. lemon juice
½ C. wine vinegar
¼ C. soy sauce
½ tsp. monosodium glutamate

Combine all ingredients. Add salt to taste. Add fresh ground pepper and herbs.

Keep in covered jar in refrigerator until ready to use.

— Rich Allison

BIM'S BARBECUE SAUCE

1 gallon ketchup
2 bottles of your favorite barbecue sauce
2 lg. cans tomato paste
Juice of 2-3 lemons, to taste
2 C. brown sugar
½ C. white Karo syrup
½ C. honey
3 bay leaves (remove after cooking)
1 jar brown mustard
1 jar yellow mustard
1 C. molasses
½ C. A-1 sauce
½ C. Worcestershire sauce

Bring to a boil and stir constantly. If mixture needs sweetened, add more honey and brown sugar.

Mixture can also be spiced up with garlic powder and Tabasco sauce.

Makes several gallons. Bake on all barbecue items during cooking.

— Denny (Bim) Burket

JOE'S STONE CRAB INN MUSTARD SAUCE

3½ tsp. Coleman's dry mustard
1 C. mayonnaise
Mix above ingredients.

Add:

2 tsp. Lea & Perrins Worcestershire sauce
1 tsp. A-1 sauce
⅛ C. table or whipped cream
Pinch of Salt (not too much)
Mix well.

Serve as a dipping sauce for seafood.

— Rich Allison

APPLE SAUCE FOR STEAK/CHICKEN

3 tbsp. butter
1 oz. olive oil
2 tbsp. brown sugar

Heat until sugar is dissolved.

Slice 1 yellow apple and add to skillet.

Add:

3 tbsp. Apple Schnapps
1 beef bouillon cube
1 tbsp. honey

Add:

½ tsp. cornstarch and ⅛ C. water (mix together before adding).

Simmer until apples are soft.
Serve over steak or chicken.

— Rich Allison

SAUCES & DRESSINGS

GALEN DIVELY'S BARBEQUE CHICKEN SAUCE

1 gallon white vinegar
2 lb. margarine (preferably Country Crock)

Melt margarine and vinegar
Add salt and pepper

Baste chicken with sauce while barbequing.

In memory of
— Galen Dively

> *Galen Dively was a high school teacher and college professor from Claysburg, PA who loved Bluegrass music. He was a legend around Claysburg. His favorite past time was cooking and his specialty was cooking barbeque chicken for fund raisers for local organizations.*

CARAMELIZED BOURBON SAUCE

4 tbsp. bourbon
Cook until alcohol cooks off.

Add:

1 C. brown sugar
1 stick margarine
Cook until caramelized.

Serve over meat or poultry.

— Rich Allison

BARBECUE DRESSING

1 C. mayonnaise
½ C. sour cream
¼ C. barbecue sauce
¼ C. honey
¼ tsp. black ground pepper
¼ tsp. cayenne pepper

Combine all ingredients until well blended.

BARBECUE SAUCE

Place one green pepper and one onion coarsely chopped in a blender with 1 C. of water.
Puree mixture. Place in a pan to cook with the following:

1 C. barbecue sauce
1 C. ketchup
2 tbsp. brown sugar
1 tsp. dry mustard
1 tbsp. Worcestershire sauce
¼ C. honey

Bring to a boil for 10 minutes. Use as a barbecue baste.

In memory of
— Grace Allison

SOUTHWEST SEASONING

2 tbsp. chili powder
2 tbsp. paprika
1 tbsp. ground coriander
1 tbsp. garlic powder
1 tbsp. salt
2 tsp. ground cumin
1 tsp. cayenne pepper
1 tsp. crushed red pepper
1 tsp. black pepper
1 tsp. dried oregano

Directions:

Combine all ingredients thoroughly and store in an airtight jar.

This can be used to season meat as a rub or sprinkle on dishes after cooking.

Yield: ½ Cup

DILL SAUCE

Make a Roux:

2 tbsp. melted butter
2 tbsp. flour

Add:

¾ C. chicken broth
1 tbsp. fresh dill
Pinch of salt

Serve over fish or cooked vegetables.

— Rich Allison

LES'S CRAB SEASONING

⅔ C. Old Bay Seasoning
⅓ C. Wye River Seasoning-Red Formula
⅓ C. coarse rock salt

Mix all together and sprinkle over crabs after cooking or use as a seasoning to dip crabmeat.

— Les Burdett

Les and Florence Burdett live on the Eastern Shore of Maryland on the Chesapeake Bay at Claiborne, MD. Their home is always open to visitors where they provide great hospitality.

SOUTHWEST FLANK STEAK MARINADE

5 tbsp. olive oil
4 tbsp. lime juice
1 tbsp. garlic, minced
2 tbsp. cilantro, minced
1 tbsp. parsley, chopped
1 tsp. cumin
1 tsp. chili powder
1 jalapeno pepper, minced

Wire whisk. Pour over flank steak and marinate over night.

Cook flank steak quickly over hot grill until desired doneness.

— Rich Allison

BASTING AND MARINADE SAUCE

1 C. brown sugar
½ C. soy sauce
½ stick margarine
2 tbsp. garlic powder
1½ tsp. ginger powder
1 oz. bourbon

Place in a saucepan and heat. Prior to boiling, place ¼ C. cornstarch in a cup of cold water and mix well.

Add cornstarch mixture to saucepan and stir constantly.

Basting sauce will thicken. Stir constantly for approximately 5 minutes after boiling starts.

Use as a base on ham, fish, etc.

— Rich Allison

PORK LOIN GLAZE

1 C. pineapple preserves
⅔ C. ketchup
½ C. barbecue sauce
1 tsp. dry mustard
¼ tsp. ground cloves

Combine above ingredients in a saucepan and heat until well blended.

Use as a baste during the last hour when smoking a pork loin or other pork items, such as ribs and pork chops.

— Rich Allison

SAUCES & DRESSINGS

CHICKEN WING SAUCES

Cook chicken wings in deep fryer depending on size of wings for 30-45 minutes until golden brown. Drain wings, but immediately coat with your favorite wing sauce or one of the sauces below. Allow 1 to 1¼ lb. wings per person.

TRADITIONAL BUFFALO WING SAUCE

½ C. margarine
½ C. Frank's Hot Sauce
½ C. cider vinegar

Heat mixture until margarine melts and then lightly coat cooked wings.

— Roger Knisely

HONEY BARBEQUE SAUCE

¾ C. barbeque sauce
½ C. honey
½ C. ketchup
6 tbsp. brown sugar

Heat until mixture comes to a boil and sugar is dissolved.

— Rich & Sandy Allison

SHANE'S HOT AND SWEET WING SAUCE

12 oz. Wing-O Hot Sauce
2 C. brown sugar
1 tsp. Italian seasoning
½ tsp. seasoning salt
½ tsp. garlic powder
½ tsp. fresh ground pepper

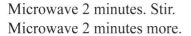

Microwave 2 minutes. Stir.
Microwave 2 minutes more.

— Shane Weyant

TIM'S WING SAUCE

½ lb. light brown sugar
¼ C. onion salt
¼ C. garlic powder

Mix well and toss with cooked wings while they are still very hot until lightly coated. Brown sugar mixture will melt and coat the wings. This serves about 3 lb. wings. Must use deep fried wings with this mixture for brown sugar to adhere to wings.

— Tim Burket

GUS' HONEY MUSTARD SAUCE

Take equal amounts of Gulden's Mustard and honey and mix well. If you like mustard flavor, add more mustard.

Heat mixture and stir well. Lightly coat deep fried wings.

— Gus Walter

WILD BILL'S BBQ SAUCE FOR WINGS

2 C. Cattlemen's Gold Sauce
4 oz. Frank's Red Hot Sauce
1 oz. honey
1 oz. brown sugar

Heat until mixture is well blended and sugar has melted. Serve on wings.

— Adapted from Bill Kargo's recipe
— Rich Allison

We have developed a love for wings of all types. Sandy's brother, Tim cooks his wings in lard — forget the cholesterol! After about 45 minutes of cooking (depending upon the size of the wings), they are flavorful, crispy and tender. All of these sauces are good, but try Tim's with the brown sugar. It is outstanding!

SALADS

Cooking from the Farm to the City

The Very Best
Recipes
of

Rich & Sandy Allison

and Their
Family and Friends

SALADS

ANTIPASTO SALAD WITH ROMANO CHEESE DRESSING

Arrange the following in a large salad bowl:

Lettuce torn in pieces for a salad
Chopped tomatoes
Chopped onions

Cut the following meat and cheeses into julienne strips and place in bowl:

Ham
Hard Salami
Provolone Cheese

Drain one jar of green olives and place on top of other salad mixture.

Drain one can of small black pitted olives and place on top of salad mixture.

Drain one can of garbanzo beans and place on top of salad mixture.

Top entire salad with 12-16 ounces of shredded mozzarella cheese.

For the dressing, take a quart jar and mix the following:

Fill ¼ full of cider vinegar
1 egg yolk, pasteurized if you prefer
2½ tbsp. garlic powder
1½ tbsp. fresh ground pepper
3-4 oz. grated Romano cheese
Fill jar to top with olive oil

Do not add salt

Shake well before serving. Pour dressing over salad immediately prior to serving the salad.

— Rich Allison & Bim Burket

"Cousin" Bim Burket loves to cook. He works hard and plays hard and usually is found cooking for a group of hungry people when he isn't working. Bim and Rich found this variation of an antipasto salad one weekend while the girls were out shopping. It has a good Romano flavor. Use any variation of meats, cheeses, greens, etc. to suit your tastes.

ALL VEGETABLE SALAD

Use all raw vegetables:

1 med. size head cauliflower
3 stalks broccoli
1 pt. mushrooms
1 pt. cherry tomatoes
1 bottle cocktail onions
4 stalks celery
2 cucumbers
1 can garbanzo beans
1 stick pepperoni, sliced thin
3 green peppers
6 carrots

Cut up all vegetables into bite size pieces.

Add 2 large bottles of Kraft Zesty Italian dressing – no substitutions. Marinate in salad dressing. Store in refrigerator and stir occasionally. Above makes a large bowl. Recipe can be cut in half for smaller amounts.

Will keep in refrigerator for 1-2 weeks.

— Anne Kimble

CAESAR SALAD

Mix in a bowl and wire whisk:

3 garlic cloves, crushed
3 anchovies, crushed
1 C. olive oil
2 pasteurized egg yolks, blended
Splash Worcestershire Sauce
1½ tsp. Dijon mustard
Splash balsamic vinegar
Juice of ½ lemon

In a separate bowl, put the following:

Torn Romaine lettuce
Croutons
Parmesan Cheese
Fresh ground pepper
Top with dressing

— Rich Allison

This is the best Caesar Salad recipe that we ever had. We found it the night of our wedding in Laughlin, Nevada. We watched the waiter make it at our table. It has been a favorite of everyone ever since.

TEXAS TWO STEP SLAW

4 C. green cabbage
1 C. red cabbage
1 can corn (with peppers)
1 red onion, chopped
Mildly hot peppers

Dressing:

¾ C. Creamy Ranch Dressing
1 tbsp. lime juice
1 tsp. cumin
Parsley
4 oz. Cheddar Cheese, grated

— Thelma Absher

TACO SALAD

1 head lettuce
2 tomatoes
2 green peppers
1 onion, optional
1 lb. hamburger
1 (8 oz.) bag of shredded cheddar or taco cheese
1 pkg. taco seasoning
1 lg. bag Doritos
1 lg. bottle Kraft Catalina French dressing

Prepare lettuce, tomatoes, peppers and onions as for a salad.

Fry hamburger, drain and add taco seasoning as per instructions on package.

Just before serving, add hamburger, cheese, dressing and crushed up Doritos to salad. Mix everything together.

— Beccie Weyant

This is a good flavorful salad that can be prepared ahead and then mixed when you are ready to serve. This works well for tailgates and parties.

COLESLAW

1 qt. Miracle Whip
1½-2 C. sugar

Whip together. Then add enough whole milk to thin out to dressing consistency. Add salt to taste.

Grate 2 heads of cabbage on hand grater. Per Jim Allison, "push real damn hard and fast" while grating. Mix dressing with grated cabbage.

In memory of
— Peggy Allison

SALADS

CRANBERRY SALAD

1 (3 oz.) box cherry jello
1 (16 oz.) can cranberry sauce
1 (15 oz.) can crushed pineapple
Diced grapes
Chopped walnuts

Add only 1 C. boiling water to jello. Mix all ingredients together and place in refrigerator to gel.

In memory of
— Donna Burket

This was a Thanksgiving and Christmas tradition made by Sandy's mom, Donna Burket.

FROZEN GRAPE SALAD

2 (3 oz.) pkg. cream cheese
2 tbsp. mayonnaise
2 tbsp. pineapple syrup
Miniature marshmallows
1 can (20 oz. or 2½ C.) pineapple bits, drained
½ pt. heavy whipping cream whipped into 1 C.
2 C. grapes, halved and seeded

Soften cream cheese. Blend in mayonnaise. Beat in pineapple juice (use from canned pineapple).

Add marshmallows and drained pineapple bits. Fold in whipped cream and grapes.

Freeze until firm. Remove from freezer ½ hour before serving. Serves 8.

— Bonnie Schultz

A cool, refreshing salad that keeps well in the freezer. Make well ahead of time and forget the rushing to make at the last minute.

POTATO SALAD

5 lb. Potatoes, peel and dice, cook until semi soft in salted water.
9 eggs, cooked, peeled and sliced
Onion and celery, diced

When potatoes are cooked, drain and add onion, celery and eggs.
Season with salt and pepper
Take ½ to ¾ qt. Miracle Whip
Add ¾ C. sugar
Add 3 tbsp. yellow mustard and mix, then add to potatoes while hot.

Add yellow food coloring

Season to taste and mix well

— Adapted from Kathy Burket's Recipe by Rich Allison

FATIGATI SALAD

1½ heads lettuce (rinsed, dried and chilled)
1 cucumber
1 large tomato
6 garlic cloves crushed
½ tbsp. salt
11 grinds of pepper
Chop salad items and toss.

Add:

¾ C. Yolanda salad oil or any vegetable oil
Toss well
Add ¼ C. cider vinegar
Toss well
Serves 8

— Rich Allison

This recipe came from a famous restaurant in the South Hills of Pittsburgh. They were well known for their Italian garlic salad. The key is lots of salt and adding the vinegar after mixing.

ST. MICHAELS SUMMER SALAD

Place ½ head washed, shredded, romaine lettuce on platter.

Slice red tomatoes, individually seasoned on both sides with kosher salt and fresh ground pepper.

Slice yellow grape tomatoes in half and season with kosher salt and fresh ground pepper.

1 large onion, sliced

Roast 1 red and 1 yellow pepper. Do on gas grill. Place peppers in paper bag and let steam for 15 minutes. Remove from bag. Peel charred skins and remove seeds. Cut in julienne slices.

To Arrange Platter:

Place ½ slice provolone cheese and then 1 slice red tomato. Continue alternating around edge of platter.

In center arrange sliced onions. Top with yellow tomatoes. Put julienne strips of pepper over platter.

Arrange green and black olives over entire platter.

Mix 5 oz. olive oil and 3 oz. balsamic vinegar. Drizzle over platter

Place crumbled gorgonzola over platter.

— Roger Knisely
— Rich Allison

Rich and Roger won the Iron Chef award in St. Michael's, MD on the Eastern Shore of the Chesapeake Bay in 2002 for this recipe. It is very easy to make.

BLACK BEANS AND RICE SALAD

1 (15 oz.) can black beans
1 C. cooked cold rice
1 medium onion, diced
3 Roma tomatoes, diced
2 stalks celery, diced

Mix Hoezel dressing with only ½ C. vinegar.

Add:

1 tsp. cumin
½ C. sugar
1 tbsp. garlic powder

Chill several hours before serving.

— Rich Allison

PASTA SALAD

3 lb. pasta (tri-colored) cooked for 12 minutes and drain.
½ lb. pepperoni chopped
1 can black olives, sliced
½ jar green olives, sliced
1 lb. grape tomatoes or others, sliced
2 stalks celery, diced
1 purple onion, diced
½ green pepper, diced
½ lb. Pepper Jack cheese, diced
½ lb. Colby cheese, diced

Add:

2 tsp. Salad Seasoning
Lots of garlic powder
Lots of Italian Seasoning
Black Pepper to taste

1½ large bottles Zesty Italian dressing

Mix well and let chill and marinate.
Add more Italian dressing if the mixture becomes dry.

— Rich Allison

SALADS

ITALIAN SALAD FOR 15 PEOPLE

Chop the following and mix in bowl:

3 heads romaine lettuce
1 red pepper
½ yellow pepper
15 mini carrots
3 stalks celery
½ onion - on side
6 plum tomatoes

Dressing:

3 oz. balsamic vinegar
9 oz. olive oil
1 tsp. (heaping) kosher salt
1 tsp. Italian seasoning
½ tsp. grated black pepper
2 tsp. garlic powder

Mix above ingredients and toss.

— Rich Allison

GREAT NORTHERN BEAN SALAD

2 cans Great Northern beans, drained and rinsed.
2 stalks celery, diced
1 medium onion, diced
5 garlic cloves, smashed and diced

Microwave ½ C. sun dried tomatoes covered with water for 1½ minutes. Then drain.

1 handful fresh parsley, minced
1 handful fresh oregano, minced
Pepper to taste
½ tsp. salt
½ tbsp. Italian seasoning
1 tbsp. sugar
2 oz. white vinegar
6 oz. olive oil

Mix all together and refrigerate over night.

— Rich Allison

SWEET & SOUR BROCCOLI SALAD

Broccoli, chopped fine
Cauliflower, chopped fine
Red Onion, sliced
Carrots, shredded

Fry bacon, drain and cut into small pieces.

Mix all items above and add mayonnaise (Hellmann's).

Add salt and pepper and a little sugar if needed.

PASTA SEASHELL SALAD

½ lb. provolone cheese
¼ lb. hard salami
½ lb. pepperoni
2 green peppers
1 small onion
2 stalks celery
3 tomatoes

Dressing: (Double this mixture)

1 tsp. oregano
½ tsp. salt
1 tsp. pepper
¾ C. oil
¼ C. white vinegar

— Sandy Allison

FRENCH DRESSING

1 can tomato soup
1 tsp. dry mustard
1 C. sugar
1½ tsp. garlic salt
1½ tsp. paprika
¾ C. vegetable oil
½ C. wine vinegar
1 tsp. Worcestershire sauce

Mix all together and serve on salads.

In memory of
— Olive Wentz

BROCCOLI SALAD

2 bunches broccoli, chopped
10 slices bacon, crumbled
½ C. onion, diced
1 C. mayonnaise
½ C. sugar
2 tbsp. vinegar

Mix well. Refrigerate.

— Sandy Allison

BLACK BEAN FIESTA SALAD

Ingredients:

1 (15 oz.) can black beans, drained
2 large ears corn cooked and kernels removed
from cob.
½ C. red onion, finely chopped
1 avocado, chopped
2-3 jalapeno peppers, minced (remove seeds and
membrane for less heat)
1 C. fresh cilantro, coarsely chopped
1½ C. cherry tomatoes or 1 large tomato chopped
¼ C. olive oil
Juice of 1 lime
1½ tsp. cumin powder
1 tsp. kosher salt
½ tsp. fresh ground black pepper
1 C. crumbled feta cheese*

Combine all ingredients in a large bowl and mix
thoroughly. Best made at least 1 hour ahead of
serving so that flavors can blend.

*You can substitute fresh mozzarella for the feta
cheese.

— Rich Allison

STEAK & CHICKEN SALADS

Take a rib eye steak and several pieces of boneless
chicken breasts and sprinkle well with granulated
garlic powder, seasoning salt and fresh ground
black pepper. Then pour Kraft Zesty Italian
dressing over them. Turn the pieces several times
and let marinate for approximately 30 minutes.

Cook on grill until desired doneness. Cut into bite
size pieces to put on your favorite salad greens
such as head lettuce, celery, carrots, onions,
cucumbers, tomatoes, green and red peppers. Top
with croutons, steak and chicken, crumbled bleu
cheese, and French fries if desired. Top with your
favorite dressing.

— Rich Allison

ORIENTAL BROCCOLI SALAD

Salad:

2 bunches broccoli, washed and cut
1 bunch romaine lettuce, washed and cut
2 packs Ramen oriental flavored noodles
½ C. margarine
½ C. sunflower seeds
¾ C. slivered almonds

Sauté the seeds, almonds and broken up noodles
(no seasoning) in the margarine until lightly
browned. Mix with the broccoli and lettuce.

Sauce:

1 packet of seasoning from noodles
1 C. light virgin olive oil
1 C. sugar
½ C. apple cider vinegar
1 tbsp. soy sauce
½ tsp. salt

Shake very well before pouring over salad. Do not
pour on salad until ready to serve.

— Pam Bowser Knisely

SALADS

GARLIC ITALIAN SALAD

Shred lettuce that is very dry in a bowl. Let the lettuce set at room temperature for at least ½ hour.

Add:

Sliced cucumbers and coarsely chopped tomatoes.

In a measuring cup, place 2 oz. red wine vinegar and 8 oz. of Crisco oil.

Immediately prior to serving, put 1 diced garlic clove per person in the lettuce mixture.

Season heavily with regular salt. Do not use salt substitute.

Pour enough oil and vinegar mixture over to cover the lettuce mixture well.

Toss and serve.

— Rich Allison

ITALIAN SALAD DRESSING

In a quart jar, mix the following:

8 oz. cider vinegar
½ tbsp. oregano
½ tbsp. basil
2 tbsp. garlic powder
½ tbsp. seasoning salt
½ tbsp. coarsely ground pepper
½ tbsp. Italian seasoning
½ tbsp. salt

Fill quart jar to top with Crisco oil.

Shake well before serving because dressing will separate quickly.

Serve over salad greens

— Rich Allison

STRAWBERRY SPINACH SALAD

Dressing:

1 C. vegetable oil
¾ C. sugar
⅓ C. white vinegar
2 tbsp. onion, minced
1 tsp. salt
1½ tsp. poppy seeds

Combine first 6 ingredients in blender, low speed for 30 seconds. Stir in poppy seeds. Chill dressing. Shake well before using.

Almond Mixture:

1 stick butter, melted
½ C. sugar
1 C. slivered almonds

Cook until lightly browned. Spoon onto waxed paper sprayed with Pam. Cool and break up.

2 bags baby spinach
1 med. red onion, thinly sliced
1 container strawberries* sliced
Add almonds and dressing. Stir well.

*May substitute red raspberries for strawberries.

— Jane Comas

BROCCOLI SALAD

2 bunches broccoli
1 head cauliflower

Chop broccoli and cauliflower into small pieces.

Add:

8 oz. shredded sharp cheddar cheese and Hormel Bacon bits.

Take 1 package Hidden Valley Ranch dressing and mix according to directions on package.

Pour dressing over mixture.

— Pam Bowser Knisely

HOT CABBAGE SLAW

Shred cabbage and place in a bowl.

In another bowl mix the following:

2 C. mayonnaise
3 oz. milk
4 tbsp. vinegar
¾ C. sugar
Salt and pepper to taste
Wire whisk this mixture.

Fry small pieces of bacon in a skillet. When bacon is almost crisp, sprinkle 2 tbsp. flour in skillet and lightly brown. Then add mayonnaise mixture to skillet and heat until it almost comes to a boil.

Pour hot mixture over shredded cabbage.

> In memory of
> — Grace Allison

BALSAMIC VINAIGRETTE

4 oz. Balsamic vinegar
4 oz. olive oil
1 tbsp. granulated garlic
½ tbsp. kosher salt
1 tsp. ground black pepper
½ tbsp. Italian seasoning
½ tbsp. oregano
½ tbsp. basil
2 tbsp. brown sugar

Wire whisk and microwave for 1 minute. Whisk and serve over salad.

Serves 2-3 people.

> — Rich Allison

CABBAGE SLAW

1 head cabbage, grated
2 carrots, grated
1 green pepper, cut fine
1 red pepper, cut fine
1 tsp. salt

Let set one hour and squeeze out juice.

In another bowl mix:

1 C. vinegar
2 C. sugar
½ C. water
1 tbsp. celery seed
1 tbsp. dry mustard

Pour vinegar mixture over cabbage and serve as a salad.

> In memory of
> — Grace Allison

This was a Pennsylvania Dutch tradition with the sweet and sour mix. We found a dish similar to this in Salzberg, Austria next to the German border near Munich, Germany with caraway seed in it.

LAYER SALAD

Layer in a small oblong baking dish:

1 head lettuce, small pieces
1 onion, sliced thin
1 box frozen peas, uncooked
1 C. celery, chopped
3 hard boiled eggs, chopped

Mix 1 pt. salad dressing with 2 tbsp. sugar and spread over mixture.

Sprinkle 1½ C. grated cheese and ¼ C. bacon bits over top. Refrigerate overnight.

> In memory of
> — Grace Allison

SALADS

CREAMY CUCUMBER SALAD

Place sliced cucumber and sliced onions in a bowl. Add 1½ tsp. salt and set aside for ½ hour. Cucumbers and onions will draw water. Drain off water.

Mix:

1 C. cream
3 oz. milk
½ C. sugar
2 tbsp. vinegar

Salt and pepper to taste.

In memory of
— Grace Allison

POTATO SALAD

Cook potatoes until soft. Peel and dice after cooking. Add the following to the potatoes:

Chopped celery
Sliced olives
Chopped onion
Chopped hard boiled eggs

Dressing:

½ C. sugar
3-4 tbsp. flour
2 eggs
2 tbsp. Miracle Whip
3 tsp. French's Yellow Mustard
Canned milk

Mix sugar, flour and eggs. Put on stove over low heat, stir and add water to thin. Then bring to a boil to thicken mixture.

Let mixture cool, add Miracle Whip and mustard, then add enough canned milk to thin mixture to pouring consistency.

Pour over potato mixture. Season with salt and pepper and sprinkle paprika over top.

In memory of
— Leota Noffsker

BEAN SALAD

Dressing:

½ C. oil
1 tsp. salt
Pepper to taste
⅔ C. dark vinegar
¾ C. sugar
½ tsp. Worcestershire sauce
Garlic salt to taste

Heat mixture until sugar melts. Cool.

Take:

1 can green beans
1 can yellow beans
1 can kidney beans
1 can garbanzo beans
1 green pepper, chopped
1 onion, chopped
1 C. celery, chopped

Drain beans and mix all together and let stand overnight.

In memory of
— Maxine Schultz

GREEK LEMON DRESSING

Lemon juice
Olive oil
¾ tbsp. garlic powder
½ tbsp. oregano
1 tsp. salt
½ tsp. pepper

— Rich Allison

MARINATED CAULIFLOWER SALAD

1⅓ C. salad oil
⅔ C. white vinegar
2 tbsp. sugar
½ tsp. salt
½ tsp. oregano leaves
½ tsp. basil
½ tsp. garlic salt

1 lg. head cauliflower, sliced
1 can pitted ripe olives, drained and sliced
1 med. green pepper, chopped

Early in the day, mix first seven ingredients for dressing and stir in cauliflower. Cover and refrigerate at least two hours or longer.

To serve:

Add olives and green pepper to cauliflower. Mix well.

— Bonnie Schultz

COLD CREAM LETTUCE

1 C. salad dressing
¼ C. sugar
½ C. milk or cream
Hard boiled eggs

Mix dressing.

Take leaf lettuce, wash and drain. Pour dressing over lettuce and top with sliced hard boiled eggs.

In memory of
— Grace Allison

We had a dish very similar to this at Sandy's cousin, Inge's house in Herbrechtingen, Germany. Again this shows our Pennsylvania Dutch origins.

TOMATO AND ONION SALAD

Cut up tomatoes and onion. Season with salt and pepper. Sprinkle with sugar and let the mixture draw juice.

Serve as a salad.

In memory of
— Maxine Schultz

SWEET/SOUR HOT VINEGAR DRESSING FOR LETTUCE

Fry small pieces of bacon until crisp. Do not drain off grease. Cool. Sprinkle approximately 1½ tbsp. flour into skillet stirring to lightly brown.

Mix:
½ C. vinegar
2 egg yolks
1 C. water
Sugar to taste, about ½ C.

Mix together and put in skillet and bring to a boil – stirring constantly. Mixture will thicken over medium heat.

Pour mixture over cut-up lettuce or endive and mix well.

This can be served with potatoes cooked in salt water and browned in a skillet.

Lettuce mixture must be served immediately or it will wilt.

In memory of
— Esther Burket &
Donna Burket

This hot bacon dressing does not have cream in it, but has the distinctive flavors of sweet and sour which is so predominant in Pennsylvania Dutch cooking.

SALADS

CABBAGE SALAD

TOSS:

1 bag Ramen Chicken Noodles (do not cook, break up)
½ C. slivered almonds, toasted
2 tsp. sesame seed
½ head cabbage, cut in little pieces
1 onion, chopped

DRESSING:

3 tbsp. vinegar
2 tbsp. sugar
½ C. oil
½ pkg. chicken flavor
½ tsp. each, salt and pepper
1 tsp. accent

Mix and pour over just before serving.

— Hope Kephart

BROCCOLI SALAD

½ lb. bacon, fried and drained
½ C. cheddar cheese, cubed
1 med. red onion, diced
1 head broccoli flowerets

Mix Sauce:

¼ C. sugar
½ C. Miracle Whip
1 tsp. vinegar

Mix all together. Do not put dressing on until ready to eat.

— Sally Weyant

This is a very good, flavorful salad. Prepare ahead of time, but put the dressing on at the last minute.

CRANBERRY SALAD

1 lb. cranberries, ground
1 C. sugar
2 oranges, ground
5 apples, ground
1 can crushed pineapple
2 small or 1 large Jello
1 C. hot water

Dissolve Jello in water and pour over ground fruit. Add nuts.

In memory of
— Donna Burket

FRUIT SALAD

1 qt. canned peaches and juice
1 qt. canned pears and juice
1 can pineapple cubes and juice
Sliced bananas
Sliced strawberries
Red seedless grapes, halved
Sliced kiwi fruit
Maraschino cherries
Fruit Fresh, sprinkle and stirred

Put in gallon jar. Will keep for one week.

— Allison Family

We start with home canned peaches and pears, but you can use store bought. Add whatever fruits are in season or whatever you like. Mix all, put in a gallon jar and refrigerate. It's easy to serve from the jar with a ladle dipper. This is another family tradition at picnics, parties and holidays.

WARM BACON DRESSING WITH LETTUCE GERMAN STYLE

½ lb. bacon cut into ½" pieces. Cook or fry in a skillet until pieces are crisp.

Keep ⅓ of bacon grease in skillet and discard the remainder.

½ C. sugar
2 tbsp. flour
½ C. vinegar
2 large eggs
2 C. chicken broth (can use 2 bouillon cubes dissolved in 2 C. water).

Combine sugar and flour in a small bowl. Gradually whisk in vinegar, then egg. Whisk in broth.

Take vinegar mixture and whisk in skillet and stir until dressing comes to a simmer and thickens. Add bacon. Season dressing with pepper. No salt is needed because of the bacon and chicken broth.

Let mixture cool to just warm and put dressing over lettuce. Do not put a hot dressing mixture on the lettuce or the lettuce will wilt. Toss well. You can use head lettuce or a mixture of salad greens or endive.

Dressing will be enough for 10 salads.

— Rich & Sandy Allison

ITALIAN SALAD DRESSING "TOO"

2 oz. red wine vinegar
1 tbsp. Italian seasoning
1 tsp. kosher salt
½ tsp. black pepper
8 garlic cloves
½ tsp. sugar

Emulsify using a hand emulsifier or a blender.

Drizzle in slowly 6 oz. olive oil

Note: Emulsify or blend lightly or mixture will turn into mayonnaise.

Serve with your favorite salad greens. Toss lightly. Dressing makes four servings.

— Rich Allison

CHOPPED SALAD WITH A GARLIC VINAIGRETTE DRESSSING

Note: All ingredients must be completely chilled. Prepare in advance.

Dressing:

1 oz. rice wine vinegar
1 oz. apple cider vinegar
3 oz. olive oil
1 garlic clove, minced
1 tsp. salt
¼ tsp. black pepper
1 tsp. sugar

Mix well, wire whisk and chill in advance.

Salad – Chop enough for 2 people:

Head lettuce
Carrots
Cucumbers
Celery
Red Peppers
Corn kernels
Heart of Palm
Red Onion
Tomatoes

Chop all ingredients into bite size pieces and chill.

When ready to serve, take salad mixture and toss with dressing. Mix well. Top with Gorgonzola cheese and serve.

— Rich & Sandy Allison

PEA SALAD

1 can peas, drained
1 onion, chopped
Sharp cheese, chopped
Sweet pickles, chopped
2 hard boiled eggs, chopped

Mix the above with Hellmann's Mayonnaise.

In memory of
— Louise Hidlebaugh

MACARONI SALAD

2 C. macaroni in salted water for 12 minutes, drain and rinse
2 eggs, hardboiled
1 stalk celery, finely diced
1 sm. onion, diced

In separate bowl, mix:

1½ C. Miracle Whip
1 tbsp. vinegar
⅓ C. milk
½ C. sugar
Pepper to taste
Seasoning salt to taste

Wire whisk all together. Add yellow food coloring.

Take macaroni, celery, onion, hard boiled eggs and add to mixture and mix well. Refrigerate.

— Rich Allison

This is as close as we can get to Grace Allison's macaroni salad recipe. She never wrote it down, but we have duplicated it fairly well.

LINGUINI SALAD

1 lb. linguini, cooked and drained

Equal amounts of:

1 sm. green pepper, chopped
1 sm. onion, chopped
½ stalk celery, chopped

8 oz. bottle Kraft Zesty Italian Dressing – no substitute.

1 jar McCormick Salad Supreme – no substitute.

Mix all together and let set overnight to marinate in the refrigerator.

— Tammy Claycomb

POTATO SALAD

Dressing:

1 can Eagle Brand Milk
½ C. vinegar
½ C. salad oil
2 egg yolks
1 tsp. salt
3-4 tbsp. French's Yellow Mustard

Place ingredients in a quart jar and shake well. Chill.

Cook diced potatoes until you can stick a fork in them, but not too soft.

Add dressing and parsley flakes, chopped celery and celery seed. Season with salt and pepper to taste.

In memory of
— Louis Hidlebaugh

SAUERKRAUT SALAD

1 (2 lb.) can sauerkraut
2 C. celery, chopped
1 C. green pepper, chopped
1 C. onion, chopped

¼ C. vinegar
½ C. oil
1 C. sugar

Heat vinegar, oil and sugar until sugar is dissolved. Pour over sauerkraut mixture.

In memory of
— Donna Burket

NO-REFRIGERATION SALAD DRESSING

2 C. oil
½ C. ReaLemon
1 C. ketchup
½ C. vinegar
Dash dry mustard
1-2 tsp. celery seed

Add artificial sweetener to taste.

Mix ingredients in a quart jar. Does not need to be refrigerated.

— Ann Kimble

FRENCH & BLEU CHEESE DRESSING

1 C. Bleu Cheese Dressing
1 C. Mullen's French Dressing

Mix the above all together. A variation of the above amounts can be done according to taste (which one you prefer more than the other).

— Rich & Sandy Allison

BROCCOLI SALAD

2 heads fresh broccoli, chopped small
1 lb. bacon, fried and crumbled
8 oz. pkg. shredded sharp cheddar
1 sm. red onion, chopped

Dressing:
1 C. mayonnaise
½ C. sugar
1 tbsp. red wine vinegar or cider vinegar

Mix the dressing together and let stand at least for 2 hours.

Combine salad ingredients in large bowl. Mix dressing into broccoli just before serving.

Note: I use a chopper to cut the broccoli, it goes faster than chopping by hand.

— Pat Holland

This French and Bleu Cheese dressing is always a hit on any salad. Also, can be used for a vegetable dip.

This recipe is a knockoff from a local restaurant back in Claysburg where they have good down home cooking.

Mullen's French dressing is really what is needed to make this, and it is sometimes difficult to find.

CHEESE TIPS

Cream and salt give cheeses their flavors so it's not surprising that cheeses are usually fairly high in fat and sodium.

Whole milk cheeses tend to have 45 percent to 55 percent butterfat and 1 percent to 2 percent sodium.

Triple cream cheeses can have as much as 75 percent butterfat content.

Most cheeses should be stored in the refrigerator but served at room temperature.

Cheeses are easier to grate when cold from the refrigerator.

Because cheeses need to breathe as they are stored, experts usually do not recommend covering them in clear plastic wrap for long term storage. Wax paper is a better choice.

If firm or semi firm cheeses develop mold, just cut it off before using.

Cheeses undergo changes in texture if frozen. The changes aren't noticeable if the cheese is used in cooking.

TURKEY TIPS

The Top 3 Most Asked Turkey Questions

How Much Should I Buy Per Serving?

Whole Turkey:	1 to 1½ lbs.
Turkey Breast:	¾ lb.
Boneless Turkey:	½ lb.
Boneless Turkey Breast:	½ lb.

How Do I Safely Thaw It?

In Refrigerator: Allow 24 hours per 5 pounds of turkey. **In Cold Water:** Change water every 30 minutes so water doesn't get too cold; minimum thawing time will be half the turkey's weight plus 1 hour. (**Example:** a 16 pound turkey will take about 9 hours.) **Note:** Leave turkey in original packaging for thawing.

How Long Do I Cook It & What Temperature?

The temperature should be 325°. The internal temperature of the turkey should be 180° when completely cooked. Below are some guidelines.

	Unstuffed	Stuffed
8-12 lbs.	2¾ to 3 hrs.	3 to 3½ hrs.
12-14 lbs.	3 to 3¾ hrs.	3½ to 4 hrs.
14-18 lbs.	3¾ to 4¼ hrs.	4 to 4¼ hrs.
18-20 lbs.	4¼ to 4½ hrs.	4¼ to 4¾ hrs.
20-24 lbs.	4½ to 5 hrs.	4¾ to 5¼ hrs.

SOUPS

Cooking from the Farm
to the City

The Very Best
Recipes
of
Rich & Sandy Allison
and Their
Family and Friends

SOUPS

CHICKEN CORN NOODLE RIVAL SOUP
TAILGATER'S SOUP

Start with a large soup pot and add the following:

4 stalks celery, diced
4 carrots, diced
1 onion, finely chopped
4 lg. potatoes, diced

Cover with enough water and bring to a boil.

In a separate pot, cook 4 chicken breasts and ½ tsp. salt until the chicken is cooked. Remove chicken to cool. Strain broth and add to the soup pot.

Add the following:

3 qts. water
15 chicken bouillon cubes
1½ tbsp. parsley, chopped
1½ tbsp. seasoning salt
1 tsp. pepper

After chicken has cooled, remove chicken from the bones and dice and add back to the soup.

Bring to a boil and add 1½ bags Kluski egg noodles. Cook for approximately 30 minutes until noodles are cooked.

Add 2 cans whole corn.

In a bowl, add 1 egg yolk and 1 C. flour. Stir with a fork until mixed well. Then drop into boiling soup broth small amounts the size of a pea. Continue cooking over medium heat and stirring constantly until the rivals are cooked which will be approximately 30 minutes.

Then continue cooking for several hours or place in the oven at 200° if needed for an early morning tailgate party.

Use additional seasoning salt and pepper to taste.

In memory of
— Grace Allison

This chicken noodle soup is a Penn State tailgate tradition. For the past 30 years we have served this soup at tailgates. Years ago, Grace would make this soup for the entire gang. She used to get up early to heat the soup, but through years of cooking it, she came up with the idea of placing this in the oven the night before on warm. In the morning, it was already heated and saved an hour of re-heating and gave us an extra hour of sleep.

Today we do it the same way, use the same Hot/Cold water cooler to keep the soup warm during the day. Believe it or not, this soup stays warm all day at a game and does not need re-heated.

This soup has all the ingredients of a true Pennsylvania Dutch food. It has the noodles, rivals or small dumplings or dough balls, chicken and the typical carrots, celery, onions and potatoes.

This recipe makes about three gallons. You can scale it down in size if it is for a smaller group.

We always think of Grace when we eat this soup and remember what a great cook she was.

You can cut, chop and precook the vegetables and chicken the day before. Then in a matter of 30-45 minutes, you can assemble and cook the noodles and have soup quickly.

WEDDING SOUP

Step 1:

3 chicken breasts
2 quarts water
½ tsp. salt

In a separate saucepan, bring chicken to a boil and then cook for 20 minutes. Remove chicken from stock to cool.

Set stock aside.

Step 2:

1 lb. ground beef, pork and veal or beef only
¼ C. Italian bread crumbs
½ C. grated Romano cheese
½ tsp. seasoning salt
1½ tsp. garlic powder
½ tsp. black pepper

Mix meat and other ingredients well and form into small meatballs about 1" in diameter. Place on a cookie sheet and place in oven at 325° for 20 minutes turning several times. They do not need to be totally cooked.

Step 3:

Take a 10 oz. box of frozen spinach, ¼ tsp. salt and enough water to cover. Bring to a boil until spinach is thawed and cooked, about 4 minutes after boiling.

Remove from heat and drain, pressing as much water out of spinach as possible.

Step 4:

In a large stock pan, place the following:

2 stalks celery, diced
1 medium onion, diced
5 carrots, diced
20 chicken bouillon cubes
2 quarts water

Bring to a boil. While this mixture is cooking, add the chicken broth from the chicken, but strain it as you pour it into the stockpot.

Add the meatballs draining as much grease as possible as you remove from the cookie sheet.

Add the drained spinach.

Add 1 lb. Acine di Pepe (Pastina Pasta) and continue cooking another 20 minutes.

Meanwhile remove chicken from bones when cool enough to handle, and dice into small pieces and place into stockpot.

Add ¼ tsp. black pepper to soup, but do not add salt. Add ½ tsp. yellow food coloring.

Step 5:

Take 5 eggs in a bowl and wire whisk until well blended. Add 1½ C. Romano cheese and wire whisk until smooth.

While soup is boiling, stir soup to make certain nothing is sticking to the bottom of the pan. Then pour the egg and cheese mixture into soup and do not stir for approximately 8 minutes. Then stir and break up the egg mixture into smaller pieces.

Continue simmering another 20 minutes until soup is ready to serve.

— Rich Allison

A great soup with many flavors. The unique thing about Wedding Soup is the garlic meatballs. You really don't taste the garlic in the soup, but when you bite into one of the meatballs, you definitely can taste the garlic.

For those who don't like spinach, we take part of the soup from the main pot before adding the spinach .

SOUPS

CRAB CHOWDER

In a large soup pan, place 2 tbsp. butter and 4 tbsp. olive oil.

Add:

½ large onion, diced
2 stalks celery, diced
1-2 carrots, diced
1 red pepper, diced
1 yellow pepper, diced.

Sauté in oil for 3-4 minutes. Add 3 potatoes, diced. Cook another 3-4 minutes.

Add:

2 C. chicken broth (2 C. water and 3 bouillon cubes).
Add ¼-½ C. flour
Add 1½ quarts half-and-half
1 (8 oz.) heavy cream
4 oz. cream sherry
1 lb. lump crabmeat
1 can cream corn

Season with:

1 tsp. Worcestershire sauce
Dash Tabasco
1 tsp. Old Bay
½ tsp. salt
½ tsp. pepper

Stir constantly and simmer for at least 30 minutes.

— Rich Allison
— Roger Knisely

Roger and Rich came up with this idea for Crab Chowder from many trips to the Eastern Shore of Maryland on the Chesapeake Bay. They decided they could make a better soup and save the price of expensive bowls of soup. They won the Iron Chef award in a St. Michael's, MD cookoff for this recipe!!

PASTA FAGIOLI

4 (16 oz.) cans great white northern beans
4 (15 oz.) cans diced Italian tomatoes
1 large onion, diced
4 stalks celery, diced
2 quarts water
20 beef bouillon cubes
2 tbsp. garlic powder
3 tbsp. Italian seasoning
1 tbsp. parsley
½ tbsp. seasoning salt
1 tsp. ground black pepper
½ lb. diced ham
1 pint spaghetti sauce
1 lb. digitalis pasta

Put all above in a stock pot and let simmer for at least 1 hour.

— Rich Allison

This pasta bean soup is very flavorful and always a hit.

FRENCH ONION SOUP

3 lg. onions – halved and sliced
1 stick butter
¼ C. brown sugar

Cook approximately 45 minutes on med/high until brown and caramelized.

Add 10 oz. Burgundy wine and deglaze pan.

Add:

2 (48 oz.) cans beef broth
1 tsp. salt
1 tsp. pepper
½ tsp. thyme

Bring to a boil and simmer. Put 1 piece Italian bread in bowl. Ladle soup over – cover with mozzarella cheese and microwave until cheese melts.

— Rich Allison

POTATO CHEESE SOUP

10 Medium potatoes – diced (skins on) and cooked in boiling water (enough to cover) and add salt.

Cook until medium soft.
Add 8 chicken bouillon cubes.

Add – shredded in processor:

1 onion
1 green pepper
1 red pepper
2 stalks celery
4 carrots

Add to Pot:

Dice 1 lb. bacon and microwave until almost crisp. Drain and add to pot. Dice ½ lb. smoked ham and add. Mix ¼ C. flour with ¾ C. water. Wire whisk and add to boiling mixture. Reduce heat to medium.

Then add:

2 lb. Velveeta Cheese
3 tbsp. cooking sherry
¼ tsp. white pepper
Simmer on low.

— Rich Allison

COLD ZUCCHINI SOUP

4 C. cut zucchini
1 C. onions
1 tbsp. dried dill
1 C. chicken broth
Salt and Pepper

Add Later: ¾ C. sour cream or milk

Peel zucchini leaving about ½ of the green on (for health and color). Cook all until tender. Place in blender with sour cream until smooth.

Chill and serve in chilled bowls. Chilled soup spoons add a special touch!

— Thelma Absher

RICH'S MINESTRONE SOUP

Take a 12 quart pot and add the following:

4 stalks celery, coarsely chopped
4 carrots, coarsely sliced
1 lg. onion, coarsely chopped
12 beef bouillon cubes
2 lg. tomatoes, coarsely chopped
1 can cannellini beans, rinsed and drained

Add water to fill pot half full. Bring to a boil and continue cooking.

In a separate skillet with a small amount of oil, add 1 lb. ground meat and season with pepper, garlic powder and seasoning salt. Fry until pink is gone. Drain and place ground meat into the pot with other ingredients.

Add following to pot:

1 qt. spaghetti or marinara sauce

Season with:

1½ tbsp. oregano
1½ tbsp. basil
1½ tbsp. parsley, chopped
2 tbsp. garlic powder
1 tbsp. seasoning salt
1 tsp. pepper
1 tsp. salt
1 tbsp. Italian seasoning

Add 1 lb. pasta – any type, and continue cooking until pasta is done – approximately 30 minutes. Add additional seasonings if necessary.

Serve with Romano cheese sprinkled on top of the bowl of soup and with Italian bread.

If you aren't going to serve immediately pre-cook pasta and add to broth later, so all of your broth isn't absorbed by the pasta.

— Rich Allison

SOUPS

WHITE HOT CHILI

2 tbsp. vegetable oil
1 med. onion, chopped
4 stalks celery, chopped
1 tsp. ground cumin
2 cloves garlic, crushed
2 chicken breasts, bone and cut into 1" pieces
1 (15 oz.) can white kidney beans
(cannellini) drained
1 (15 oz.) can whole kernel corn, drained
2 (6 oz.) cans chopped mild green chilies
1 (15 oz.) can chicken broth
3 tbsp. flour
½ C. sugar
Hot pepper sauce to taste

Heat vegetable oil in skillet. Sauté onions, celery, garlic and cumin until soft.

Combine this mixture with chicken, beans, corn, chilies and broth in a large pot.

Cook on low heat for about ½ hour or until chicken is tender. Add sugar and mix flour with a C. of broth and put in chili mixture.

Stir in pepper sauce to taste. Serve over cooked rice. Yields 6-8 main dish servings.

— Sandy Allison

CHICKEN OR BEEF PASTINA SOUP

Cook beef or chicken in water with salt until you have a broth. Strain broth. Add diced celery, carrots and onions. Chop up finely pieces of chicken or beef and add to the broth.

Separately cook ½ C. or more of pastina until done. Drain and add to the soup. Season to taste.

In memory of
— Margie Binotto

MANHATTAN STYLE CLAM CHOWDER

3 slices bacon, diced
1 tsp. dried thyme
1 C. onions, sliced
3 C. pared potatoes, cubed
½ C. celery, diced
5 C. hot water
2 tsp. salt
⅛ tsp. pepper
1 (3½ C.) 2 lb. can tomatoes
1½ C. pared carrots, diced
3 C. clam liquid
2 dz. hard shell clams, shucked
1 tbsp. parsley, chopped
½ tsp. oregano, dried

In deep kettle sauté bacon until crisp. Stir in 1 tsp. thyme and onions. Cook, stirring occasionally until tender. Add potatoes, celery, water, salt and pepper. Cover and simmer 5 minutes.

Add tomatoes, carrots, and clam liquid. Simmer uncovered over very low heat for 1 hour.

Cut clams into small pieces. Add clams, parsley and ½ tsp. thyme to soup. Bring to a boil and simmer uncovered for 10 minutes. Add salt to taste. Add oregano to soup when serving.

In memory of
— Maxine Schultz

Margie Binotto, a sweet little Italian lady from the south hills of Pittsburgh taught us so much about Italian cooking including wedding soup, brasciole, homemade pasta, salads, meatballs, etc. Her Italian cooking was superb. Her smile and generosity will always be remembered. She was also known as the "corn lady" along Route 19 in Canonsburg where she and her husband, Phillip sold corn that helped put four sons through college and whom are now quite successful.

NEW ENGLAND CLAM CHOWDER

Start with a very large soup pot:

1 qt. potatoes, diced
1 pt. carrots, diced
1 pt. celery, diced
1 C. onions, diced

Cook above in hot water (potatoes will not get mushy in hot water). Cook until they start becoming soft.

While vegetables are cooking, in a skillet, melt 1 stick of margarine, add salt and pepper to taste and sauté a box of fresh mushrooms until slightly soft.

In another skillet fry one pound of diced bacon. Drain grease.

Put margarine, mushrooms and bacon in with vegetables,

Add ½ gallon of canned chicken broth, ½ gallon milk and one quart of minced clams. Add another quart of minced clams for additional flavor.

Before mixture comes to a boil, mix ½ C. flour with water to make a thickening for the soup and add to the soup mixture. Bring to a boil to thicken.

Season to taste with seasoning salt, pepper and parsley. Cook on low heat for 1-2 hours.

Will serve a minimum of 15 people.

— Rich Allison

This hearty clam chowder is rich in bacon flavor as well as clams.

CRAB & ASPARAGUS CHOWDER

2 tbsp. butter
4 tbsp. olive oil

Put above in pan and add:

½ large onion, diced
2 stalks celery, diced
1-2 carrots, diced
1 red pepper, diced
1 yellow pepper, diced

Sauté in oil for 3-4 minutes.

Add 3 potatoes, diced
Cook another 3-4 minutes

Add:

2 C. chicken broth (2 C. water and 3 bouillon cubes)
1 lb. asparagus, chopped
½ C. flour
1½ qt. half and half
1 (8 oz.) heavy whipping cream
4 oz. cream sherry
1 lb. lump crab meat

Season with:

1 tsp. Worcestershire sauce
Dash Tabasco
1 tsp. old bay
½ tsp. salt
½ tsp. pepper

Stir constantly. Simmer for at least 30 minutes.

— Rich Allison
— Roger Knisely

This is another version of crab chowder that Roger and Rich came up with at the Bay. It was an early spring day when fresh asparagus was readily available and relatively inexpensive. It added great flavor to the soup.

SOUPS

TOMATO CREAM BASIL SOUP

2 (10¾ oz.) cans Campbell's Classic Tomato Soup
1 (8oz.) container heavy cream – pour in can and fill to top with milk
1 additional can of milk

Heat the above in saucepan.

In Skillet:

2 tbsp. olive oil
¼ onion, diced
Sauté until light brown.

Add to Soup:

Minced fresh basil, parsley, chives, salt and pepper. Cook 1 hour.

Serve with croutons (Flavor better 2ⁿᵈ day)!

— Rich Allison

TORTILLA SOUP

2 lb. Ground beef (lean)
1 onion, chopped
1 bell pepper, chopped
(Brown meat, onion and pepper)

Add:

1 pkg. Hidden Valley ranch dressing mix or dip mix.
1 pkg. taco seasoning

Add following cans (do not drain juice):

1 (32 oz.) can crushed tomatoes
2 (15 oz.) cans kidney beans
1 (14 oz.) can tomato sauce
2 cans water
1 (15 oz.) can pinto beans w/jalapenos
1 (10 oz.) can Rotel tomatoes w/chilies
2 (15 oz.) cans whole kernel corn

Bring to boil and simmer at least 1 hour.

To Serve:

Crush tortilla chips in bowls, spoon soup into bowl, then top with sour cream and cheese.

— Rich Allison

This tomato cream soup is ready to eat in 5 minutes but simmering for an hour makes it better. Keeping for the second day makes it even better. If you don't have fresh herbs, add dried herbs. It will still have good flavor.

CHEESEBURGER SOUP

½ lb. ground beef
¾ C. onion, chopped
¾ C. carrots, shredded
1 tsp. dried basil
1 tsp. dried parsley flakes
4 tbsp. butter or margarine (divided)
3 C. chicken broth
4 C. diced peeled potatoes (1¾ pounds)
¼ C. all purpose flour
8 oz. processed American cheese (cubed 2 C.)
1½ C. milk
¾ tsp. salt
¼ to ½ tsp. pepper
⅓ C. sour cream

In a 3 qt. saucepan brown beef, drain and set aside. In same saucepan sauté onion, carrots, celery, basil and parsley in 1 tbsp. butter until vegetables are tender, about 10 minutes. Add broth, potatoes and beef, bring to a boil. Reduce heat, cover and simmer for 10-12 minutes or until potatoes are tender. Meanwhile, in a small skillet, melt remaining butter. Add flour, cook and stir for 3-5 minutes or until bubbly. Add to soup, bring to a boil. Cook and stir for 2 minutes. Reduce heat to low, add cheese, milk, salt and pepper. Cook and stir until cheese melts. Remove from the heat, blend in sour cream.

Yield: 8 Servings (2¼ quarts).

— Cindy Marks

BLACK BEAN SOUP WITH HAM, SAUSAGE & BACON

Soak 2 lb. black beans overnight in water. Make certain that beans are completely covered.

The next day:

Start with a 12 qt. soup pot and add the following:

1 lb. cubed ham and a hambone if available. Fill pot ½ full of water. Begin cooking.

Take 1 lb. Italian link sausage and cut into 1" pieces. In a separate skillet with a small amount of oil, brown the sausage until cooked. Add to the soup pot.

Add:

½ lb. bacon cut into 1" pieces
3 stalks celery, diced
3 carrots, diced
1 lg. onion, diced
2 (16 oz.) cans whole Italian tomatoes
1 tbsp. seasoning salt
1½ tbsp. parsley, chopped
1½ tbsp. garlic powder
1 tbsp. ground cumin
1 tsp. oregano
1 tsp. basil

Add:

2 lb. black beans and continue cooking for 3-4 hours.

Serve in bowls with a heaping teaspoon of sour cream on top with cornbread.

— Rich Allison

CHEESE SOUP

5 slices bacon
½ C. carrots, grated
½ C. celery, chopped fine
½ C. green pepper, chopped fine
¼ C. flour
4 C. chicken broth
3+ C. Velveeta Cheese, shredded
2 C. milk
2 tbsp. dry sherry

In a large saucepan cook bacon until crisp. Drain on a paper towel and crumble.

Sauté carrot, celery and green pepper in bacon drippings on low heat until tender, but still crisp – don't brown.

Blend flour, then gradually add broth. Cover over low heat until mixture thickens and boils.

Cook for 5 minutes. Add cheese and stir until cheese is melted. Stir in milk and sherry. Simmer 10 minutes. Season to taste with pepper.

Serve garnished with crumbled bacon and parsley. Makes two quarts.

— Beth Martin Garafalo

If you like black beans, then you will probably like this soup. It has ham, bacon and sausage for extra flavor. If you want it hotter, you can add jalapeno peppers, but we recommend that you serve them on the side with sour cream in case some people don't like it hot. Like all soups, this develops more flavor the longer it cooks.

SOUPS

ROASTED GARLIC AND WHITE CHEDDAR SOUP

2 to 3 lg. heads garlic
½ C. (1 stick) butter, melted
2 C. leeks, chopped, white parts only
(3 to 4 large leeks)
3 lb. medium all-purpose potatoes, peel and cut into ½" cubes (about 9-10 potatoes)
6 C. ready-to-serve chicken broth
½ tsp. salt
¼ tsp. coarsely ground black pepper
2 C. milk
1½ C. (6 oz.) shredded white cheddar cheese, divided
Cooked shrimp, thinly sliced, cooked smoked sausage, strips of prosciutto or cooked ham (optional).
Chopped fresh chives or parsley

Preheat oven to 400°. Separate heads of garlic into cloves and peel off papery skin. Place garlic cloves in medium ovenproof ramekin, soufflé dish or baking dish. Pour butter over garlic; cover tightly with a double thickness of aluminum foil. Place on center rack in oven and bake 35 to 40 minutes or until garlic is very tender. Remove garlic with slotted spoon, reserving butter.

In large saucepan or Dutch oven, heat 3 tbsp. reserved butter over medium-high heat until hot.* Add leeks and cook, stirring constantly until leeks are softened, about 2 minutes. Add potatoes and cook 2 minutes more. Add chicken broth, salt and pepper; bring to a boil. Reduce heat and simmer uncovered 25 to 30 minutes or until potatoes are tender. Remove from heat, add roasted garlic.

Place half of soup in blender or food processor container; blend until smooth. Repeat with remaining soup. Return soup to saucepan and place over low heat. Add milk and heat, stirring occasionally, until soup is hot. Add 1 C. cheese, ½ C. at a time, and heat 3 to 5 minutes or until cheese is melted, stirring constantly.** If desired, stir in shrimp, sausage, prosciutto or ham. Garnish each serving with chopped chives and remaining ½ C. cheese. Serve immediately.

*Reserve remaining garlic butter for another use.

** If desired, soup can be prepared to this point, covered and refrigerated up to 2 days.

WHITE CHILI

4 cans great northern beans, undrained
4 C. cooked chicken breasts, chopped (6 split breasts)
2 tbsp. olive oil
2 med. onions, chopped
4 cloves garlic, minced
2 (4 oz.) cans green chilies, chopped
2 tsp. ground cumin
½ tsp. dried oregano
¼ tsp. cayenne pepper

3 C. Monterey Jack cheese (12 oz. grated)
12 oz. sour cream
6 C. chicken broth, or canned broth
12 oz. hot pepper cheese

Place chicken in a heavy large pot. Add enough cold water to cover and bring to a simmer and cook until tender; about 15 minutes. Drain and cool. Remove skin and cut chicken into cubes.

Heat oil in heavy large pot over medium heat. Add onions and sauté until translucent; about 10 minutes. Stir in garlic, chilies, cumin, oregano and cayenne pepper and sauté for 2 minutes. Add beans, chicken broth and chicken. Bring to a boil, simmer for 30 minutes. Add cheese to soup and cook until melted. Season to taste with salt and pepper. Add sour cream.

— Hope Kephart

TWO ALARM CHILI

Cook 2 lb. pinto beans until soft with 2 lb. cured ham and hambone if available. Cook until only a small amount of water is remaining.

Separately fry 2-3 lb. of lean ground beef, 1 large chopped onion and 1 large chopped green pepper until the pink is gone from the meat.

Add hamburger to the pinto beans. Also, add approximately 2 quarts of whole canned tomatoes and enough of the juice to thin the chili to consistency desired. Add 2 pkgs. of Wick Fowler's Two Alarm Chili kit, but do not use all the cayenne pepper and salt packets.

Add cumin and garlic powder to taste. Remove the seeds form 1-2 jalapeno peppers and dice them up. Add to the chili. Slow cook until ready to serve. Season as needed.

In memory of
— Louise Hidlebaugh

HAM & BEANS COOKED IN AN IRON KETTLE

Cook one ham and cut up the day before you plan to make your beans.

Soak 12 lb. of Great Northern beans the evening before you plan to cook them.

In the morning, drain the beans. Then put the beans, cut up ham and broth in the kettle along with the hambone. Put enough water in kettle to cover the bean mixture.

Cook until soft and add 3 lb. bacon diced up. Cook beans until they are soft.

Season with seasoning salt and pepper.

Cook over a slow fire for an entire day for the best flavor.

— Rich Allison

LASAGNA SOUP

1 lb. Italian sausage
2 C. onions, chopped
2 C. mushrooms, sliced
2 tbsp. fresh garlic, minced
4 C. chicken broth
1 (14½ oz.) can Italian style stewed tomatoes
1 (10¾ oz.) can tomato sauce
1 C. mafalda (little lasagnas) pasta
2 C. fresh spinach, chopped (frozen can be used)
¼ C. Parmesan cheese, shredded
Fresh mozzarella or provolone cheese

Brown sausage in a large saucepan. Add onions, sauté 3 minutes. Stir in mushrooms and garlic, sauté another 3 minutes. Add broth, stewing tomatoes and tomato sauce and bring to a boil.

Drop in pasta and simmer about 10 minutes. Stir in spinach and Parmesan cheese. Cook till spinach has wilted. Season to taste with salt and pepper.

Place cubed mozzarella cheese in to serving bowl and top with soup.

— Chris Wilkins

RECIPE FOR A HAPPY HOME

4 C. Love
5 tsp. Hope
2 C. Loyalty
2 tbsp. Tenderness
3 C. Forgiveness
4 qt. Faith
1 C. Friendship
1 Barrel of Laughter

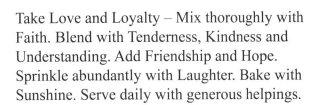

Take Love and Loyalty – Mix thoroughly with Faith. Blend with Tenderness, Kindness and Understanding. Add Friendship and Hope. Sprinkle abundantly with Laughter. Bake with Sunshine. Serve daily with generous helpings.

INSTANT SUPPER

1 Hectic day
A pinch of a headache
2 Tired feet
1 Frantic cook
1 Hungry spouse
Several starving children

Combine ingredients in any order desired. Drive to nearest grocery store. At frozen food aisle, select one T.V. dinner per person. Rush home and cook in oven according to directions on package. Serve while hot.

RECIPE FOR HAPPINESS

1 C. Good Thoughts
3 C. Forgiveness
1 C. Kind Deeds
1 C. Consideration for Others
2 C. Well Beaten Thoughts
2 C. Sacrifice for Others

Mix thoroughly and add Tears of Joy, Sorrow and Sympathy. Fold in 4 C. of Prayer and Faith to lighten all the other ingredients and raise texture to great heights of character. After flowering this into daily life, bake well with Human Kindness. Serve with a Smile anytime and it will satisfy the hunger of starved souls.

PARENTING SURVIVAL KIT

Using these simple items, collected in fun, should help you with the most difficult job in the universe…that of being a parent!

Candy Kiss – To remind you of the importance of a hug and kiss.

Button – To remind you to button your lip and listen.

Toothpick – To help you "pick out" the positive qualities in your children.

Safety Pin – To help hold you together in stressful situations.

Band-Aid – To help heal all of your children's hurts (feelings included).

Eraser – To remind you to erase all mistakes and start over again.

Flower – To remind you to take time to relax, reflect on yesterday, anticipate tomorrow and live today!

Rope – To remind you that if you get to the end of your rope, just tie a knot and hang on! This too will pass.

SEAFOOD

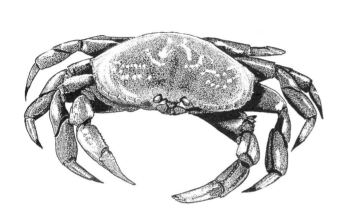

Cooking from the Farm
to the City

The Very Best

Recipes

of

Rich & Sandy Allison

and Their

Family and Friends

SEAFOOD

LOW COUNTRY BOIL

3 sm. red potatoes, per person
3 (2") pcs. kielbasa, per person
1½ ears of corn, per person, cut in half
5 lg. shrimp, shelled and de-veined, per person

In a large pot, boil water, add 1 box crab boil seasoning.

Add new potatoes and boil about 10 minutes. Do not overcook.

Add kielbasa and corn at the same time and cook another 10 minutes.

Add shrimp last and cook approximately 5 minutes until pink and done.

Drain from pot and serve with lemon wedges and cocktail sauce.

Serve with cornbread.

Instead of using shrimp you can substitute chicken.

— From Myrtle Beach Vacations

CRABMEAT HOEZEL

¼ C. olive oil
¾ C. light vegetable oil
¼ C. tarragon vinegar
¾ C. cider vinegar
2 tsp. salt
3 tsp. crushed black peppercorns

Mix well and pour over crabmeat for an appetizer.

— Rich Allison

This classic recipe comes from a business club in Pittsburgh. It is outstanding!!

CRABCAKES

2 lb. lump crabmeat
2 tsp. Old Bay Seasoning
½ tsp. dry mustard
2 tbsp. mayonnaise
2 tbsp. Worcestershire Sauce
½ tsp. salt
2 tbsp. parsley, chopped
2 eggs – beaten
1 C. bread crumbs

Mix all ingredients together and form small crab cakes or small crab balls.

Pan fry the crab cakes in a small amount of oil until golden brown, or deep fry the crab balls in oil until golden brown. Makes approximately 10-12 large or 16-20 small crab cakes.

— Minnie Ridgeway

Minnie and Jim Ridgeway live on the Eastern Shore of Maryland on the Chesapeake Bay. It is a great place to visit for a retreat and her crab cakes are the best!

STEAMED SHRIMP

Take a large pot and add enough water to cover 1" of the bottom. Then add:

12 oz. of beer
6 oz. cider vinegar
3 tbsp. pepper
1½ tsp. Tabasco Sauce
Add 5 lb. shrimp with shell on and bring to a boil.

As soon as the shrimp turn pink – approximately 10 minutes after boiling begins, taste test one. If done, drain water and place shrimp in ice water to stop the cooking. Serve with cocktail sauce and lemon wedges.

— Rich Allison

SEAFOOD PAN ROAST

Melt one stick margarine in skillet. Sauté one small diced onion in skillet and remove onion.

Sauté ½ lb. bay scallops until they lose their glistening appearance.

Dice ½ lb. shrimp and add to mixture.

Add 1½ C. of oysters without the juice or 1 lb. crabmeat whichever is in season.

Add 1 qt. half and half and 1 qt. of regular milk. Also, add 1 pt. of heavy cream.

Add ½ C. of flour before mixture becomes hot.

Increase heat until mixture almost comes to a boil. Then add one can Campbell's Tomato Soup.

Season With:

1 tbsp. Old Bay Seasoning
1 tbsp. seasoning salt
Sprinkle lightly with pepper
½ tsp. basil
½ tsp. oregano
½ tsp. garlic powder

Simmer on low for approximately 3 hours for flavor to go through the mixture.

Add more of the above seasoning if needed for extra flavor.

Can be served as soup or over linguini.

— Rich Allison & Roger Knisely

This is a take-off from a Pittsburgh restaurant sitting on the Monogahela River. The key to the good flavor is the tomato soup.

CRAB MUFFINS

Melt one stick margarine.

Add:

2 tbsp. mayonnaise
Salt and pepper
1 tbsp. garlic powder
1 jar Cheese Whiz at room temperature
1 lb. crabmeat.

Mix together and spread on 10 halves of English Muffins.

Bake at 400° for 15 minutes.

— Minnie Ridgeway

BAKED OYSTERS

1½ pints oysters and ¾ C. juice
¼ lb. margarine
1½ sleeves saltines, crumbled
½ C. milk
Salt and pepper to taste

Layer in baking dish
Pour in milk.
Bake at 350° until brown
(approximately 30-45 minutes)

In memory of
— Donna Burket

Jim and Min Ridgeway live on the Eastern Shore of Maryland on the Chesapeake Bay in Wittman, MD. Jim was a great boss and has always been a good friend. Min has always welcomed everyone into their home. We have been blessed wih fresh seafood at the Bay. We love to visit the Bay and cook the seafood and they love to eat. What a match!!

SHRIMP & PASTA WITH PESTO AGLIO-OLIO

1 red pepper, diced
2 stalks celery, diced
½ red onion, diced

Heat ½ stick butter with 1 C. olive oil in medium skillet. Sauté onion, pepper and celery for 3 to 5 minutes. Add 4 heaping tsp. minced garlic, 2 tsp. pesto sauce and 2 medium yellow squash, sliced and quartered.

Season with:

1 tbsp. season salt
3 tbsp. parsley
1½ tbsp. Italian seasoning

Add:

15 medium shrimp, cleaned and de-veined. Sauté additional 5 minutes. Turn off heat and add 1 C. Romano cheese.

Meanwhile:

Cook 1 lb. pasta in salted water for 12 minutes. Drain and put back in cooking pan and add oil mixture. Toss well and place on pasta platter. Sprinkle with Romano cheese.

— Rich Allison

IMPERIAL CRAB

1 lb. jumbo lump crabmeat
1 lg. egg
1 C. grated extra-sharp cheddar cheese
¼ C. mayonnaise
Salt & pepper to taste

Preheat the oven to 350°. Combine all ingredients and divide mixture evenly among 6 oven-proof ramekins or shells.

Bake 15 minutes or until bubbly and browned. Makes 6 servings.

LINGUINE WITH WHITE CLAM SAUCE

Cook 1 lb. linguine. Drain and set aside.

Meanwhile:

Sauté ¼ C. onion, diced
4 cloves garlic, minced
⅓ stick butter
¼ C. olive oil
Sauté all above for 5 minutes.

Add:

1 (8 oz.) bottle clam juice
Bring to a boil

Mix 1 tbsp. corn starch in 3 tbsp. water and pour into skillet. Sauce will begin to thicken. Add two 6½ oz. cans of minced clams. Season with ¼ tsp. salt, ¼ tsp. pepper and 1 tbsp. minced parsley.

Drain pasta and add ¾ C. grated Romano cheese, clam mixture and toss well.

Serves 4

— Rich Allison

SHRIMP BATTER

2 eggs
4 tbsp. cornstarch
¼ tsp. baking powder
Salt and pepper
Sprinkle Old Bay seasoning

Blend altogether to make a batter

Put ½ C. flour in a bowl. Dredge shrimp in flour, then in batter.

Deep fry in hot grease

— Rich Allison

CRAB IMPERIAL

Mix:

8 tbsp. mayonnaise
1 egg
½ tsp. white pepper
½ tsp. Accent
Juice of one lemon
Add 2 lb. crabmeat in big chunks

Put in casserole or back in shell. Brush top of mixture with 1 egg yolk and 1 tbsp. water. Sprinkle with paprika and bake for 10 minutes at 400°. Serves 6.

— Minnie Ridgeway

OYSTERS ROCKEFELLER

Put oysters in baking dish. Sprinkle with garlic powder. Put chopped spinach with water squeezed out on top. Top with Monterey Jack and cheddar cheese, shredded. Place bacon on top and broil.

— Rich Allison

SOFT SHELL CRABS

Use fresh or thawed soft shell crabs that have been cleaned.

Dredge soft shells in flour and season generously with salt and pepper. You can also use lemon pepper.

Put 1 tbsp. bacon grease in a skillet with margarine and sauté until the soft shells are golden brown – approximately 7 minutes.

— Minnie Ridgeway

SAUTEED SCALLOPS

Heat butter in a skillet and add scallops along with garlic powder or freshly pressed garlic.

Sauté scallops until they lose their glistening appearance.

Add ½ C. white wine and let scallops simmer another 2 minutes.

Top with seasoned bread crumbs. Remove from skillet and sprinkle a few more bread crumbs on top along with some Romano cheese.

— Rich Allison

SAUCE FOR 2 LB. STEAMED MUSSELS

Sauté:

1 stick margarine
3 tbsp. garlic cloves, minced
¼ C. onion, finely minced

Add:

Juice from 2 whole lemons
8 oz. heavy cream
4 tbsp. white wine, Pernod
⅛ tsp. white pepper
½ tsp. kosher salt
Fresh basil

To prepare 2 lb. mussels, wash and de-beard mussels.

Place in pot with about ¾" water for steaming. Add ¾ C. white wine. Once they come to a boil, cook approximately 3 minutes stirring during cooking. Mussels are cooked once they open. Do not overcook or they will become mushy.

Place mussels in a bowl, pour sauce over them and serve with Italian bread for dipping.

Serves approximately 3-4 people.

— Roger Knisely
— Rich Allison

SEAFOOD

CRABMEAT AU GRATIN

Sauté small amount of onion in margarine and put in casserole.

Add:

1 lb. Crab meat
Old Bay seasoning
Lemon pepper
Parsley
Dash hot sauce

Mix well.
Blend in 8 oz. heavy cream

Add:

1 C. cheddar cheese, shredded
½ C. Velveeta cheese, in small chunks

Bake at 325° for 45 minutes.

— Rich Allison

OYSTERS CASINO

Put shucked oysters in a casserole.

Sprinkle with garlic powder and Romano cheese. Cover with finely chopped red bell pepper and onion. Place pats of margarine on peppers and onions. Cover with seasoned bread crumbs. Place cut pieces of bacon on top.

Broil at medium level about 12 minutes.

— Rich Allison

OYSTERS BIENVILLE

Put oysters in shells or in a baking dish. Sprinkle with garlic powder. Put crumbled, fried sausage that was seasoned with salt and pepper during frying on top of oysters. Top with Monterey Jack and cheddar cheese, shredded. Place under broiler until cheese melts.

— Rich Allison

HERMAN HARRISON'S FAVORITE CRABCAKES

2 eggs
½ C. cracker crumbs
2 tbsp. mayonnaise
1 tbsp. yellow mustard
1 tbsp. Worcestershire Sauce
sprinkle with Old Bay

Fold in:

1 lb. fresh lump crabmeat

Roll into golf ball size meatballs and fry in peanut oil until brown.

— Dale Hicks

MINNIE'S OYSTER CASSEROLE

1 pint oysters
1 sleeve Town House crackers crushed
½ C. melted butter
2 strips bacon, cooked and cut into small pieces
2 heaping tbsp. diced red peppers
2 tsp. capers in vinegar (not salted ones)
½ C. shredded sharp cheddar cheese

Layer in 1½ quart greased dish using:
½ of oysters on the bottom, then ½ red peppers and ½ of bacon and ½ capers. Then put ½ of cracker crumbs and ½ of butter and repeat with remaining mixture.

Bake at 375° for 30 minutes. Five minutes before done, sprinkle cheese on top and finish baking.

— Minnie Ridgeway

SEAFOOD CASSEROLE IN PHYLLO DOUGH

½ onion, chopped
1 stalk celery, diced

Sauté in 2 tbsp. margarine and 2 oz. olive oil.

Add:

1 (8 oz.) pkg. sliced mushrooms (Use a combination of porcini, oyster and shitake, if possible)

Sauté all of the above.

In a separate skilled, sauté ½ lb. bay scallops in margarine and ½ lb. diced shrimp (uncooked). If shrimp are cooked, dice and add after you sauté scallops.

Add:

8 oz. light cream to onion, celery and mushroom mixture. Reduce until slightly thickened. Add scallops and shrimp, drained (no juices). Season mixture with pepper, lemon pepper, oregano and a small amount of seasoning salt and sherry.

Layer phyllo dough in a casserole dish spraying each layer with Pam. Put approximately 5 layers in the bottom of the casserole with the edges extending over the edges of the dish. Pour mixture in casserole. Layer 5 more layers of phyllo on top and pull edges back into casserole and crimp and press down.

Bake at 325° for approximately 35 minutes or until golden brown.

— Rich Allison

FRIED OYSTERS

Using fresh shucked oysters, coat with 1 C. Bisquick flour mixed with ½ tsp. baking soda and fry in a skilled in Crisco oil until golden brown.

— Jim Ridgeway

OYSTER STEW

Sauté:

1½ pints oysters (drain ½ juice) in margarine until edges curl. Remove from heat and add:

2 qts. Half and Half
2 (8 oz.) containers heavy cream

Put back on burner and cook at medium heat until it slowly cooks. Do not cook at too hot of a boil.

Season With:

Seasoning salt
Coarse ground pepper
Old Bay seasoning

Simmer for approximately 2 hours.

ASPARAGUS OYSTER STEW

Sauté:

1 bunch finely chopped asparagus in margarine and seasoning salt. Then follow oyster stew recipe above.

— Rich Allison & Roger Knisely

OYSTERS WITH BACON

Take freshly shucked oysters and lay on a broiler pan. Top with a small piece of raw bacon and place under the oven broiler until the bacon is cooked.

— Jim Ridgeway

DECANTING OYSTERS

As you shuck oysters, place them in a deep plastic container. Let shells and other dirt sink to the bottom. Slowly scoop the oysters to another similar bowl with a slotted spoon. After all oysters are removed, slowly pour juice into another container except for sediment on the bottom of the bowl. Repeat this three or four times to clean the oysters.

— Jim Ridgeway

STEAMED CRABS

Place live crabs in a large pot that has a cage. Place a brick or something heavy on the bottom of the pot to keep the cage out of the water.

Place some clothes pins around the cover of the pot, this keeps the live crabs in the pot and also keeps the steam in. Steam the crabs for approximately ½ hour. Turn off gas and remove clothes pins and lid.

In a large pan place a layer of steamed crabs. Sprinkle with a little water and dust crabs with Old Bay seasoning. Keep layering crabs and Old Bay seasoning.

Start picking and eating. Clean hot pot as soon as possible after the steaming process, the longer you let it sit the harder it is to clean.

— Jim Ridgeway

CLEANING SOFT SHELL CRABS

To clean soft shell crabs, you must start with live soft shell crabs. If they have died, throw them away.

Take live soft shell crabs and with scissors, cut out the eyes and mouth. Lift the apron and clean out the lungs. Lift the tab and snip with scissors.

Rinse and place on a paper towel to dry. To cook, refer to recipe on page 75 for cooking.

— Jim Ridgeway

FRESH SHRIMP SALAD

1 lb. fresh medium shrimp, cooked, peeled and deveined
½ C. mayonnaise
⅓ C. chopped celery
2 tsp. Old Bay seasoning
2 tsp. fresh lemon juice
¼ tsp. Worcestershire Sauce
¼ tsp. curry powder

Cut shrimp in half and combine with remaining ingredients. Cover and refrigerate 30 minutes or more.

Stir before serving on a bed of lettuce or croissant or sandwich roll.

Makes 4 servings.

— Rich Allison

GRILLED FISH

Take fillets of fish and season with garlic powder, seasoning salt and freshly ground black pepper. Pour Kraft Zesty Italian dressing over fish. Let marinate a few minutes.

Grill over medium heat preferably on grilling tray so fish does not fall through grill grates. Grill for approximately 2-3 minutes on each side or until fish is flakey.

If grilling tuna, cook until medium rare.

— Sandy Allison

PAN FRIED HADDOCK

Take pieces of frozen or fresh haddock, thawed and do the following:

Dip in flour seasoned with salt and pepper to coat.

Then dip in a batter of three eggs beaten with ¼ tsp. baking powder added and mixed well.

Dip back in flour to coat.

Pan fry in a small amount of Crisco oil until golden brown. Fish should flake apart when a fork is cut into them.

In memory of
— Grace Allison

MEATS & VEGETABLES

Cooking from the Farm to the City

The Very Best
Recipes
of

Rich & Sandy Allison

and Their

Family and Friends

REUBEN CASSEROLE

1 (1 lb. 11 oz.) can sauerkraut, drained
2 med. tomatoes, sliced
2 tbsp. Thousand Island dressing
2 tbsp. margarine
2 (12 oz.) cans corned beef
2 (8 oz.) C. shredded or sliced Swiss cheese
1 pkg. Pillsbury Butterflake Rolls

Place sauerkraut in bottom of 13"x 9" baking dish.

Top with tomato slices. Spread Thousand Island dressing and margarine.

Cover with corned beef and cheese.

Bake at 425° for 25 minutes covered.

Remove from oven and separate biscuits and lay on top. Bake 20 minutes uncovered until biscuits are brown.

In memory of
— Louise Hidlebaugh

LASAGNA

1 lb. ground beef
1 lb. sweet Italian sausage

(2 lb. ground beef and 2 lb. sausage makes two large and one small casserole).

Fry sausage and ground beef until pinkness is gone. Drain and cool.

2 eggs
1 C. bread crumbs
1 C. milk

Mix eggs, bread crumbs and milk. Add drained meat when cooled.

Cook 1 box lasagna noodles in salted water. Be careful not to overcook noodles or tear them apart.

(3 lb. Lasagna noodles makes two large and one small casseroles).

Salt and Pepper
1 (29 oz.) can Contadina tomato puree
¾ C. water
1 (12 oz.) can Contadina tomato paste
Garlic powder
Sage/oregano
2 (16 oz.) cans spaghetti sauce

Combine sauces and spices and bring to a boil and cook for ½ hour covered. Then cook for an additional hour without the lid on.

Grease a 13"x9"x2" casserole dish.

16 oz. Kraft mozzarella shredded cheese
15 oz. Maggio ricotta cheese

Using the above ingredients, begin layering casserole dish first with sauce on the bottom of the dish. Then place a layer of meat, cooked noodles, mozzarella cheese, ricotta cheese, more sauce, meat and noodles, etc.

Top with sauce and cheese.

Bake 1 hour at 325°. If frozen and thawed, bake at 325° or 1½-2 hours. Check to make certain the center is hot. May need more time.

Makes 2 – 13"x9"x2" casseroles.

— Sandy Allison

Everyone will love this hearty lasagna. It is great to make in large quantities and freeze and send with the kids to school. Also, it is great after a busy day at work. With one day of thawing in the refrigerator, it can be cooked and you have fresh pasta in 1-2 hours.

PAM'S POTATOES

Bake eight potatoes one hour at 325°. Slice top off and scoop out insides and place in a mixing bowl.

To the potatoes in the bowl add:

1 stick margarine
1 container sour cream
12 oz. grated cheddar cheese
½ C. bacon bits

Season with:

Chives
Pepper
Seasoning salt
Garlic powder

Mix well and put back in shells. Sprinkle with paprika and bake for 30 more minutes at 325°.

— Pam Bowser Knisely

These are great. Make ahead of time!

SOUR CREAM ENCHILADAS

Place 1 tbsp. oil in skillet and brown 2 lb. lean ground meat. Drain and set aside.

Hot Sauce Mixture:

1 tsp. salt
½ tsp. black pepper
1 med. onion, finely chopped
1 med. bell pepper, chopped
1 tbsp. chili powder
½ tsp. garlic powder
4 tbsp. ripe olives, sliced
¼ tsp. cumin powder
¼ tsp. coriander
1 tbsp. hot sauce
4 drops Tabasco
1 tbsp. Worcestershire sauce
1 sm. can chili without beans

Mix cooked ground meat and hot sauce mixture together.

Sour Cream Sauce:

Melt one stick oleo and add 2 tbsp. flour.

Add 1½ C. milk at room temperature and 1½ pints of sour cream. Mix sour cream sauce well.

Have ready 1 lb. grated sharp cheddar cheese.

Put large layer of sour cream sauce in bottom of buttered baking dish. Place 2 tbsp. meat and hot sauce mixture on a flour tortilla and sprinkle with cheese. Fold tortilla

Make only one layer of tortillas; do not stack on top of each other.

Cover with hot sauce mixture and remaining sour cream mixture if any is left.

Sprinkle the remaining cheese and ripe olives. Cover and bake at 375° for 15-20 minutes until bubbly.

Can be frozen, baked or unbaked.

In memory of
— Louise Hidlebaugh

This is a little time consuming but definitely worth the work. Our dear friend, Louise Hidlebaugh who lived in Pasadena, TX. Originally from Roaring Spring, PA, she is a great cook and has given us many good recipes that you will find throughout this book.

MEATS & VEGETABLES

BREAKFAST BISCUITS APPLES

1 (10 oz.) pkg. buttermilk biscuits, cut into pieces
1½ C. Macintosh apples, chopped
⅓ C. brown sugar, packed
2 tbsp. margarine
1 egg
⅓ C. light corn syrup
¼ tsp. cinnamon
Nuts and raisins, optional (cook raisins soft first)

Cut apples into pieces. Put onto bottom of square greased baking dish. Cut biscuits into pieces and put on top of apples. Mix remaining ingredients together and pour over top of biscuits. Bake at 350° for 35-45 minutes.

Cool. Mix a glaze of ⅓ C. sugar, ¼ tsp. vanilla and 1-2 tsp. milk and spoon over cooled biscuits/ apples.

— Donna Claar

BREAKFAST CHEESE CASSEROLE

Take a 9"x13" casserole pan and place 10 slices of white bread, buttered and cubed in the bottom of the pan.

Sprinkle 1 lb. grated sharp cheddar cheese over bread.

Mix with a beater and pour over bread:

6 eggs
1 qt. milk
1 tsp. salt
2 tbsp. dry mustard

Sprinkle over the top ½ lb. diced fried bacon, ham or other meat. This must be refrigerated overnight. Bake at 350° uncovered for 45 minutes or until brown.

In memory of
— Louise Hidlebaugh

HOT LETTUCE/ENDIVE DRESSING

1 C. mayonnaise
½ C. sugar
2 tbsp. cider vinegar
Salt and pepper to taste

Fry diced bacon in a skillet until crispy. Add 1 tbsp. flour to skillet and brown, then add above ingredients to skillet on medium heat along with enough milk to thin mixture. Continue stirring until mixture becomes hot and bubbly.

Remove mixture from stove and pour over head lettuce or endive which has been cut-up. Chopped onions can also be included if desired.

Serve with fried ham as the meat dish and cooked, fried potatoes.

Serves 2-3 people. Double for 4-6 people.

In memory of
— Grace Allison

This is another Pennsylvania Dutch recipe that has been handed down through the generations. We think that you will only find this in central Pennsylvania. It has a distinct flavor of sweet and sour. While it may not sound appetizing, it is very good. This has always been served in our family as the main course. However, it could be served as a hot salad.

This same dressing can be used with dandelion, endive or lettuce.

CORN & NOODLES CASSEROLE

Cook 1 lb. bag wide noodles, drain

Warm:

2 cans creamed corn
1 stick margarine
Salt to taste
Sugar to taste
1 lb. Velveeta Cheese, cut up
3 oz. milk

Warm mixture until cheese dissolves. Combine with noodles in a casserole dish. Bake at 300° for 45 minutes.

In memory of
— Peggy Allison
— Evelyn Dodson

This dish is always a hit with the cheese and noodle combination. Originally this dish was made by Evelyn Dodson. This recipe has now been made by many people, because everyone loves this dish. It is also an easy dish to take to a party.

VODKA PINK PASTA SICILIAN STYLE

In a sauce pan:

1 med. onion, coarsely chopped
2 stalks celery, diced
1 roasted red pepper, julienned

Sauté in ¼ C. olive oil until onion is glistening. Add 2 tbsp. minced garlic and sauté another 2 minutes.

Add 1 shot vodka. Cook 1 minute.

Add:

1 (26 oz.) can tomato sauce
1 (16 oz.) can diced tomatoes
1 (8 oz) can tomato paste
2 (8 oz.) cans water
2½ tsp. salt
¾ tsp. pepper
2 bay leaves, crumbled
1 tbsp. dried basil
2 tbsp. Italian seasoning

Bring to a boil and cook 5 minutes.

Add ⅛ tsp. baking soda, to remove acidity, and continue stirring for about 5 minutes.

Add either meatballs or fried and seasoned ground beef while simmering. Simmer for another 30 minutes on low.

Turn off heat and add 1 (8 oz.) container of heavy whipping cream and stir well. Add a handful of chopped fresh basil and parsley if desired.

Cook 2 lb. Trio Pasta for 12 minutes in salted boiling water. Drain.

Toss pasta with sauce and add ¾ C. Romano cheese, toss again and serve.

— Rich Allison

CARAMELIZED ONIONS

2 lg. onions, sliced
1½ sticks margarine
½ C. brown sugar
Salt and pepper

Cook on high until onions are soft (approximately 15 minutes)

— Rich Allison

Serve on potatoes, meats or salads.

MEATS & VEGETABLES

CHICKEN CORDON BLEU

6 boneless chicken breasts, flatten with mallet.
6 slices baked ham
6 slices Swiss cheese
3 tbsp. flour
2 tsp. paprika
1 chicken bouillon
6 tbsp. margarine
½ C. white wine
1 tbsp. cornstarch
1 C. whipping cream

Wrap cheese and ham in breasts. (Fasten with a toothpick). Add wine and bouillon and simmer 15-20 minutes with lid on.

Remove chicken and add cream and corn starch to juice in pan and heat until thick. Pour over chicken.

— Sandy Kardos

LOW COUNTRY BOIL WITH CHICKEN

1 box crab boil seasoning
6 lb. red potatoes
4 lb. kielbasa
4 lb. boneless chicken
2½ dz. ears of corn

In a large pot, boil water and crab seasoning. Add new potatoes and boil about 10 minutes. Do not over cook.

Add chicken, kielbasa and corn at the same time and cook another 10 minutes.

Drain from pot and serve with cornbread and butter.

Serves 14.

— Claysburg Myrtle Beach Gang

KASS' BAKED BEANS

2 cans great northern beans
1½ C. ketchup
¾ C. white sugar
½ C. brown sugar
2 tsp. mustard
2 tbsp. syrup
Bacon

Bake at 350° for 45 minutes

In memory of
— (Aunt Kass) Kathleen Claar

These are great baked beans!!

PINK PASTA

3 tbsp. olive oil
1 small onion, diced
1½ tbsp. garlic, minced
1 C. spaghetti sauce
8 oz. heavy cream
¾ tsp. seasoning salt
¼ tsp. pepper
1 lb. pasta
½ C. Romano cheese

Place oil in skillet and sauté onion until translucent. Add garlic and sauté for another minute. Add spaghetti sauce and heavy cream. Bring to a simmer. Add salt and pepper. Simmer for approximately 15 minutes until mixture reduces slightly and thickens.

Meanwhile, make your meat of choice: meatballs, sausage or boneless chicken cut into strips and place in sauce while simmering.

Also, while sauce is simmering, cook 1 lb. of pasta in salted water. Boil for 14 minutes. Drain pasta water, put pasta back in pan, add sauce and toss it. Then add Romano cheese and toss again. Serve on a large platter or in a bowl.

— Rich Allison

CHICKEN AND TORTELLINI IN CREAM SAUCE

2 lb. fresh tortellini stuffed with cheese or some other pasta.

3 tbsp. olive oil

3 boneless, skinless chicken breasts, sliced into julienne strips seasoned with pepper, seasoning salt and garlic powder.

Sauté chicken in large skillet with olive oil until partially cooked. Remove from skillet.

Begin boiling water for pasta and cook according to pasta directions.

Cream Sauce:

3 tbsp. olive oil

½ stick butter

1 C. onions, diced

2 tbsp. garlic, minced

2 (8 oz.) container heavy cream

2 chicken bouillon cubes in 2 oz. water

½ tsp. black pepper

½ tsp. seasoning salt

¾ C. Romano cheese, grated

In skillet where chicken was cooked, add oil and butter and when butter is melted, add onions and sauté for 1 minute or until translucent. Add garlic and cook another minute.

Place bouillon cubes in a cup with 2 oz. of hot water and microwave for 1 minute to dissolve while onions are cooking. Add bouillon mixture and cream to skillet.

Add chicken back into skillet. Add salt and pepper and continue cooking on medium high until mixture reduces and thickens – about 7 minutes. Add Romano when you remove sauce from the stove.

Drain pasta well and add cream sauce. Toss well and serve.

— Rich Allison

SHRIMP ARTICHOKE PASTA

4 tbsp. basil olive oil

4 tbsp. Pepperolio

½ C. olive oil

Sauté cleaned shrimp in oil over medium heat. Season with seasoning salt and garlic powder. Remove shrimp after 3 minutes.

Sauté:

1 sm. onion, chopped

2 stalks celery, diced

½ red bell pepper, diced

Sauté above for 2 to 3 minutes until tender crisp. Leave in skillet.

Add to Skillet:

1 can artichoke hearts, drained

½ can black olives, sliced

Heat for 1 to 2 more minutes.

Add:

½ C. Romano cheese

Continue cooking.

Add shrimp. Season with oregano, basil, more garlic powder, seasoning salt and pepper.

Cook 2 to 3 more minutes.

Cook pasta and drain. Add to skillet mixture, toss well and serve.

— Rich Allison

This pasta dish has a great Mediterranean flavor. We first had this in Venice, Italy.

If you aren't crazy about artichokes, simply eliminate them from the recipe.

ROAST PORK LOIN WITH HERB SPINACH STUFFING

1 pork loin (10-12 lb.)
3 tbsp. olive oil
1 small onion, diced
2 tbsp. garlic, minced
1 box frozen chopped spinach (thawed)
8 tbsp. mixture of fresh minced herbs –
(Combination of any of following: parsley, marjoram, sage, rosemary)
½ C. Romano cheese
¾ C. Italian style bread crumbs
3 C. flour
Garlic powder
Seasoning salt
Black pepper

Sauté diced onion in olive oil over medium heat until onion is translucent. Add minced garlic. Cook for one minute. Add spinach and minced herbs.

Cook for three minutes.

Remove from heat. Add cheese and bread crumbs. Mix well. Let cool.

Butterfly pork loin across the length but do not cut through totally. Also cut the pork loin into two pieces for ease of handling.

Pull other piece off and secure with cooking string. Tie loin in both directions to keep stuffing from falling out. Repeat with other piece of loin.

Take flour, garlic powder, seasoning salt and pepper and mix well and place on a tray. Take one pork loin and coat entire loin with flour mixture. Do this several times until totally coated. Do the same with the other piece.

Place about ½" of olive oil in a skillet and heat on high until hot. Brown meat on all sides including ends until browned. Repeat with other piece of loin.

Place both pieces of loin in a baking pan on a metal rack. Insert a meat thermometer into the thickest section of meat. Bake at 375° until meat thermometer reaches 170° or approximately two hours.

Remove meat from oven and from pan, let stand for approximately 1 hour before slicing.

Take pan drippings and remove fat. Make a brown gravy with a mixture of 4 tbsp. flour and 2 C. water and five beef bouillon. Add to pan drippings with ¼ tsp. Gravymaster for color. Cook until mixture thickens. Add 2 ounces of Appleschnapps and continue to cook for another 5-10 minutes.

Serve pork loin with gravy on the side.

— Rich Allison

HAM LOAF

1½ lb. ground ham
1½ lb. ground beef
1 C. milk
2 eggs
3 C. corn flakes
1 can pineapple

Grind corn flakes in food processor. Then mix everything together and form into a roll.

Bake at 350° for 1½ hours

— Roger Knisely

SAUCE FOR HAM

1 C. brown sugar
½ C. white vinegar
1 C. water
1 tbsp. yellow mustard
1 C. raisins

Heat until sugar dissolves. Let cool before using.

— Roger Knisely

BEEF BRISKET SANDWICHES

1 beef brisket (not corned beef) – about 4½ lbs.
1 tbsp. vegetable oil
1 C. celery, chopped
1 C. onion, chopped
6 beef bouillon cubes in ¾ C. water
1 C. tomato sauce
½ C. water
½ C. sugar
1 packet Lipton Onion Soup Mix
2 tbsp. vinegar
24 hamburger buns

In a large skillet brown the brisket on all sides in oil. Transfer to a slow cooker.

In the same skillet, sauté celery and onion for one minute. Gradually add the bouillon and water as well as tomato sauce and water.

Bring to a boil to deglaze the pan and remove the bits from the bottom of the pan.

Add sugar, soup mix and vinegar and bring to another boil. Pour over brisket and cover and cook on slow or low cook (about 275°) for 4-5 hours or until tender.

Remove meat form mixture and let set for five minutes before slicing. Let juice set until you can skim fat from the top. Reheat juice if necessary after skimming fat. Serve meat in buns with juices. Yield is approximately 24 sandwiches.

— Rich & Sandy Allison

These beef brisket sandwiches work great at a tailgate party. The vinegar flavor is a take-off on barbeque cooking from the Carolinas. This can be made a day or two ahead for a party or picnic.

SUE ROTELLA'S SPAGHETTI SAUCE

Place ½ C. vegetable oil in a sauce pot

In a blender place:

¼ large onion
6 cloves garlic, peeled
1½ tsp. salt
1 tsp. pepper
2 bay leaves
3½ tsp. basil

Add enough water to process to liquid.

Put in vegetable oil and sauté.

Add:

1 (18 oz.) can tomato paste
2 (18 oz.) cans water
1 (26 oz.) crushed tomatoes

Bring to a boil. Cook five minutes. Add ⅛ tsp. baking soda to remove acidity. Continue to stir.

Cook at least ½ hour more and add meat if desired.

In memory of
— Sue Rotella

HOT CHICKEN SALAD

1 C. diced chicken
1 tbsp. chopped onions
½ tsp. salt
3 tbsp. lemon juice
¾ C. Hellmann's mayonnaise
1 can cream chicken soup
1 C. cooked rice
1 C. diced celery
3 hard boiled eggs (chopped)

Mix all of the above together. Put in casserole dish and cover with Rice Krispies or potato chips.

Bake at 375° for 30 minutes.

MEATS & VEGETABLES

CASSOULETT

1 stalk celery
1 carrot, diced
¾ large onion, diced
2 qts. water
1 tsp. kosher salt
½ tsp. coarsely ground pepper
6 chicken bouillon cubes

Bring to a boil and reduce heat and cook about 15 minutes.

Meanwhile in a skillet with:

2 tbsp. olive oil
½ lb. sweet Italian sausage sliced
½ lb. smoked sausage, sliced
1 boneless chicken breast, cubed
1 boneless pork chop, cubed

Fry on medium heat approximately 5 minutes.

Season with salt and pepper.

Add 15 cloves minced garlic to the skillet and sauté another 10 minutes.

Drain meat and garlic and add to the stock pot with celery, carrots and onions. Add 3-15 oz. cans cannellini white beans, rinsed and drained and 1 15 oz. can diced tomatoes.

In the skillet with the remaining oil, sauté ¼ lb. endive or escarole, chopped. Place in cassoulett.

Add:

¼ C. fresh parsley, chopped
⅛ C. fresh thyme
2 bay leaves

Bring to a boil. Place in 375° oven for 1 hour without lid on pan.

Serve with Italian bread. Season with additional salt and pepper if needed.

— Rich Allison

COUSIN INGE'S SPAETZLE

2 C. flour
2 eggs
1 egg yolk
½ tsp. salt
½ C. water

Wire whisk eggs until blended and add all other ingredients.

Have pot of boiling salted water cooking. If you have a spaetzle maker, put dough in spaetzle maker and squeeze noodle type dough through. Cut off in approximately 4" pieces.

As soon as dough rises to the top of the boiling water, remove. It cooks quickly in approximately 1½ minutes.

For more flavor cook spaetzle in chicken bouillon broth and then make a chicken gravy from the water by adding a thickening of corn starch and water and some yellow food coloring. Serve the gravy over the spaetzle.

In Germany they sprinkle the spaetzle with bread crumbs and put melted butter over the bread crumbs and spaetzle.

— Inge Schiller
— Rich & Sandy Allison

We found Sandy's cousin, Inge Schiller and her family, Helmut, Joachim and Thomas in Herbrechtingen, Germany in 1995 just by chance while doing research on Sandy's Burket family genealogy. Inge welcomed six of us, total strangers into her house. It was the day after Easter and what a feast of desserts we had. Several years later, we went back for a visit and was treated to a feast of all types of great German foods. We love her Spaetzle! We stay in touch on a regular basis.

SAUSAGE & WILD RICE CASSEROLE

¾ lb. bulk pork sausage
1 tbsp. bell pepper flakes
½ C. celery, chopped
1 (4 oz.) can pimento
1 C. wild rice
2 tsp. chicken seasoned stock base
1½ C. hot water
1 (10 oz.) can condensed cream of mushroom soup
1 (2 oz.) can mushrooms
1 tbsp. instant minced onion
½ tsp. marjoram leaves
½ tsp. thyme leaves
1 C. grated American cheese (9 slices)

Crumble sausage and brown in large skillet. Add pepper flakes and celery; continue cooking until celery is soft. Drain off excess fat. Drain and chop pimento; add to sausage mixture along with remaining ingredients, mixing well. Pour into a 3 qt. casserole. Cover.

Bake at 325° for 1½ hours or until rice is tender and dry.

Serves 4 people.

— Sandy Allison

CAJUN STUFFING

8 oz. sausage, fried
8 oz. smoked sausage, fried
Put in food processor.
Sauté in margarine; onion, celery, green pepper and mushrooms. Add cream to thicken.

Add:
Sage
Oregano
Seasoning Salt
Pepper
Parsley

Remove from heat and add bread cubes and sausage. Bake in crock pot for 1-2 hours.

— Rich Allison

RICE & BROCCOLI CASSEROLE

1 can mushroom soup
½ can milk
1 (8 oz.) Velveeta Cheese, melted together
1 (10 oz.) frozen broccoli, cooked
1 C. rice, cooked

Mix all ingredients together.
Bake at 350° for 10-15 minutes or until thoroughly heated through.

— Sandy Allison

BROCCOLI CASSEROLE

1 pkg. stuffing mix for chicken
1 (10 oz.) box frozen broccoli cuts
1 (10 oz.) box cauliflower cuts
1 can cream of celery soup (undiluted)
1½ C. grated cheddar cheese

Follow stuffing mix directions and set aside. Partially cook vegetables, then combine soup and vegetables with stuffing.

Grease a 2 qt. casserole bowl, put mixture in and top with grated cheese.

Bake at 350° for ½ hour.

PIZZA BURGER

1 lb. jumbo bologna, chopped
1 lb. sharp cheese
2 lb. hamburger, fried and drained
Salt and pepper
2tsp. oregano
2 small cans pizza sauce
⅛ C. parsley

Mix above all together.
Spread on bread.
Lay on cookie sheet

Bake at 400-450° for 10 minutes.

In memory of
— Louise Hidlebaugh

MEATS & VEGETABLES

HAM BAR B-QUE

½ C. chili sauce
3 tbsp. water
2 tbsp. brown sugar
1 tbsp. prepared yellow mustard

Simmer 5 minutes and add 1 lb. chipped ham. Stir. Serve on round buns.

Makes 5-8 sandwiches

In memory of
— (Aunt Kass) Kathleen Claar

THELMA'S PASTA

1 (1 lb.) pkg. penne pasta, cooked and drained, keep pasta water.
1 pkg. asparagus, cut diagonally. Cook in pasta water until soft.
3 tbsp. olive oil
4 garlic cloves, crushed
2 C. mushrooms, chopped
4 slices proscutti ham, slivered thin
½ C. mozzarella cheese
½ C. parmesan cheese
2 tbsp. fresh basil, chopped

Sauté mushrooms and garlic.

Mix all together. Sprinkle extra cheese over pasta and serve.

Add a little Italian seasoning and pepper for taste.

— Thelma Absher

Thelma and Wade Absher live on the Eastern Shore of Maryland on the Chesapeake Bay in Claiborne, MD. They are tremendous hosts always greeting people at their home. Thelma is an excellent cook as you will see from her recipe.

Great Aunt Kass Claar was always a great cook and continued cooking until her death at age 98. This ham bar-b-que and also her baked beans are outstanding. Both recipes are in this book. She was always a second mother to Rich, sister Sally and brother Jimmy. We hope that we have the mental sharpness later in life that she had. She was a very independent person who loved to cook and loved to talk to people. She was a lovely lady.

CHICKEN FRIED STEAK

¼ C. all-purpose flour
½ tsp. salt
½ tsp. pepper
1 (1 lb.) pkg. cubed beef steaks
1 lg. egg, lightly beaten
2 tbsp. milk
1 C. saltine cracker crumbs
Vegetable oil
3 tbsp. all-purpose flour
1¼ C. chicken broth
½ C. milk
Dash of Worcestershire Sauce
Dash of hot sauce (Red Hot)

Combine first 3 ingredients; sprinkle on both sides of steaks. Combine egg and 2 tbsp. milk in a shallow dish. Dip steaks in egg mixture; dredge in cracker crumbs. Pour oil to depth of ½" into a large, heavy skillet. Fry steaks in hot oil over medium heat until browned, turning once. Cover; reduce heat and simmer, turning occasionally for 15 minutes or until tender. Remove steaks and drain on paper towels. Keep warm.

(Continued on Page 91)

(Continued from Page 90)

Drain off drippings, reserving tbsp. in skillet. Add 3 tbsp. flour, stirring until smooth. Cook 1 minute, stirring constantly. Gradually add broth and ½ C. milk; cook over medium heat, stirring constantly until thickened and bubbly. Stir in Worcestershire sauce and hot sauce.

Serve gravy with steaks and rice or potatoes.

(Do not put meat in oven with gravy over it. The meat soaks the gravy up and the crunchy crust on meat gets soft).

Yield: 4 Servings

— Sandy Allison

This is a really good chicken fried steak recipe. It takes a little time, but it is definitely worth doing. It is far better than what you will find in a restaurant. And the gravy is also very good and goes well over garlic mashed potatoes.

PESTO SAUCE

¼ stick butter
¼ C. olive oil

Sauté ½ diced onion on medium heat
Add 6 cloves diced garlic and sauté.

Add 4 tbsp. pesto and add another ½ C. olive oil. Season with seasoned salt and freshly ground pepper. Add 3 tbsp. pepperolio.

Serve with 1 lb. pasta.

— Rich Allison

BUTTERMILK PANCAKES

1 C. all-purpose flour
2 tbsp. sugar
½ tsp. baking soda
½ tsp. salt
1 C. buttermilk (or 1 tbsp. lemon juice to 1 C. milk and let stand 5 minutes)
2 tbsp. melted butter
1 egg

Mix all ingredients together. Don't over mix. Batter should have lumps.

Pancakes are light and airy.

Bake in skillet on low setting or they will burn.

PEPPEROLIO PASTA

Sauté in a skillet 10-12 cloves of garlic crushed through a garlic press with an 8½ oz. bottle of Pepperolio oil. Heat until mixture is hot.

Meanwhile, cook 1 lb. pasta, preferably zitis. Drain.

Sprinkle basil over pasta along with plenty of Romano cheese and Parmesan cheese. Pour oil mixture over pasta and toss. Serve warm.

— Irene Cibrone

FLADLEY

1 C. flour
1 C. milk
1 tsp. salt
1 egg

Make a thin pancake batter. Pour batter into frying pan, as thin as paper. Brown on both sides, fry until crisp.

Cut into narrow noodles before they cool. Drop into boiling broth. You can use pork, ham, and chicken or beef broth.

— Doris Knisely

FARFALLE PASTA

1 C. olive oil, heated in skillet

Add:

2 C. fresh tomatoes, chopped
¼ C. parsley, chopped
¼ C. basil leaves, chopped
3 tbsp. minced garlic

Cook above ingredients in oil for 2 minutes.

Add:

9 oz. Brie cheese with rind removed. Stir.
Let melt to blend.
Add 2 chicken breasts, grilled and chopped.

Cook 1 lb. Farfalle bowties in salted water until done, (12 minutes). Drain.

Add sauce and toss to coat. Season with seasoning salt and pepper. Add ½ C. Romano cheese.

Toss well and serve.

— Rich Allison

CHILIES RELLENOS

Can be stuffed with ground beef or cheese.

If stuffed with ground beef:

Cook ground beef with a little salt, pepper, onions (diced very small) and potatoes. Can also add raisins.

If stuffed with cheese:

Oaxaca, mozzarella or jack cheese.

To prepare chili peppers:

Wash peppers and sear them in a pan, turning over once or twice. Do not let them get burned. Put the chilies in a Ziploc bag for about ½ hour so they can sweat. Take out of the bag and peel off the burnt skin. After this put on some gloves to clean the chilies. Open the chilies and clean all the seeds out.

On a large plate put some flour with a little salt and pepper. In separate bowl beat some egg whites. When starting to stiffen or harden, add the yolks and mix all together.

Stuff the chilies with either cheese or the ground beef. Cover the chilies with flour mixture, then dip them in the egg batter.

You can either fry them in oil or bake them in the oven a little less than ½ hour. If you bake in oven, make a cream sauce to pour over the chilies.

— Aide Ruiz

CREAM SAUCE FOR BAKED CHILIES

Sour cream
Walnuts

Blend both and pour over the chilies.

— Aide Ruiz

CHEESE SANDWICHES

16-20 hamburger rolls
1 lb. chopped chipped ham
1 lb. Velveeta Cheese, chopped
6 hard boiled eggs, chopped
16-20 olives, chopped
½ C. ketchup
½ C. mayonnaise
3 tsp. onion, chopped
3 tbsp. relish

Mix well.

Fill hamburger rolls and wrap in foil.
Bake at 350° for 15-20 minutes.

Can be made ahead and kept in freezer, then popped in oven.

In memory of
— Louise Hidlebaugh

CHICKEN QUESADILLAS

4 boneless chicken breasts

Season with seasoned salt, garlic powder, pepper and cumin. Marinate in zesty Italian dressing and juice of 1 lime.

Cook 12 minutes on grill and cube into small pieces.

Filling of Quesadillas:

1 lg. tomato, diced
½ lg. onion, diced
½ jalapeno pepper
½ red pepper

Add:

Salt & pepper
Juice of 1 lime
Sprinkle with cumin
Minced parsley
Minced cilantro
Minced chives
Stir well.

To Make Quesadillas:

Brush 1 side of large flour tortilla with olive oil and place down on griddle/grill until heated and some small black spots appear. Remove and place on grille on aluminum foil. Add diced chicken, tomatoes, onion, jalapeno pepper and red pepper. Top with grated Monterey Jack/cheddar cheese. Place another flour tortilla on top and press down with cake turner.

Repeat for 6 to 8 quesadillas and let heat on grill for approximately 10 minutes.
Serve with salsa.

— Rich Allison

Try the Monte Cristo sandwich with or without the Crab Imperial mix. Both ways are good.

COMBINATION LO MEIN

½ C. Crisco oil
7 tbsp. soy sauce
½ large onion, chopped
2 celery stalks, chopped
3 tbsp. sesame oil
1 tbsp. chili oil
1 can baby corn
6-8 raw shrimp (medium size) chopped into small strips
1 whole boneless pork chop, cut into small strips
2 chicken breast halves, cut into small strips
2 tbsp. garlic powder
1 lb. pasta (enough for 4 people)

Add Crisco oil to pan or wok. Add soy sauce, onion, celery, sesame oil and chili oil. Stir constantly on high heat. Add chopped meat and seafood. Add garlic powder, 1 can corn. Stir fry for approximately 10 minutes.

Cook pasta in ½ tsp. salted water. When done strain well.

Add to stir fry and mix well.

— Rich Allison

MONTE CRISTO SANDWICH CHESAPEAKE

½ lb. crabmeat
¾ C. mayonnaise
1 tsp. Dijon mustard
Coarse black pepper
½ tsp. Old Bay
¼ tsp. salt
Mix well

Place mix on Italian bread (enough to make 6 sandwiches) with ham, turkey, Swiss cheese and roasted red peppers. Dip in egg batter and fry slowly until golden brown.

— Rich Allison

GRILLED TOURNEDOS OF BEEF

⅓ C. A-1 Steak Sauce
¼ C. tomato ketchup
¼ C. orange marmalade
2 tbsp. lemon juice
2 tbsp. minced onions
1 clove garlic, crushed
8 slices bacon
8 beef tenderloins – 1" thick

Mix sauce in a small bowl. Wrap a bacon slice around edge of each steak and secure with a toothpick.

Grill over medium high heat – 4" from heat source – about 10 minutes for rare or until desired doneness. Turn occasionally and brush frequently with sauce.

— Aimee Schultz

CHICKEN CHEESE LASAGNA

1 medium onion, chopped
1 garlic clove, minced
½ C. butter
½ C. all-purpose flour
1 tsp. salt
1½ C. milk
4 C. (16 oz.) shredded mozzarella cheese, divided
1 C. grated parmesan cheese, divided
1 tsp. dried basil
1 tsp. dried oregano
½ tsp. white pepper
1 (15 oz.) carton ricotta
1 tbsp. fresh parsley, minced
9 lasagna noodles, cooked and drained (or use the ones already cooked)
2 pkgs. frozen spinach; thawed and well drained
2 C. cooked chicken, cubed

In a saucepan, sauté onion and garlic in butter until tender. Stir in flour and salt; cook until bubbly. Gradually stir in broth and milk. Bring to a boil, stirring constantly. Boil 1 minute. Stir in 2 C. mozzarella, ½ C. parmesan cheese, basil, oregano and pepper. Set aside in a bowl. Combine ricotta, parsley and remaining mozzarella; set aside. Spread ¼ of the cheese sauce into a greased 13"x9"x2" baking dish; cover with ⅓ of the noodles. Top with half of ricotta mixture, half of spinach and half of chicken. Cover with ¼ of cheese sauce and ⅓ of noodles. Repeat layers of ricotta mixture, spinach, chicken and ¼ cheese sauce. Cover with remaining noodles and cheese sauce. Sprinkle the remaining parmesan cheese over all.

Bake at 350° uncovered for 35-40 minutes. Let stand 15 minutes.

— Kay Burket

JALAPENO POTATOES

4 lb. red potatoes, salt and pepper to taste
8 green onions, chopped
1 green bell pepper, chopped
1 jar pimento, drained
1 C. butter
2 C. milk
1 roll (6 oz.) jalapeno cheese, chopped

Boil potatoes, peel and slice in flat buttered dish. Layer potatoes, salt and pepper.

Sauté peppers and onions in ½ of the butter. Melt the other ½ of butter in milk and stir in flour to make a sauce. Add cheese, melt. Add peppers, onions and pimentos. Pour over potatoes.

Bake at 350° for 45 minutes.

It is best if this is made the day before and kept overnight.

In memory of
— Louise Hidlebaugh

BREAKFAST CASSEROLE

1½ C. milk
½ C. sugar
½ tsp. vanilla
¼ tsp. salt
2 tsp. cinnamon
6 eggs
Loaf of French bread cut into 1" slices
1 (8 oz.) cream cheese (softened)

Generously grease 2½ quart casserole or rectangular baking dish, 13"x9"x2". Beat milk, sugar, vanilla, cinnamon, salt and eggs in large bowl with hand beater until smooth.

Take 2 bread slices and make a sandwich with the cream cheese. Line the casserole dish with cream cheese sandwiches. Pour egg mixture over top. Wait 5 minutes and turn sandwiches over so they're coated on top and bottom with egg mixture. Cover and refrigerate at least 8 hours but no longer than 24 hours.

Heat oven to 400°. Uncover and bake 20 to 25 minutes or until golden brown. Sprinkle with powdered sugar. Serve with syrup.

— Sandy Kardos

STUFFED SHELLS –
STUFFING AND CHICKEN

1 box jumbo shells
3 cooked chicken breasts, cut into small pieces
2 (6 oz.) boxes Stove Top Stuffing (chicken)
1½ C. mayonnaise
3 cans cream of chicken soup
1½ cans water

Cook shells until tender; drain and set aside. Mix Stove Top stuffing as directed; combine stuffing, chicken and mayo – set aside.

Combine soup and water. Place small amount of soup in the bottom of a greased 13"x9" pan.

Stuff shells with stuffing, chicken and mayo mixture. Place in pan.

Spread more soup on top. Add shredded mozzarella cheese after soup.

Bake at 350° for 45 minutes in covered dish, then bake an additional 15 minutes uncovered.

— Chris Wilkins

GUS' BAKED BEANS

1 gallon Bush's Baked Beans, drained

Add:

KC Masterpiece BBQ Sauce until coated
Brown sugar to taste
½ C. Jim Beam

Mix well. Bake at 325° for 1 hour.

— Gus Walter

STEWED TOMATOES
EASTERN SHORE
CHESAPEAKE BAY STYLE

1 medium onion, diced
½ stick margarine
1 (29 oz.) can stewed tomatoes
4 tbsp. brown sugar
4 slices white bread, cubed
Salt and pepper to taste

Sauté onion in margarine until onion is soft.

Add stewed tomatoes and brown sugar and bring to a slow boil. Season well with salt and pepper

Add four slices of cubed bread. Mix well and continue cooking until bread absorbs tomato juice and is thoroughly heated.

— Rich Allison

MEATS & VEGETABLES

STEAK OR TUNA AU POIVRE

2 tbsp. black peppercorns
2 tsp. white peppercorns
2 tsp. green peppercorns
2 tsp. fennel seeds
2 tbsp. unsalted butter
2 tbsp. vegetable oil
3 tbsp. chopped shallots
½ C. beef broth
¼ C. plus 2 tbsp. heavy cream
¼ C. Cognac or Brandy
2 tsp. Dijon mustard
Salt

In a heavy-duty sealable plastic bag or between 2 sheets of waxed paper, crush peppercorns and fennel seeds coarsely with bottom of a heavy skillet. Pat steaks dry and coat both sides with salt and the peppercorn mixture. In a 10" heavy skillet heat butter and oil over moderate heat until hot but not smoking. Cook steaks for 4 to 5 minutes on each side for medium rare. Transfer to plates and cover to keep warm.

Pour off excess fat from skillet and add shallots and ½ C. broth and deglaze pan. Add cream and cognac. Boil mixture, scraping up browned bits, until sauce thickens and coats back of spoon, about 1 minute. Finish sauce by whisking in mustard. Taste and season sauce with salt if necessary and spoon over steaks.

— Charmayne Holland

CREAMED CHIPPED BEEF ON TOAST

Take 1 lb. chipped beef purchased from deli section of grocery store and fry slowly in a little oil. Sprinkle a little flour over the beef. Add enough milk to make creamy and heat until mixture thickens.

Serve over buttered toast.

— Sandy Allison

CHICKEN SALTIMBACCA

8 large, boneless, skinless chicken breasts
½ lb. soft Fontina cheese cut into rectangular pieces about ¼" thick – 8 pieces
½ lb. or 8 slices of maple ham or Virginia ham slices

Lay chicken breast flat on counter and cut pockets in the side of each chicken breast. Use a knife and cut almost to the outer edge of each chicken breast creating the pocket.

Take a piece of Fontina cheese and wrap a piece of ham around it enclosing the cheese with ham.

Place the ham and cheese piece inside the chicken pocket. Secure with toothpicks if a piece falls out.

Take 1 C. flour and season liberally with seasoning salt, garlic powder and black pepper. Mix well. Dredge chicken pieces in flour.

Heat skillet to medium high heat and put Crisco oil in skillet to cover the bottom of the pan. Fry chicken until lightly browned. Chicken will not be fully cooked. Remove from skillet and place in a baking dish.

Bake in the oven at 325° for 18 minutes.

Empty most of the grease from the skillet and sauté sliced mushrooms in a stick of margarine with the rest of the drippings. Sprinkle 1 tbsp. flour over mushrooms. Add 2 crumbled chicken bouillon cubes and add 1½ C. marsala wine. Wire whisk until flour and ingredients are mixed well.

Season with granulated garlic and black pepper. Do not add salt.

Cook the sauce until it thickens. Plate chicken on a platter and pour sauce over chicken platter.

— Rich Allison

TURKEY MEATBALLS AND MUSHROOM GRAVY OVER NOODLES

1 lb. lean ground turkey
1 egg
Breadcrumbs
¼ C. onions, chopped
Parsley, salt and pepper

Mix altogether and form into meatballs. Fry in skillet with some vegetable oil. Scoop meatballs and set aside. Drain all grease except 1 tbsp. Add enough flour to coat oil. Add 2 cans mushroom soup plus 2 cans full of milk, or half milk and half water. Add 4 chicken bouillon cubes. Stir constantly until cooked.

Cook 1 lb. wide noodles, as per package and drain. Place in a deep dish and cover with meatballs and gravy.

Serves 4.

In memory of
— Louise Hidlebaugh

SPAGHETTI SAUCE

½ C. canola oil
4 lb. stewing beef, cubed (trim all the fat off)
4 (29 oz.) cans Contadina tomato sauce
1 (18 oz.) can Contadina tomato paste
Oregano
Parsley
1 bay leaf
2 heaping tbsp. garlic, minced

Place canola oil in sauce pot.
Add stewing beef and cook until redness is gone. Add oregano, parsley and minced garlic; cook for about 2 minutes stirring so the garlic doesn't burn. Then add tomato paste, sauce, 2 (18 oz.) cans of water and 1 level tbsp. of sugar.

Bring to a boil. Turn heat on low and simmer for 2 to 2½ hours.

— Pat Holland

CABBAGE ROLLS

1 head cabbage, cored
1 lb. ground chuck, raw and uncooked
1 lb. ground pork, raw and uncooked
1 medium onion, chopped
2 C. rice, uncooked
Salt
Pepper
Garlic powder
Parsley
1 lg. can tomato paste + 1 can water or
1 lg. can stewed tomatoes and juice
Brown sugar to season (add to tomato paste)

Cook cabbage until soft, pull apart.
Mix together; ground beef, pork, rice and onion. Season.

Take cabbage leaf, scoop meat mixture onto it. Roll and stick a toothpick in it to hold together.

Pour sauce and brown sugar mixture over cabbage rolls.

Bake in oven until done at 350°. Check frequently to see if you need to add more sauce. Don't let them dry out.

You can freeze cabbage rolls individually on a cookie sheet then put in freezer bag. Don't add sauce until you cook them to serve.

— Eleanor Nesky

MACARONI AND CHEESE

Cook 1½ C. macaroni until soft. Drain.

Spray Pam in casserole.

Layer macaroni with margarine, American and Velveeta cheese, season with salt and pepper.

Pour 1 C. milk over casserole.

Bake at 350°. Serves two.

— Sandy Allison

TRI-COLORED TORTELLINI WITH CHICKEN & ASIAGO CHEESE

Dice:

1 red pepper
1 stalk celery
¼ medium onion
3 plum tomatoes

Cut 2 chicken breasts into strips. Season with seasoned salt, garlic powder and black pepper. Toss and marinate in ¼ C. Italian dressing.

Take a hot skillet and put in chicken with Italian dressing. Sauté 4 minutes. Remove from skillet.

Add:

4 tbsp. olive oil and 2 tbsp. margarine. Add pepper, celery and onion. Cook 3 minutes. Add 2 chicken bouillon cubes. Add 1 tbsp. minced garlic and fresh ground black pepper. Continue cooking for 2 minutes. Add the plum tomatoes.

Add:

Chicken back to skillet and cook on high. Add 1 C. half and half and cook reducing to medium heat until slightly thickened, and reduced.

Add:

Fresh basil, oregano and parsley. Continue cooking, then add ½ C. Romano cheese.

Meanwhile:

Cook 2 C. tortellini for 8 minutes. Drain well and add to the skillet – toss well.

Add ¼ C. Asiago cheese over top and place in a 250° oven for 5 minutes.

—'Rich Allison

> *This dish can be prepared in less than 30 minutes if you have all the ingredients readily available.*

GENERAL TSO'S CHICKEN

3 chicken legs, de-boned and skinned
½ tsp. salt
1 medium egg
5 tbsp. water
¾ C. cornstarch + 1 tbsp.
3 C. vegetable oil + 3 tbsp.
2 tbsp. green onion, chopped
1 tbsp. garlic, minced
⅔ C. chicken broth
2 tbsp. soy sauce
4 tbsp. sugar
½ to 1 tsp. chili oil to taste
1 tbsp. cooking wine or sherry
1 tbsp. white vinegar

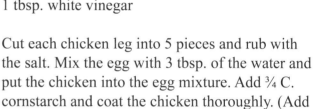

Cut each chicken leg into 5 pieces and rub with the salt. Mix the egg with 3 tbsp. of the water and put the chicken into the egg mixture. Add ¾ C. cornstarch and coat the chicken thoroughly. (Add cornstarch to egg mixture then dip).

Heat 3 C. of the oil in a wok or skillet, on high. Add the chicken until it turns golden brown. Remove from oil and drain. Remove the oil from the skillet and replace with the remaining 3 tbsp. of oil. Add green onion and garlic; when the garlic turns clear add the chicken broth, soy sauce and sugar, and stir.

Mix the remaining 2 tbsp. of water with the remaining tbsp. of cornstarch and pour into the stock mixture; stir well. Add the chicken and continue stirring. Add the chili oil and from the edge of the pan add the wine and vinegar, stirring gently.

Transfer to plates and serve immediately.

Serves 2 as a main course.

Recipe should be doubled. Do not add chicken to sauce until a few minutes before you serve.

— Aimee Schultz

JAMBALAYA

4 C. white rice
2 C. each, green peppers, celery and green onions, all diced
4 bay leaves
1½ tbsp. Cajun spice, preferably Zatarains
1 C. Tasso ham or regular ham, diced
12 Roma tomatoes, diced
1 (12 oz.) can tomato sauce
2 C. Andouille or smoked sausage, cut into slices.
2 C. shrimp, peeled and de-veined
1¼ qt. chicken or shrimp stock
4 tbsp. salad oil
2 lb. chicken tenders or breasts, cut into diced pieces
8 cloves garlic, chopped
1 (6 oz.) can (5 tbsp.) tomato paste

Heat oil in a Dutch oven, brown chicken and ham. Add peppers, onions, celery, garlic, tomatoes and sausage. Cook approximately 20 minutes.Add tomato sauce, tomato paste and Cajun spice. Cook 2 minutes, stirring constantly. Add rice and stock. Simmer 10 minutes, stir often. Add shrimp and bay leaf. Cover with a tight-fitting lid. Bake at 350° for 25 minutes, until rice is tender. Add more broth if rice mixture is dry.

— Rich Allison

GREEN BEAN-MUSHROOM CASSEROLE

16 oz. can green beans, drained
10¾ oz. can cream of mushroom soup
1 can fried onion rings

Spray casserole dish. Mix green beans and can of mushroom soup. Season with pepper - no salt. Onion rings already have salt added.

Bake at 350° for approximately 30 minutes. Cover with a lid. Place onion rings on top of casserole last 10-15 minutes of baking.

— Sandy Allison

RICE PILAF

1 med. onion
½ C. margarine
2 C. Minute Rice
2+ C. of beef bouillon
1 (8 oz.) can mushrooms and juice

Sauté onion and margarine in pan. When soft, place in a casserole dish and add rice and beef bouillon. Add mushrooms and juice.

Microwave for approximately 15 minutes or until done, or bake at 350° for approximately 45 minutes.

Check frequently and stir. It may need extra bouillon and water. However, don't stir too much since it causes rice to crumble apart.

— Connie Burket

CAJUN CHICKEN PASTA

2 boneless, skinless chicken breasts, cut into strips
2 tsp. Cajun seasoning
2 tbsp. butter
1 green pepper, sliced
1 red pepper, sliced
4 lg. fresh mushrooms, sliced
1 green onion, sliced
2 C. heavy cream
¼ tsp. dried basil
¼ tsp. garlic powder
¼ tsp. lemon pepper
½ tsp. Cajun seasoning
½ tsp. seasoning salt
8 oz. linguine, cooked and drained
¼ C. grated Parmesan cheese

Place chicken and Cajun seasoning in bowl. Toss to coat. In a large skillet over medium heat, sauté chicken in butter for 7-10 minutes until almost tender. Add peppers, mushrooms and onion. Cook and stir for 7-10 minutes. Reduce heat. Add cream and seasonings. Heat through, until sauce starts to thicken. Add linguine and toss. Heat through. Sprinkle with Parmesan Cheese.

— Kera Knisely

CHICKEN STUFFING CASSEROLE

4 chicken breasts
1 (8 oz.) can mushrooms
4 tbsp. butter
4 tbsp. flour
1 C. chicken broth
1 C. milk
1 can cream of chicken soup
1 box Stove Top Stuffing

Cook chicken until tender. Remove skin and bones and cut into large chunks. Sauté mushrooms in butter. Add flour and blend.

Add broth, milk and soup. Cook until thickened. Mix stuffing by directions on box. Layer chicken, sauce and stuffing. Bake at 350° for ½ hour.

— Joan Leach

CHICKEN RICE CASSEROLE

¼ C. margarine
5 tbsp. flour
1½ tsp. salt
⅛ tsp. pepper
1½ C. milk
1½ C. cooked rice
1 C. chicken broth
2 C. cooked cut-up chicken
⅓ C. chopped green pepper
¾ C. mushrooms or 4 oz. can
2 tbsp. pimento

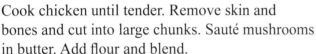

Melt margarine in pan over low heat. Blend in flour, salt and pepper. Cook until smooth and bubbly. Remove from heat. Stir in broth and milk. Bring to a boil and boil one minute stirring constantly.

Mix this sauce with remaining ingredients. Pour in greased 10"x6"x1½" baking dish. Bake 40-45 minutes at 350°. Freezes well.
Serves 8.

In memory of
— Grace Allison

BROCCOLI-CHICKEN CASSEROLE

2 pkg. frozen chopped broccoli
2-3 C. chopped cooked chicken
1 can cream of mushroom soup
1 can cream of chicken soup
1 C. mayonnaise
1 tsp. lemon juice
8 oz. sharp shredded cheddar cheese
½ C. bread crumbs, Italian
1 tsp. margarine

Layer broccoli and chicken. Mix soups, mayonnaise and lemon juice together and pour over broccoli and chicken.

Sprinkle cheese over this. Melt margarine and mix bread crumbs and sprinkle over casserole.

Bake 30-40 minutes at 350° in long casserole pan.

— Pam Bowser Knisely

GNOCCHI

2 C. mashed potatoes, stiff
Approximately 2-3 C. flour
2 eggs

Mix together. Add enough flour so mixture is dough like. Roll into long pretzel log shape. Cut into small pieces and flour well.

Lay on a cookie sheet and freeze. Take out of freezer and bag. Freeze.

To cook Gnocchi:

Bring pot of water to a boil. Put gnocchi in water.

Boil approximately 5 minutes until gnocchi start rising to surface. Gently stir and cook another minute. Drain and add sauce.

In memory of
— Margie Binotto

BAKED BEANS

½ lb. hamburger
1 med. onion, diced
½ lb. bacon, diced
½ green pepper, diced

Fry in small amount of oil until hamburger is cooked. Drain.

In a casserole add the above mixture with the following:

1 can green beans, drained
1 can butter beans, drained
1 can pork and beans
1 can kidney beans, drained
½ C. brown sugar
⅔ C. white sugar
½ C. ketchup
1 tbsp. mustard
1 tsp. salt
3 tbsp. vinegar

Bake at 350° for 45 minutes.

— Sally Weyant

Rich's sister, Sally Weyant has always been a good cook. She learned from one of the best, our mother, Grace Allison.

Sally did a lot of the cooking on the farm when we were young so Grace could work outside on the farm.

This baked bean recipe is very flavorful and has ground beef in it. It can be made ahead and re-heated for serving later.

REBELQUE
NORTH CAROLINA BARBEQUE

1 pork Boston butt roast
Aluminum roasting bag
Salt and pepper to taste
Cider vinegar
Barbeque sauce
Kaiser rolls
Cole slaw
Hot sauce

Put roast in aluminum roasting bag. Season with salt and pepper. Add small amount of water to bag. Seal and place in oven.

Bake at 300° for 4 to 4½ hours, until meat begins to fall apart.

Remove from oven. Remove bones. Pull apart with your hands until in small pieces. Add salt and pepper to taste.

Sauce:

Mix 2 parts vinegar with 1 part barbeque sauce. Add to pork.

Serve on toasted Kaiser roll with cole slaw and topped with hot sauce.

— Michael Hagan

BAKED CORN

1 tbsp. cornstarch
2 tbsp. sugar
1 tsp. salt
3 eggs, well beaten
1 can cream style corn
2 C. milk
2 tbsp. melted butter

Mix together the first four ingredients. Add corn and remaining ingredients. Mix well.

Bake at 350° for 45 minutes.

— Margaret Langham

HAMBURGER AND VEGETABLE CASSEROLE

Fry 1 lb. hamburger, diced green peppers and diced onions. Drain.

Place the following in a casserole dish.

Mushrooms, cut-up
Green peppers, sliced
Onion, sliced
Potatoes, sliced
Carrots, sliced

Stir ingredients Add hamburger mixture. Pour a quart jar of canned tomatoes, peppers, and onions over mixture and stir. See recipe on page 212.

Bake at 350° until vegetables are cooked soft – approximately one hour.

Salt and pepper to taste. Season with garlic powder and seasoning salt.

In memory of
— Donna Burket

BROCCOLI BEEF

¼ C. cornstarch
¼ C. soy sauce
1 tsp. ground ginger
5 tbsp. vegetable oil
1 lb. boneless round steak, sliced diagonally into ¼" strips
1 bunch fresh broccoli, trimmed and cut into 2" pieces, about 4 C.
3 tbsp. water
1½ C. canned beef broth, not condensed

Hot cooked rice.

Combine 2 tbsp. cornstarch, 2 tbsp. soy sauce and ginger in a medium sized bowl, and mix well. Add 2 tbsp. oil and the beef. Toss to coat. Let stand 15 minutes or refrigerate several hours.

Heat 2 more tbsp. oil in Wok or skillet. Sauté broccoli over high heat stirring for 3 minutes until bright green, but crispy. Add water, cover and steam 1 minute. Drain broccoli and remove from Wok.

Add remaining 1 tbsp. oil to Wok. Add meat and cook over high heat stirring about 4 minutes.

Remove and place with broccoli.

Add broth to Wok and bring to a boil. Combine remaining corn starch and 2 tbsp. soy sauce in a small cup. Stir into broth.

Add broccoli and beef. Cover and cook 4 minutes or until sauce is thickened and meat is tender.

Serve over hot cooked rice.

— Jean Stefanski

MACARONI-CHICKEN CASSEROLE

8 oz. macaroni, uncooked
½ lb. cheddar cheese, shredded
14 oz. cooked chicken, diced
4 hard boiled eggs, diced
2 C. milk
2 C. mushroom soup, 1 can
1 sm. can mushrooms, drained
Bread crumbs

Mix altogether in greased casserole dish.

Refrigerate overnight.

Cover with bread crumbs. Bake at 350° for one hour uncovered.

— Linda Glass

BRASCIOLE

2 round steaks-thin cut and bone at end of steak.

Trim fat and cut steaks in half lengthwise. Salt and pepper steaks. Generously place chopped garlic cloves on steaks.

Spread a generous portion of chopped fresh flat leaf parsley on steak. Grate old bread into crumbs and mix with grated Romano cheese and add enough vegetable oil to add some moisture.

Put crumb mixture in middle of steak lengthwise. Roll up steaks (jellyroll style). Tie with string and brown in skillet with oil.

Put in casserole dish with spaghetti sauce and oil from skillet. Bake at 300° for 3 hours.

In memory of
— Margie Binotto

Home Cooked Meals

> *Another great Italian meal that we learned to make from Margie Binotto. She always told us, "lots of freshly chopped garlic and fresh parsley". This is easy to make and very good.*

CHICKEN PARMESAN

1½ lb. chicken breasts, boneless and skinless
½ C. seasoned dry bread crumbs
½ C. Parmesan cheese
1 egg, well beaten
2 tbsp. olive oil
1 C. mozzarella cheese, shredded
1 can (8 oz.) tomato sauce
¼ tsp. dried oregano

Combine bread crumbs and Parmesan cheese. Dip chicken in egg and roll in bread and cheese mixture.

Heat oil in preferably a corning ware skillet and brown chicken on both sides.

Remove from stove and sprinkle with mozzarella cheese. Combine oregano and tomato sauce and spoon over chicken.

Heat covered at 350° for 45 minutes. Sprinkle with Parmesan cheese a few minutes prior to serving.

— Shirley Knisely

SCALLOPED CORN SUPREME

1 can (1 lb. 1 oz.) cream style corn
1 C. milk
1 egg, well beaten
1 C. cracker crumbs
¼ C. onion, finely chopped
3 tbsp. pimento, chopped
½ tsp. salt
½ C. buttered cracker crumbs

Heat corn and milk. Gradually stir in egg. Add next four ingredients and a dash of pepper.

Mix well. Pour into greased 8-inch round baking dish.

Top with buttered crumbs. Bake at 350° for 20 minutes. Serves 6.

— Sandy Allison

> *Try this variation of creamed corn for a casserole type dish. The pimentos give extra flavor. Can be baked ahead and reheated.*

BROCCOLI CASSEROLE

3 pkg. chopped broccoli
¾ lb. Velveeta Cheese
½ C. milk
½ C. Town House Crackers, crushed
½ C. melted butter

Cook and drain broccoli.

Melt cheese and add milk. Fold into broccoli. Layer broccoli with crumbs and butter in greased baking dish. Top with crumbs.

Bake at 350° for 20-25 minutes.

In memory of
— June Campbell

ONION PIE

2 lb. Spanish onions, thinly sliced
1 stick butter (no substitutes)
3 eggs, well beaten
1 C. sour cream
¼ tsp. salt
½ tsp. white pepper
Dash Tabasco
1 pastry shell, unbaked
Grated Parmesan cheese

Sauté onions in butter. Combine eggs and sour cream. Add to onion mixture. Season mixture and pour in pastry shell.

Top with cheese. Bake at 450° for 20 minutes then 325° for 20 minutes more.

Good with steak or roast beef.

Serves 6.

— Sandy Allison

Onion Pie? Sounds strange, but it is really very good.

SQUASH CASSEROLE

6 to 7 squash (half zucchini and half yellow squash) – cut into slices
1 lg. onion, chopped fine
1½ C. carrots, chopped

Sauté onions and carrots in some margarine while boiling squash in salted water. Do not overcook squash, then drain.

To the carrots and onions add:

1 can cream of chicken soup
1 C. sour cream

Then fold in squash to the mixture.

In a separate bowl, mix:

1 box Stove Top stuffing-chicken
½ C. melted butter or margarine

Layer in casserole dish starting with dressing, then squash, ending with dressing on top. Bake at 350° for 30-40 minutes.

In memory of
— Louise Hidlebaugh

ORIENTAL ASPARAGUS

1 tbsp. soy sauce
¾ tsp. ground ginger
1 clove garlic, crushed
1 lb. asparagus
2 tbsp. salad oil

Combine soy sauce, ginger and garlic; mix well. Let stand 30 minutes.

Wash asparagus, removing tough ends. Cut on slant into 1" pieces.

In skillet heat salad oil over high heat. Add sauce and asparagus. Stir fry 2 minutes, then cover and steam until asparagus is tender, approximately 3-5 minutes. Serve at once.

— Roger Knisely

GREEN TOMATO PIE

3½ C. green tomatoes, sliced
¾ C. seedless raisins, washed
1½ tsp. lemon grind, grated
2 tbsp. lemon juice
1 tbsp. cider vinegar
½ tsp. salt
1⅓ C. sugar
3 tbsp. flour
½ tsp. cinnamon
⅛ tsp. ginger
1 tbsp. tapioca
2 tbsp. butter

Wash tomatoes, remove stems, cut into eighths and slice thinly on cutting board.

Put into a 3 quart bowl and stir in the next five ingredients. Set aside.

In a second bowl, blend flour, sugar, spices and tapioca.

Use a 9" unbaked pie pastry crust and sprinkle with 2 tbsp. of the sugar mixture over pastry in the pie pan.

Fold rest of the sugar mixture into tomatoes. Add to the pie plate and dot with butter.

Cover with a top unbaked pastry. Bake 15 minutes at 400° then 50 minutes at 325°.

— Sandy Allison

Cinnamon, ginger and raisins give this casserole pie a different flavor.

PEPPER STEAK

1½ lb. top beef round or sirloin steak about 1" thick
¼ C. salad oil
1 C. water
1 med. onion cut into ¼" slices
½ tsp. garlic salt
¼ tsp. ginger, optional
2 med. green peppers cut into slices
Instant rice
1 tbsp. cornstarch
2-3 tsp. sugar
2 tbsp. soy sauce
2 med. tomatoes

Trim fat from meat. Cut meat into strips approximately 2"x1"x¼". Heat oil in large skillet. Add meat. Cook turning frequently until brown – about 5 minutes.

Stir in water, onion, garlic salt and ginger. Heat to boiling. Reduce heat. Cook and simmer 12-15 minutes for round steak and 5-8 minutes for sirloin.

Add green pepper strips during last five minutes of simmering. While meat simmers, cook instant rice as directed on package.

Blend cornstarch, sugar and soy sauce. Stir into meat mixture. Cook stirring constantly until mixture thickens and boils. Boil and stir one minute.

Cut each tomato into eighths and place on meat mixture. Cover and cook over low heat just until tomatoes are heated through – about three minutes. Serve with rice.

— Sandy Allison

This is a version of a stir fry dish with ginger and soy sauce. Serve over rice.

MEATS & VEGETABLES

POT PIE DOUGH

2 eggs, beaten
1 C. water
Sprinkle of salt
Approximately 2 C. flour

Use enough flour to hold together – approximately 2 C. Roll out <u>thin</u>, <u>very</u> <u>thin</u>.

When partially dry, cut into squares and let finish drying by laying on thin dry towels on a table.

Cook in either ham or chicken broth.

In memory of
— Grace Allison

> *Ham pot pie was a weekend tradition at the farm. It was served every Friday evening. This is not the pie type food that many people are used to eating. It is a dough cut into squares similar to large pieces of pasta and cooked in a broth of either ham or chicken. The Pennsylvania Dutch serve this. This is very much a central Pennsylvania dish, and you will rarely see it other places. Many people put chopped onions on top of their plate of pot pie. You can find a dough in the pasta or noodle section at the grocery store called Bott Boi (German). If you cannot find Bott Boi, use Haluski noodles.*

SUGAR PEAS & POTATOES
IN CREAM SAUCE

Cook new potatoes in water until they are tender. Then add sugar peas and cook until peas are tender.

Make a sauce with 3 tbsp. flour and 1 C. milk and add to mixture while mixture is not boiling. Bring to a boil to thicken, add a chunk of butter, salt and pepper to taste.

In memory of
— Grace Allison

CHICKEN, TURKEY
OR VEAL ROMANO

3 eggs
⅓ C. vegetable oil
Seasoning salt and pepper to taste
1 C. Italian bread crumbs
Romano cheese
¼ C. flour
Garlic powder to taste

Beat eggs and oil with seasoning salt, pepper and garlic powder in one bowl. Put ¼ C. flour in another bowl and season with seasoning salt, pepper and garlic powder. Place bread crumbs and Romano cheese in the third bowl.

Dredge boneless turkey breast, chicken or veal with flour. Cut into strips and dip in egg mixture, then in bread crumbs to make it Romano style.

Fry slowly over medium heat in a skillet with vegetable oil until brown. Finish cooking in oven at 325° for 12 minutes. Can be served with spaghetti sauce and pasta on the side.

— Rich Allison

> *We use this recipe mainly for chicken, but also have used it for turkey or veal romano. It is slightly messy to make, because of the three step process of dipping in flour, then egg and then bread and Romano cheese. The key is to keep one hand to dip into the flour and bread crumb mixture and use the other hand to dip into the egg mixture. Otherwise you will have two hands coated with the mixture. This is very flavorful. The key is to season the flour, season the eggs and use seasoned Italian bread crumbs.*

ITALIAN MEAT AND CHEESE ROLL

1½ lb. ground chuck hamburger, sausage and pepperoni
⅓ C. onion, chopped
½ tsp. oregano
Salt and pepper to taste
½ C. processed cheese spread
1 egg
1 pkg. (15-3/8 oz.) cheese pizza mix
2 tbsp. shortening
2 tsp. butter, melted
Chopped parsley

Brown meat and onion together in a hot skillet. Season with oregano, salt and pepper. Stir in cheese spread, egg and grated cheese from pizza mix.

Combine pizza dough mix and shortening. Mix with a fork until well combined. Stir in ½ C. very warm water. Mix to form a smooth dough. Cover and let stand 5 minutes. Knead dough on well-floured board until it is no longer sticky. Roll out into a rectangle about 12"x14".

Spread filling out on dough except for a 1½" strip on two long sides. Fold over dough and continue to roll up log. Pinch edges together.

Place roll on greased cookie sheet. Brush with melted butter and sprinkle with chopped parsley.

Bake at 425° for 15 minutes

Slice and serve with hot pizza sauce.

In memory of
— Grace Allison

DRIED CORN

Using dried corn from the canning section or by purchasing dried corn, do the following to prepare for eating:

Place corn in a pan covered with water and let set on counter all night.

Next day drain water and add fresh water covering the corn. Cook until soft and add salt, pepper and a little sugar to taste.

You can also make a flour thickening with water and flour and add to the corn and cook until thickened on medium heat, stirring often.

In memory of
— Vivian Lingenfelter

SUMMER SAUSAGE

4 lb. ground meat-lean (use hamburger or deer meat)
¼ C. or less Morton's Tender Quick Curing Salt
⅛ tsp. garlic, minced
1 tbsp. mustard seed
2 tsp. pepper
3 tsp. sugar
2 tsp. hot pepper seeds

Mix well and refrigerate over night.

Next Day:

Add 5 tsp. liquid smoke. Shape into loaves. (1 lb. each).

Bake on a cookie sheet for 1 hour at 300°. Do not over bake.

In memory of
— Donna Burket

GLAZED CARROTS

⅓ C. brown sugar
2 tbsp. butter
8 cooked carrots-sliced, or 1 can carrots

Heat together brown sugar and butter until sugar dissolves. Add carrots and cook until glazed and tender.

— Sandy Allison

MEATS & VEGETABLES

SOUR DOUGH PANCAKES

In the evening, put:

2 C. warm water in a bowl
Sprinkle 1 pkg. dry yeast and stir
Add 2 C. flour. Beat with a fork

Put a plate on top and let set until morning.

In the morning:

Add 1 tsp. salt
1 tbsp. sugar
2 eggs
½ tsp. baking soda dissolved in tbsp. water

Beat well and bake into pancakes.

In memory of
— Grace Allison

BROCCOLI CHEDDAR ROLLS

1 (36 oz.) frozen bread dough
1 (10 oz.) frozen broccoli, chopped, thawed and drained
1 C. cheddar cheese, grated
¼ C. instant minced onions
1 egg
1 tsp. onion salt
2 tbsp. grated parmesan cheese
2 tbsp. margarine melted

Let dough thaw. Roll out dough onto a rectangle. Mix broccoli and all other ingredients except margarine. Spread over dough. Roll dough up tightly in jelly roll fashion.

Use a little water on your fingertips and pinch edge firmly to seal dough. Cut into 24 slices and place in muffin pans. Brush dough with melted butter. Let rise until double. Bake at 375° for 10-15 minutes. Remove from pan immediately.

— Aimee Schultz

CHINESE COLD ROAST PORK

1 lb. pork tenderloin or lean boneless pork
¼ C. Kikkoman Soy Sauce
2 tbsp. dry sherry
2 tsp. brown sugar
1 tbsp. Hoison sauce
½ tsp. salt
½ tsp. sesame seed oil
1 garlic clove, crushed
¼ C. honey

Make 4 long cuts the entire length of the tenderloin about ½" deep. Combine remaining ingredients except honey and mix well. Add pork and marinade overnight periodically turning to coat.

Line a baking pan with aluminum foil. Place pork loin on a rack in the pan and roast at 400° for 10 minutes. Reduce heat to 300° and roast for another 45 minutes.

Brush honey heavily on all sides of pork and roast for 5-10 minutes longer at 400°.

Slice cooled pork into thin slices and arrange on a platter. Serve with the following:

Garlic Dipping Sauce:

¼ C. Kikkoman Soy Sauce
1 tbsp. dry sherry
1 tsp. brown sugar
2 cloves garlic, minced
¼ tsp. dried ginger or dash fresh ginger

Combine all ingredients and let stand ½ hour before serving. Strain out garlic.

Toasted Sesame Seeds:

3 tbsp. sesame seeds

Place seeds in a shallow baking pan and toast lightly at 325° for 10-12 minutes. Pork should be dipped in sauce then sesame seeds.

BAKED EGGPLANT OR SQUASH PARMIGIANA

Grease baking dish. Preheat oven to 350°.

1 med. sized eggplant-peeled or 1 med. squash – unpeeled. Slice either into thin slices.
2 med. onions, sliced
2 med. tomatoes, sliced
Salt and pepper
Parmesan, mozzarella and white cheddar cheese
Spaghetti sauce

Layer eggplant or squash, onions, tomatoes, spaghetti sauce and cheese. Sprinkle with salt, pepper and a dash of oregano.

Bake at 350° until eggplant or squash is soft. Add some cheese on the top for the last 15 minutes of baking. Drain off excess liquid.

— Sandy Allison

SLOPPY JOES

3 lb. ground beef
1½ tsp. salt
½ tsp. pepper
1½ C. onion, chopped
½ C. green pepper, chopped
½ C. celery, chopped
2 (15 oz.) or 1 (29 oz.) can Hunt's Tomato Sauce
1 C. water
½ C. ketchup
2 tbsp. Worcestershire sauce
1 tbsp. prepared mustard
1-2 tbsp. brown sugar, firmly packed
20 hamburger buns

Cook beef until it loses its redness. Drain fat. Add salt, pepper, onion, green pepper and celery. Cook approximately 5 minutes to soften vegetables. Stir occasionally.

Stir in remaining ingredients. Simmer 10-15 minutes. Can be frozen.

In memory of
— Maxine Schultz

FRENCH TOAST

Mix:

6 eggs
1 C. milk
1 tsp. vanilla
¼ tsp. nutmeg
½ tsp. cinnamon

Wire whisk and then dip thick sliced bread (preferably a sour dough bread) in mixture and turn and coat well.

Place in a skillet over medium heat until brown on both sides. Serve with margarine and maple syrup.

— Sandy Allison

HAM LOAF

1½ lb. fresh ground ham
2 eggs
Salt and pepper to taste
¼ C. green pepper, chopped
¼ C. celery, chopped
¼ C. onion, chopped

Mix above and shape into a ham loaf.

Make a basting mixture as follows:

1 C. sugar
½ C. water
½ C. vinegar
½ tsp. dry mustard

Boil 5 minutes and pour over ham loaf and reserve ½ C. to baste several times during baking. Bake at 350° for 1 hour.

In memory of
— Grace Allison

This ham loaf recipe has been in the family for many, many years.

MEATS & VEGETABLES

BREAD STUFFING

Dice 3 stalks celery, 2 carrots and 1 medium onion and place in a small saucepan with enough water to cover it. Bring to a boil and cook until soft. When soft, add 1 stick of margarine.

In a large pan or mixing bowl, add two loaves of cubed old bread. Sprinkle generously with seasoning salt, poultry seasoning and black pepper.

Add the celery, carrot and onion mixture and mix well.

Place in a crock pot with the lid on, cook on high for 2 hours and then on medium for approximately 2 hours stirring occasionally.

After two hours, add chicken, turkey or beef broth from whatever meat or poultry you are cooking and stir occasionally.

In memory of
— Grace Allison

PORK MARINARA

Take a piece of boneless pork and punch holes with a sharp knife in it. Stuff approximately 10 garlic cloves into the roast at various places.

Flour, salt and pepper roast. With a small amount of olive oil in a large pot, brown roast on all sides over medium heat.

When roast is browned, add either homemade marinara sauce or spaghetti sauce. Bring sauce up to a low boil. Remove from top of stove and place in oven and bake for approximately 4-5 hours at 300° until done.

Cook pasta of your choice and serve with pork and sauce.

In memory of
— Sue Rotella

STUFFED FLANK OR ROUND STEAK

Take one large flank steak or two round steaks. Make a stuffing mixture from recipe on previous column.

Place the stuffing mixture on one side of a flank steak or on one of the round steaks.

Fold over flank steak or place the round steaks on top of one another with stuffing in the middle. Sew with thread to seal in stuffing.

Place in a baking pan with a small amount of water in the bottom of pan along with 2 stalks of celery.

Season steak on outside with seasoning salt and pepper.

Bake at 325° for approximately 4 hours. Make brown gravy from broth and serve gravy over sliced pieces of steak.

In memory of
— Grace Allison

This was always a meal that we looked forward to having. The stuffing was always very moist because it was sealed inside the flank or round steak and baked and the stuffing would have lots of internal steam to make it moist and flavorful. Finding large pieces of flank steak is difficult unless you know a good butcher. We have found that two large slices of thin round steak (the type used for brasciole) works well.

Sue Rotella of Canonsburg, PA also taught us how to make many great Italian dishes. Pork marinara was one of her specialties. The long roasting time in the oven gives it good flavor.

STUFFED BANANA PEPPERS

Take 24 banana peppers, washed, seeded and sliced in half, lengthwise.

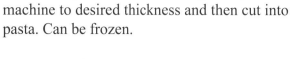

Meat Mixture:

3 lb. hamburger
3 lb. bulk Italian sausage
5 eggs
1½ C. seasoned bread crumbs or bread cubes
1½ C. Romano cheese
1 small onion, diced

Mix above mixture and then season well with garlic powder, black pepper and seasoning salt. Mix well again.

Take meat mixture and fill banana peppers with meat mixture. Lay on a waxed paper tray and cover with Saran wrap and place in the freezer until frozen firm.

Then place in Ziploc bags and put in freezer. When ready to eat, place number of peppers needed in a baking dish, cover with spaghetti sauce and some Romano cheese. Bake at 325° for one hour.

— Rich Allison
(Adapted from Margie Binotto's recipe)

HOME MADE SPAGHETTI PASTA

4 C. flour
4 lg. eggs
¼ C. water
1-2 tbsp. oil
1-2 tbsp. salt

Mix above and place under a bowl for 5-10 minutes. Remove from under bowl. Cut into smaller pieces and roll out each piece with a rolling pin to approximately ¼" thickness.

Take these pieces and run through the pasta machine to desired thickness and then cut into pasta. Can be frozen.

In memory of
— Margie Binotto

PAN FRIED BAKED STEAK

Take round steak and cut into pieces approximately 5"x5". Dredge in flour and season heavily with garlic powder, seasoning salt and black pepper.

Pan fry steak in Crisco oil in a large iron skillet, if available, until steak is brown on the outside

Transfer steak to a large baking pan. When done frying all the steak, add 2 C. water to the skillet with ½ C. flour. Bring to a boil to thicken. Add Gravy Master to give it a brown color. Season with more of the above seasonings. Pour gravy over steak and bake in the oven at 325° for approximately 3 hours, or until fork tender.

In memory of
— Grace Allison

PORK LOIN WITH SAUERKRAUT IN SLOW COOKER

Take a pork loin and place in a slow cooker (not a crock pot). Heavily season with garlic powder and black pepper. Do not add water.

Start pork loin on medium until heated through. Reduce heat to low and let cook for approximately 12 hours.

Approximately 2 hours before serving, add 2 cans sauerkraut, rinsed without the juice to the pork loin. Continue cooking until ready to serve. Add kielbasa and caraway seed if desired.

— Sandy Kardos

BEEF RIVAL SOUP

Take a medium sized beef roast and place in a pan with approximately 2" water season with salt and pepper and add 2 stalks of celery. Roast in the oven for approximately 4 hours at 325°.

When roast is done, remove roast and celery from broth. Strain the broth and place in a large pan on the stove.

Add 8 bouillon cubes to broth and add 4 C. of water. Dissolve the bouillon by boiling. Add black pepper and later add salt to taste.

Rivals:

Take 2 C. flour and break in 3 egg yolks. Mix with a fork until all flour is blended well. When broth is in a rolling boil, break the rival dough apart and drop into boiling water. Turn down stove to medium heat and stir constantly to avoid sticking. Cook until they are soft; approximately 30-45 minutes.

— Sandy Allison

FRIENDSHIP POTATOES

1 bag (32 oz.) frozen hash brown potatoes, thawed
1 C. sour cream
1 can cream chicken soup
1½ C. shredded cheddar cheese
1 small onion, diced
1 tsp. salt
1 C. butter or oleo, melted
1 C. corn flakes, crushed

Butter baking dish.

In a large bowl, combine hash browns, sour cream, cream of chicken soup, cheddar cheese, diced onion and salt.

Put mixture in baking dish.

In a skillet melt the butter and add cornflakes and mix well.

Spread corn flakes on top covering all of mixture.

Bake in preheated oven at 350° for 60-70 minutes.

In memory of
— Louise Hidlebaugh

RAVIOLI

Dough:

3 eggs
4 C. flour, sifted
¼ C. water

Sift flour into medium size mixing bowl and form a well. Place eggs and water inside well and beat lightly. Gradually mix flour and egg batter by hand.

When dough mixture becomes moderately stiff, roll out on a lightly floured board with a rolling pin.

Cut dough with a round cookie cutter and place 1 tsp. filling below in each piece of dough. Fold over dough and press edges with tine of fork to seal making a half moon.

Filling:

Fry 1 lb. hamburger seasoned with garlic powder, seasoning salt and black pepper. Mix with 1 lb. ricotta cheese, 2 eggs, 2 tbsp. parsley, ¾ C. Romano cheese.

To Cook Ravioli:

Add 3 tbsp. salt to boiling water. Place ravioli in pot and cook 8-10 minutes. Place in colander and drain thoroughly. Place ravioli on platter, sprinkle with Romano cheese and cover with spaghetti sauce.

In memory of
— Grace Allison

SMOKED STUFFED PORK LOIN

Take two pieces of pork loin. Make a stuffing mixture as per Page 110. Take one pork loin and lay flat on the counter. Lay stuffing across pork loin in a "tent" or "pyramid" fashion.

Put other pork loin on top and tie with cord to hold in place. Locate cord netting used by butcher shops to tie roasts and place the two loins inside the netting.

Season outside of pork loin with seasoning salt, pepper and garlic powder. Insert meat thermometer.

Place in the smoker with a pan of water in the bottom of the smoker. Start pork out on higher temperature and reduce to ideal level. Cook until meat registers 170° on thermometer. Baste with one of the barbecue or fruit sauces listed in the sauce section.

— Rich Allison

We love cooking on the smoker, and our favorite food is roast smoked pork loin stuffed with a bread stuffing. The stuffing becomes very moist because of being sealed inside the pork loin.

Season the loin with lots of garlic powder, seasoning salt and black pepper. Always use a meat thermometer to eliminate the guesswork and to avoid robbing the juices from the meat from overcooking.

MARGIE BINOTTO'S MEATBALL RECIPE

1 lb. Hamburger (not real lean). Use 80% lean – 20% fat.

3-4 slices of old bread, crust removed. (Soak in milk and squeeze excess milk out.) Crumble in hamburger meat.

Mix with hamburger and add:

1 small onion, diced
2 cloves minced garlic
1 egg
Salt and pepper
½ C. Romano cheese
1-2 tbsp. parsley flakes (use fresh flat leaf parsley, if available).

Fry meatballs in skillet in olive oil until browned. Place in sauce and let finish cooking.

In memory of
— Margie Binotto

At Margie Binotto's table there was always a large bowl of homemade meatballs. The romano cheese, fresh parsley and fresh garlic give these meatballs great flavor. The old bread soaked in milk give extra moisture to the meatballs. These meatballs were always considered a side dish to several types of pasta and also several other meats, salads and always lots of Italian bread and butter.

ALFREDO SAUCE

¼ stick butter
¼ C. olive oil
½ diced onion

Sauté above on medium heat until translucent.

Add 6 cloves minced garlic and sauté.

Add 12 oz. whipping cream and reduce until thickened.

Season With:

Seasoned salt
Freshly ground pepper
Parsley flakes

Continue Simmering and Add:

½ C. Romano cheese
Toss with 1 lb. cooked pasta

— Rich Allison

GARLIC MASHED POTATOES

4 lb. red skinned potatoes-peeled and cubed (1")
9 lg. garlic cloves
2 tbsp. unsalted butter
2 tbsp. chopped fresh rosemary
1 C. (or more) chicken stock
½ C. grated parmesan cheese
Fresh rosemary sprigs for garnish

Directions:

Cook the potatoes and garlic in a large pot of boiling salted water until both are very tender, about 30 minutes. Drain. Transfer the potatoes to a large bowl. Using an electric mixer, beat potatoes and garlic. Add butter and chopped rosemary; beat until smooth. Bring 1 C. of chicken stock to a simmer. Gradually mix broth into potato mixture. Stir in parmesan cheese. Season with salt and pepper to taste. Transfer potatoes to a serving bowl. Garnish with rosemary.

Serves: 8

SWEET POTATO CASSEROLE

3 C. sweet potatoes or yams (canned) drained
2 eggs
½ C. milk
½ C. melted margarine
¼ C. sugar
1 tsp. vanilla
*Mix above ingredients well with mixer. Pour into buttered 9"x13" baking dish

⅓ C. melted margarine (5 tbsp.)
1 C. brown sugar
½ C. flour
1 C. chopped pecans or walnuts
*Mix together to form a fine sprinkle and put on top of sweet potato mixture

Bake uncovered at 350° for 30-40 minutes.

— Sandy Kardos

COLORFUL VEGGIE BAKE

2 packages (16 oz. each) frozen California blend veggies
8 oz. Velveeta Cheese, cubed
6 tbsp. butter or margarine, divided
½ C. crushed butter flavored crackers

Prepare veggies according to package directions. Drain.

Place half in ungreased 9"x13" baking dish.

In small pan (or microwave) combine cheese and 4 tbsp. butter, melt slowly. Pour half over veggies; layer again with veggies, then cheese

Melt remaining butter, toss with cracker crumbs and sprinkle over top.

Bake uncovered at 325° for 20-25 minutes or until golden brown.

— Sandy Kardos

GREEN BEANS-MUSHROOMS AND RED PEPPERS

2 tbsp. margarine
2 tbsp. olive oil

Add:

1 tbsp. garlic powder
Lightly season with seasoning salt

Add:

Red peppers
¼ C. soy sauce
Mushrooms
Green beans

Sauté until partially crunchy

— Rich Allison

MUSHROOMS-YELLOW SQUASH AND RED PEPPERS

In skillet:

2 tbsp. margarine
2 tbsp. olive oil

Sauté:

Mushrooms
Yellow squash
Red peppers

Add:

1½ tbsp. Italian seasoning
1 tbsp. garlic powder
Salt and pepper

Near the end of cooking squeeze the juice of 1 whole lemon over and remove from heat.

— Rich Allison

GRILLED ITALIAN VEGETABLES

Wash and Slice:

½ zucchini
½ eggplant
2 red peppers
1 onion

Mince 3 garlic cloves and add 3 tbsp. olive oil. Add vegetables and toss mixture.

Grill in wire basket until tender and crisp.

While Grilling:

Fresh parsley and oregano, chopped
2 garlic cloves, minced
¼ C. olive oil

Microwave above for 45 seconds

Put cooked vegetables in bowl, add oil mixture with garlic, parsley and oregano.

Season with salt and pepper. Toss well and serve.

— Rich Allison

GRILLED VEGETABLES

Take your favorite fresh vegetables or any combination of items below:

Red pepper cut into ⅛ pieces
Large onion, cut into ⅛ pieces
Yellow squash, cut into large julienne strips
Zucchini, cut into large julienne strips
Mushroons, cut in half
Baby carrots, partially boiled to soften

Season with kosher salt and fresh ground pepper. Drizzle with olive oil.

Place in a vegetable grill basket over medium high grill heat. Cook approximately 7 minutes until slightly tender but not soft. Vegetables may smoke and catch on fire, but that will give them additonal smoky flavor.

— Rich Allison

MEATS & VEGETABLES

NATALIA'S RUSSIAN VEGETABLE PIE

6 medium potatoes
2 small to medium red beets
2 medium carrots
2 eggs – hard boiled

Boil vegetables separately, skin and shred.

Layer:

½ potatoes. Top with chopped onion, mayonnaise, sour cream and salt.

Continue layers and topping:

2nd layer - beets
3rd layer - carrots
4th layer - remainder of potatoes

Separate hard boiled egg whites and yolks
Shred whites as vegetables
Shred yolks finer

Use eggs to decorate top.
Garnish with dill, parsley and cucumber curls.

Serves 6-8

— Sally Kaufman

BROCCOLI AND RED PEPPERS

1 head broccoli, chopped
1 red pepper, sliced julienne
2 tbsp. margarine
2 tbsp. olive oil
Seasoning salt to taste
Granulated garlic to taste
Black pepper to taste
6 tbsp. sesame oil

Stir fry broccoli and peppers in margarine and oil. Add seasonings and sesame oil. Cook approximately 3 minutes. Remove vegetables from heat while still crunchy

— Rich Allison

SMALL BOILING ONIONS & PEAS

Sauté sugar peas in 2 tbsp. each of margarine and olive oil, approximately 2 minutes. Salt and pepper

Add:

1 container (8 oz.) heavy cream

Bring to a boil and reduce the cream
Mix 1 tsp. cornstarch with water and add to thicken.

— Rich Allison

PICADILLO (PICA-D-O)

2 lb. lean ground beef
¼ tsp. oregano
¼ tsp. cumin
1 bay leaf
½ C. raisins
1 C. cooking wine
½ C. stuffed olives
1 small onion, chopped
½ green pepper, chopped
½ tsp. garlic powder
1 can (15½ oz.) tomato sauce
Salt to taste

Put meat in pan. Add garlic powder, green pepper, oregano, cumin, bay leaf and tomato sauce in pan and cook for 30 minutes on low heat. Then add cooking wine, olives and raisins. Cook for 5 more minutes.

Serve over white rice.

— Grant and Millie Jackson

Grant and Millie Jackson live south of Pittsburgh, PA not too far from us. Grant was a former Pittsburgh Pirate pitcher, and we frequent the same watering hole and restaurant in the area. This was originally Millie's mother's recipe. Both Grant and Millie are excellent cooks especially in Latino specialties.

The Very Best Recipes of Rich & Sandy Allison

PASTA WITH CHICKEN

8 pieces chicken tenders

Season with garlic powder, season salt, and black pepper. Marinate in Zesty Italian dressing.

Sauté chicken in olive oil in skillet on medium-high until browned. Remove from skillet and drain all but 2 tbsp. oil.

Sauté ¾ C. diced onions and 2 tbsp. minced garlic for 2 minutes. Add a 29 oz. can of tomato sauce.

Add:

1 tbsp. parsley
½ tbsp. basil
1 tsp. kosher salt
¼ tsp. fresh grated pepper

Add chicken back to skillet. Simmer for 15 minutes.

Meanwhile; cook 1 lb. pasta in salted water for 12 minutes.

Drain and add to skillet with ¾ C. Romano cheese.

Serves 4.

— Rich Allison

BAKED BEANS

4 lb. navy beans
1 lg. bottle ketchup
1 sm. bottle dark Karo syrup
4 lg. onions
2 cans tomato soup
2 lb. brown sugar
2 tbsp. yellow mustard
3 lb. bacon, fried and dried

Cook beans until soft. Then drain. Mix all ingredients together.

Bake at 350° for approximately 2 hours. Add 1 tbsp. ginger to other ingredients.

— Margaret Langham

CLAIBORNE CHICKEN

2 whole chicken breasts, skinless and boneless
3 tbsp. olive oil
2 cloves garlic, minced
½ tsp. basil
½ tsp. marjoram
1 med. red onion, chopped
2 ripe tomatoes, chopped
1 green pepper, cut in bite-size pieces
¼ lb. mushrooms, halved or quartered
8 oz. Feta cheese, crumbled
½ C. chopped fresh parsley

Marinate bite-size chicken pieces in olive oil, garlic and herbs for a few hours. Sauté onions in olive oil; add chicken (and its marinade) and sauté until done. Toss in large serving bowl with ¾ lb. of hot fettuccine and all remaining ingredients. The Feta cheese will melt a bit.

— Janice Steff

CHICKEN OR PORK SCHNITZEL

Take boneless chicken breasts and pound to ¼" thickness. Cut into small pieces of about 2½" square. Or take a boneless pork loin and cut ¼" thick slices of loin and then cut into two pieces of about 2½" square.

Take flour and place in bowl and season with seasoning salt, garlic powder and black pepper.

In another bowl, beat three eggs; season with seasoning salt and pepper.

In another bowl, place seasoned Italian bread crumbs.

Dredge meat or poultry into flour, then into egg batter and then into bread crumbs. Pan fry in Crisco oil at medium high until golden brown. Meat will not be cooked inside. Place cookie sheet and put in oven at 325° for 12 minutes to finish.

— Rich Allison

MEATS & VEGETABLES

MEAT LOAF

1 lb. hamburger
1 lb. ground pork
1 egg
1 C. bread crumbs
1 tsp. garlic, minced
½ C. Romano cheese
1 sm. can Hunts tomato sauce
1 onion, chopped
Salt and Pepper
Mix all above ingredients together.

Bake at 300° for 2½ to 3 hours.

— Hope Kephart

PIZZA BURGERS

1 lb. Jumbo bologna
1 lb. chopped ham
1 lb. hamburger
½ lb. yellow American cheese, grated
½ lb. mozzarella cheese, shredded
1½ jars spaghetti sauce (reg. size)
Pinch of sage, oregano, Italian seasoning and parsley

Fry hamburger.
Grind meats.
Mix cold meats and cheese.
Add warm hamburger.
Add spices and sauce; mix all together.
Spread on hamburger rolls.

Bake at 350° for 20 minutes.

— Beccie Weyant

TACO STUFFED SHELLS

18 jumbo shells
1 lb. ground beef, chicken or turkey
1 (8 oz.) cream cheese
1 tsp. chili powder
1 tsp. chives
1 can (4 oz.) green chilies
2 bottles (8 oz.) taco sauce
1 C. cheddar cheese
1 C. Monterey Jack cheese
1 C. tortilla chips, broken up
Garnish with green onions (optional)

Preheat oven to 350°. Cook shells. Brown meat.
Add cream cheese, chilies and spices to meat.
Fill shells. Place in greased 13"x9" baking dish.
Spoon taco sauce over and bake 15 minutes
covered. Uncover and top with cheeses and chips.
Bake another 15 minutes. Sprinkle with onions.

— Tammy Claycomb

SWEET POT PIE

Use pot pie dough recipe on Page 106.

Take a quart jar of canned peaches or canned
oxheart cherries with the juice and pour into a
large pot, or take 1 C. raisins and 2-3 C. water.
Pick the fruit of your choice.

Bring this to a boil on medium heat. Cook slowly
for approximately 10 minutes stirring constantly.

Add 2-3 tbsp. margarine and 3-4 C. water. Bring
to a boil. Add the pot pie dough and stir constantly
until the dough softens.

Near the end of cooking, add sugar to taste.

Do not make this to a broth. Use fruit juice and
water only.

In memory of
— Linnie Knipple

CHICKEN SHEPHERDS PIE

Cook 6 chicken breasts for 20 minutes. Chop chicken into bite size pieces and strain broth to use in pie.

Coarsely chop:

4 stalks celery
1 lb. Carrots
2 onions
12 potatoes with skins left on

Cook vegetable mixture in just enough water to cover. Cook until partially soft, approx. 30 minutes. Add strained broth to mixture.

Then add:

1 lb. box mushrooms, sliced
2 cans whole corn, undrained
2 cans peas, undrained
18 chicken bouillon cubes
3 tbsp. parsley
1 tbsp. seasoning salt
1 tsp. Pepper
Yellow food coloring

Take 18 tbsp. cornstarch and 2 C. cold water to make a thickening and add to the above mixture. Cook another 5 minutes until mixture thickens.

Line a two (2) 13"x17" pans with your favorite pie crust recipe or use the pastry recipe on page 126 or purchase store made pie crust pastry. Pour in chicken / vegetable mixture on top of pastry.

Cook another 4 lbs.of potatoes, drain and mash and mix like you would for mashed potatoes. Top mixture with potatoes and cover with a top pie crust.

Bake 350° for 45 minutes or until top crust is golden brown.

— Rich & Sandy Allison

GUINESS STOUT IRISH STEW PIE

3 lbs. stewing beef, cubed

Toss beef in flour seasoned with seasoning salt, pepper and garlic powder. Fry in Crisco oil until browned and remove from oil. Remove all oil except for approx ½ C. Add 12 oz. dark Guiness beer, deglaze pan and simmer.

Coarsely chop:

4 stalks celery
1 lb. carrots
2 onions, chopped fine
5 lbs. potatoes, washed, cut into pieces with skins left on
1 box (12 oz.) mushrooms, cut into larger chunks

Toss all vegetables with seasoning salt and pepper. Put vegetables into pan with Guiness beer mixture and cover with water and add 10 beef bouillon cubes. Add beef chunks. Let mixture cook for one hour. Make a "dark roux" of ¼ C. flour and ¼ C. butter. Add to pan.

Add 1 tbsp. Gravy Master to darken broth. Add 2 tbsp. parsley and ½ tsp. thyme. Place in oven at 350° and cook for 3 additional hours. If not thick enough, add more cornstarch to thicken. Cook 4 lbs. more potatoes, drain and mash and mix like you would for mashed potatoes. . Set aside.

Place your favorite pie crust recipe or use the pastry crust recipe on page 126 or purchase store-made pie crust pastry in bottom of two (2) 13"x17" pans. Add vegetable / beef mixture and top with mashed potatoes. Cover with a top pie crust. Bake 350° for 45 minutes or until top crust is golden brown.

— Rich & Sandy Allison

The back cover of this book shows a shepherd's pie similar to the recipes above. These recipes are large and each will serve 25-30 people. You can cut this recipe in half or quarter.

MEATS & VEGETABLES

PIEROGI

2 C. flour
1 whole egg + 1 yolk
1 tsp. butter
½ C. warm milk
½ tsp. salt
2 tbsp. sour cream

Mix ingredients and knead until dough is soft and pliable. Let rest 10 minutes covered with a warm bowl. Divide dough into halves and roll thin. Cut circles with large biscuit cutter. Place a small spoonful of filling to one side. Moisten edge with water, fold over and press edges together firmly. Be sure they are well sealed. Drop pierogi into salted boiling water. Cook gently for 5 minutes. Lift out of water with slotted spoon. Sauté in butter and onions.

Sauerkraut filling:

2 C. sauerkraut, cooked with butter and salt.

Potato and Cheese filling:

1 C. mashed potatoes
Salt and pepper
American cheese, melted

— Sandy Allison

SPINACH-BROCCOLI AND CAULIFLOWER SOUFFLE

1 box Stouffers Spinach Soufflé
1 box Bird's Eye Broccoli and Cheese
1 box Bird's Eye Cauliflower and Cheese

Mix the above all together.
Thaw and place in a casserole dish.

Bake at 350° until bubbly.

— Kathy Dudro

RED CABBAGE

1 head red cabbage
4 red tart apples
¼ C. white vinegar + 3 C. (to taste)
1 C. brown sugar
2 tbsp. margarine
½ tsp. salt
½ tsp. caraway seeds

Shred cabbage and place in saucepan. Add 4 apples that have been cored and sliced thin. Do not peel. Add vinegar, brown sugar, margarine and salt.

Cook slowly until tender.

— Rich Allison

KEY WEST GREEN BEANS

Caramelize one large onion sliced in ½ stick margarine in a skillet until golden brown, about 20 minutes.

In a separate pan, fry 1 lb. diced bacon until done. Remove bacon and add 2 lb. green beans and 1 diced red pepper to bacon grease along with 2 tbsp. olive oil. Add ¼ to ½ C. teriyaki sauce to mixture.

Sauté until the beans are slightly crunchy. Then add 2 tbsp. chili Sichuan sauce and 2 tbsp. sesame seeds.

Add bacon back into pot and drain the caramelized onions and add the onions to the pot. Cook another minute stirring to blend.

— Rich & Sandy Allison
— Bim and Kay Burket

We found this recipe on one of our trips to Key West at a little bar on a side street that had a poly tarp for a roof.

MEAT LOAF

1 lb. lean ground beef
¾ lb. lean ground pork
1 egg
½ C. bread crumbs
1 tsp. granulated garlic powder
½ tsp. seasoning salt
¼ tsp. pepper
1 tsp. parsley flakes
½ C. chopped onions

Mix above ingredients together. Place in greased casserole dish. Refrigerate 4-6 hours to blend flavors. Pour ketchup over top. Put 3 tsp. margarine over top.

Bake at 350° for 1 to 1½ hours.

Serves 4.

— Sandy Allison

POTATOES OREGANO

Wash 8 potatoes leaving skins on. Cut potatoes into approximately 6 pieces per potato or 6 large wedges.

Cook in a pot of salted water until almost soft, but not mashed potato quality of softness.

Drain water. While potatoes are still hot, add 1 stick margarine, 8 ounces of sour cream, 2 tbsp. of dried oregano, seasoning salt, garlic powder and black pepper. Mix well trying not to mash the potatoes.

Serves 8 people. You should use 1 potato per person.

— Rich Allison

BAKED HAM

With a sharp knife, cut scores into the ham diagonally making a diamond pattern.

Bake ham covered at 350° for 2½ hours with a small amount of water in the bottom of the pan. Remove from oven and drain off broth and save for another use.

Coat the ham with yellow mustard brushing it into the crevices of the diamond pattern. Baste with honey and coat with brown sugar packing the brown sugar all over the ham.

Put canned pineapple slices and maraschino cherries on ham securing with toothpicks if necessary. Mix the pineapple and cherry juice and place in the bottom of the pan. Bake one additional hour and baste the last 15 minutes using a turkey baster leaving the ham uncovered for the last 15 minutes.

— Rich Allison

GRILLED POTATOES

Cook 1 potato per person in salted water until partially soft but not mushy.

Drain water. Season with seasoning salt, garlic powder and black pepper. Toss to coat. Add olive oil to coat the potatoes.

Place the potatoes in a grill basket and cook over medium high heat for about 5 minutes until they begin browning.

Remove from grill before they become too soft.

Can be served as a side dish or on chicken or steak salads.

— Rich Allison

MEATS & VEGETABLES

POT ROAST

2 lb. beef roast
6-8 potatoes, peeled and cut into pieces
6-8 carrots, cut into pieces
2 medium onions, peeled and quartered

Cook the beef roast in water in the oven at 350° for approximately 3 hours.

When beef is done, place on a plate and strain the broth. Put the broth back into the pot and add more water along with 6-8 beef bouillon cubes. Add cut-up vegetables. Cook in broth on top of stove until soft about 30-40 minutes.

When the vegetables become soft, you can thicken the broth with a mixture of flour and water. Use approximately ¼ C. of flour mixed with 8 ounces of cold water and stir until smooth. Add this mixture to the pot and continue to stir until the mixture comes to a boil. Cook for another 10 minutes for the flour mixture to thicken and cook. Continue stirring regularly to prevent the flour mixture from sticking to the bottom of the pan.

Taste the broth mixture, and if desired, you can add more beef bouillon for more flavor.

— Sandy Allison

STUFFED PEPPERS

3 large red peppers, clean and washed with tops cut off. (Red peppers are sweeter and add more flavor than green peppers.)
½ lb. ground beef and ½ lb. ground pork
1 egg
Bread crumbs
1 small chopped onion

Mix meat, egg, bread crumbs and onion together. Sprinkle garlic powder, seasoning salt, parsley flakes and ground pepper over mixture and mix well.

Stuff red peppers with mixture. Place in casserole dish. Pour spaghetti sauce over peppers.

Cover casserole dish with lid or aluminum foil. Bake at 325° for one hour.

— Sandy Allison

BAKED APPLES

2 lb. apples, preferably McIntosh or another baking type apple
1 C. brown sugar
1 stick margarine
Cinnamon

Peel, core and slice apples and place in a bowl. Add cinnamon to lightly coat apples. Add brown sugar and slices of margarine. Toss well to coat.

Place in a greased baking dish, cover and bake at 325° for 30-45 minutes until soft.

— Rich & Sandy Allison

CHIPPED HAM WITH BARBECUE SAUCE

1 (14 oz.) bottle ketchup
1½ bottles water
¼ C. light brown sugar
Salt and pepper

Fry together: ½ C. chopped celery, 1 whole pepper, chopped fine and 1 onion, chopped fine.

Add:

2 tbsp. Worcestershire sauce
2 tbsp. vinegar
1 tbsp. mustard
8 whole cloves (remove when sauce is cooked)

Cook sauce 1 hour than add chopped ham. Simmer.

— Marianne Erhart

DESSERTS

Cooking from the Farm to the City

The Very Best

Recipes

of

Rich & Sandy Allison

and Their

Family and Friends

DESSERTS

STRAWBERRY & GRAND MARNIER SABAYON TRIFLE

8 lg. egg yolks
½ C. plus 2 tbsp. (or more) sugar
Pinch of salt
½ C. Grand Marnier, Galliano or other Orange liqueur
¼ C. orange juice

1 C. chilled whipping cream
3 containers (1 pint) strawberries, hulled

⅔ of 12 oz. purchased pound cake, cut into ½" cubes

Whisk yolks, ½ C. sugar and salt in medium metal bowl. Whisk in Grand Marnier and orange juice. Set bowl over a pot of simmering water (do not let bowl touch water). Using electric mixer, beat until mixture is thick and thermometer registers 160° - about 7 minutes. Place bowl over larger bowl filled with ice and water, Whisk until sabayon is cool.

Beat cream in another medium bowl until stiff peaks form. Gently fold into sabayon in 2 additions. Coarsely chop strawberries with 2 tbsp. sugar in processor. Stir in additional sugar to taste, if desired.

Spoon ½ C. strawberries onto bottom of 2½ qt. glass bowl. Spoon ¾ C. sabayon evenly over. Top with enough pound cake to cover. Spoon 1 C. strawberries over cake. Spoon 1 C. sabayon over strawberries. Top with remaining pound cake. Spoon remaining strawberries over pound cake. Spread remaining sabayon evenly over strawberries. Cover and refrigerate at least 8 hours or overnight.

— Rich Allison

This dessert takes a considerable amount of time, but it is definitely worth doing. It has rich flavors from the freshly made sabayon or pudding.

CRÈME BRULEE

3 C. heavy cream
¾ C. milk
1½ tsp. almond extract or vanilla
10 egg yolks
¾ C. sifted confectioner's sugar

Preheat oven to 300°.

In a 2 quart saucepan over medium heat combine cream, milk and flavoring. Bring just to a boil and remove from heat.

Place yolks in a bowl and whisk in sifted confectionery sugar. Beat until pale yellow and slightly thickened.

Slowly whisk the cream mixture into yolk mixture. Be careful not to do it too quickly. Strain into a 2 qt. pitcher and skim foam.

Place 8 molds (5 oz.) in a baking pan and blot any bubbles with paper towel. Place pan in oven and fill with hot water halfway up molds. Cover with foil and bake 60-65 minutes until a paring knife comes out slightly sticky. Do not overcook.

Take custard out of water and cool to room temperature. Wrap with Saran Wrap and refrigerate custard. Sprinkle each custard with 1 tbsp. granulated sugar. Wipe excess from rims and light blow torch on medium and brown sugar with torch.

— Rich Allison

We picked up this variation of Creme Brulee while in Europe one time. We had our best tasting and smoothest creme brulee in Paris, France. Later we found a recipe that was good, but not quite as good as what we had near the Eiffel Tower.

TIRAMISU

3 tbsp. sugar
2 egg yolks
2 oz. cream cheese
6 oz. mascarpone cheese
3 tsp. Marsala wine
7 oz. heavy whipping cream, whipped
2 C. espresso or strong coffee
1 oz. additional Marsala wine
2 tbsp. additional sugar
½ C. warm water
24 French style ladyfinger cookies
3 tbsp. powdered sweetened cocoa mix

Step One:

Prepare cream mixture in an electric mixer by whipping sugar and egg yolks on high speed until pale yellow and thick. With mixer on medium speed, add cream cheese and whip until smooth. Add mascarpone and Marsala. Mix until incorporated. Fold in whipped cream. Refrigerate.

Step Two:

To prepare espresso mixture, combine espresso, additional Marsala, sugar and warm water.

Step Three:

To assemble, dip ladyfingers in espresso mixture. Place one layer of dipped ladyfingers on bottom of serving platter. Top with one layer of cream mixture. Add another layer of dipped ladyfingers, topped with second layer of cream mixture. Sift cocoa over top.

Prepare several hours before serving.

Makes 6 servings

— Rich & Sandy Allison

This tiramisu recipe comes very close to what we tasted in Rome, Italy.

APPLE BUTTER PIES

½ C. warm water
3 pkgs. dry yeast
Mix together.

Take 1 can evaporated milk and add enough warm water to make 3 C.

To this add:

½ C. sugar
2 tsp. salt
3 eggs
½ C. shortening
7½ C. flour

Mix this with yeast mixture and let raise.

Make small balls. Roll into circles and place one tbsp. of apple butter on one side of the dough. Fold over the other half and crimp shut. Make certain they are crimped well. Jab the pies with a fork before deep frying. Also, these can be rolled out thick, cut into donuts and deep fried.

Fry in a deep fryer with the pinched side down in oil at 350° until golden brown.

These are very hot in the middle when they are cooked.

Makes approximately 35 pies. Also, you can use other fruit fillings in them.

In memory of
— Grace Allison

These applebutter pies were a tradition in Claysburg. They were sold at street fairs and community celebrations through the years.

CHOCOLATE PIE

Pie Crust:

Mix:

1 stick (½ C.) oleo
1 C. flour
1 tsp. sugar
1 C. nuts, chopped

Bake at 300° for 15-20 minutes.

Mix:

8 oz. cream cheese, softened
1 C. Cool Whip

Spread on cooled crust.

Mix:

2 pkgs. instant chocolate pudding
3 C. milk

Pour over cream cheese. Top with Cool Whip and nuts.

Keep refrigerated.

— Anne Kimble

VEGETABLE OIL PASTRY

2 C. sifted flour
1¼ tsp. salt
½ C. Crisco vegetable oil
¼ C. plus 2 tbsp. icy cold water

Sift flour and salt together.

Pour vegetable oil and water into a measuring cup and beat until frothy.

Sprinkle 1 tbsp. oil mixture over flour mixture, toss lightly with a fork. Continue adding oil mixture gradually and tossing quickly until dough holds together.

Divide dough in half and roll each half into a smooth ball.

Roll dough between two 12" squares of waxed paper. Remove top sheet of paper and place dough in pan and peel off bottom paper.
Roll dough for top crust the same way.
Makes 2 (9") crusts.

Bake at 450° for 10-12 minutes.

If crust is for unfilled pies, prick the shell before baking.

If crust is for filled pie, brush the bottom crust with egg whites one minute before done baking.

— Sandy Allison

This pie dough always makes good, consistent pie dough that is flakey. Icy cold water is the key to the success of this. Sandy learned this recipe in high school in home economics class.

BANANA LOAF

¾ C. sugar
¼ C. shortening
3 tbsp. sour milk
1 egg
1 C. mashed bananas
½ tsp. baking powder
½ tsp. baking soda
¼ tsp. salt
2 C. sifted flour
1 C. nuts, chopped
2 tsp. vanilla

Cream sugar, shortening, egg, bananas and sour milk. Add dry ingredients and vanilla.
Double recipe makes 2 loaves.

Bake at 350° for 50 minutes.

In memory of
— Louise Hidlebaugh

GLAZED FRESH STRAWBERRY PIE

1 pastry shell (9"), baked
1½ qt. fresh strawberries washed and sliced.
1 C. granulated sugar
3½ tbsp. cornstarch
½ C. cold water
Few drops of red food coloring
Cool Whip

After strawberries have drained well, take one pint and mash them. Set others aside.

Mix sugar and cornstarch in a saucepan and stir in cold water along with mashed strawberries.

Cook mixture over medium heat, stirring constantly until mixture comes to a full boil. Boil for 2 minutes.

Remove from heat, stir in food coloring and cool.

Fold in remaining 2 pints of sliced strawberries into cooled mixture.

Pour into baked pastry shell. Cover pie with Cool Whip. Garnish with a strawberry on top.

Serve immediately because crust will get soggy.

— Sandy Allison

RITZ ICE CREAM DESSERT

2 stacks Ritz crackers, crushed (or one 8 oz. box)
1½ sticks margarine, melted

Mix above and pat into a 9"x13" cake pan.

Mix 2 pkgs. toasted coconut or coconut cream instant pudding with 1½ C. milk with mixer.

Add ¾ of ½ gallon of French Vanilla ice cream softened and mix.

Place mixture in pan and refrigerate several hours. Frost with Cool Whip and garnish with toasted coconut.

— Shirley Knisely

GOBS

1 box chocolate cake mix (mix as on box)

Add:

1 C. flour
½ C. sugar
2 tbsp. cocoa
1 tsp. baking powder
2 egg yolks (save whites for filling)

Mix all above and spoon out a heaping tablespoonful onto cookie sheets.
Bake at 350° for 10 minutes.

Gob Filling:

½ C. Crisco
2 tbsp. butter
2 egg whites
2 tbsp. flour
2 tbsp. milk
2 tsp. vanilla
2 C. powdered sugar

Beat egg whites stiff, add other ingredients keeping milk until last. Add milk, but do not let it get too thin. 1 tbsp. may be enough.

For peanut butter filling:

Add enough peanut butter to the Gob filling to give it flavor. Ice cooled cake cookie and place another one on top of icing.

In memory of
— Annie Blazevich

Annie Blazevich has always made the best gobs ever. The ones with the peanut butter filling are really outstanding.

This ice cream dessert has been made for years. The combination of coconut pudding and French vanilla ice cream give this dessert a very rich and flavorful taste.

STRAWBERRY PRETZEL DESSERT

2+ C. crushed pretzels
3 tbsp. sugar
¾ C. butter

Mix and pat into bottom of 13"x9" pan.
Bake at 350° for 10 minutes.
Cool.

1 lg. Cool Whip (8 oz. or 12 oz.)
¾ C. sugar
8 oz. cream cheese

Mix together with beaters and spread over pretzel crust.

1 lg. box strawberry Jello
1½ C. boiling water
Add strawberries after jello starts to jell.
2 pkgs. (10 oz.) frozen strawberries

Blend above, cool until almost jelled. Pour over cream mixture. Refrigerate until serving.

— Beccie (Allison) Weyant

CLOUDS

This recipe makes (2) 9"x12" pans of cake for the clouds. Use cake pans only.

Cloud Bottoms:

½ lb. softened butter
1 C. sugar
6 egg yolks
1½ C. flour
1 tbsp. baking powder
1 C. milk

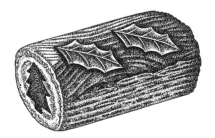

Whip butter and sugar adding sugar slowly. Then add egg yolks one at a time. Add alternately flour, baking powder and milk. Scrape sides of bowl and then divide evenly into 2 pans with wax paper lining spreading evenly. This should be approximately 4 C. of batter or two per cake pan.

Meringue Top:

6 egg whites, chilled ice cold
Small pinch of cream of tartar
1½ C. sugar
1 C. almonds
1 tsp. vanilla

Whip egg whites and cream of tartar. Add sugar, vanilla and stir in almonds if desired. Spread evenly on top of cake mixture.

Bake cake mixture till brown about 10-15 minutes at 350°.

CHOCOLATE MOUSSE FILLING

(Enough for 2 clouds)

3 C. chocolate chips
½ C. hot water
1 tbsp. instant coffee
¼ C. triple sec or Galliano liquor
4 egg yolks

Melt in double boiler starting with chocolate chips and water. Add coffee and triple sec. Blend in one egg yolk at a time. Cool.

2½ C. whipping cream
¼ C. powdered sugar
Small pinch cream of tartar
4 egg whites

Whip cream until stiff. Add sugar, whipped egg whites and cream of tartar. Then fold into mixture. Chill until cold. About 8 hours.

(Continued on Page 129)

(Continued from Page 128)

LEMON CURD

2 large eggs
2 large egg yolks
¾ C. sugar
⅓ C. fresh lemon juice
2 tsp. lemon peel, grated
3 tbsp. butter, cut into small pieces

Whisk eggs, yolks and sugar in heavy saucepan until well blended and slightly thickened. Whisk in juice and peel. Add butter. Stir over low heat until thickened and comes to a boil – about 5 minutes. Transfer to bowl and refrigerate until well chilled – about 8 hours.

COCONUT CREAM FILLING

(Enough for two clouds)

1½ C. whipping cream
¼ C. powdered sugar
Small pinch cream of tartar
4 egg whites
1 C. shredded coconut
½ C. Coco Lopez
½ tsp. coconut extract

Whip cream until stiff. Add sugar, whipped egg whites and cream of tartar. Add coconut and Coco Lopez. Then fold into mixture. Chill until cold.

To Assemble Clouds:

Turn cake out of pan onto a dishtowel with cake on top. The meringue portion is now on the bottom.

Spread with your choice of cream filling. Roll up jelly roll style starting to roll the cake on the longer portion. Refrigerate until well chilled prior to serving.

— Sandy Allison

> *These clouds are a lot of work but worth it.*

HOMEMADE ECLAIRS

1 pkg. (17¼ oz.) puffed pastry thawed
13 oz. pkg. instant vanilla pudding
2 C. milk
1 C. whipping cream
1 tsp. vanilla
1 C. confectioner's sugar
2 tbsp. water
½ tsp. almond extract
½ C. semisweet chocolate chips
1 tsp. shortening

Unroll each sheet of puff pastry – total of two. Cut each pastry into nine pieces or a total of 18 pieces for both pastries. Place on ungreased cookie sheets and bake at 400° for about 12 minutes until lightly golden brown. Remove from oven and from cookie sheets to cool.

Meanwhile mix pudding and milk for 2 minutes on low speed.

In a separate bowl, whip chilled whipping cream and ½ tsp. vanilla. Fold the whipped cream mixture gently into the pudding mixture. Refrigerate until the puffed pastries are cold.

Take a serrated knife and slice each puffed pastry into a top and bottom.

On a waxed paper tray, place a bottom of puffed pastry, spoon a layer of pudding on top of pastry. Add another pastry, spoon another layer and then add another pastry and spoon another layer of pudding. Be certain that you keep a top, not a bottom, of puffed pastry for the top piece. Assemble all 9 eclairs in the same manner.

Then mix ½ tsp. vanilla, confectioner's sugar, water and almond extract in a measuring cup and wire whisk. Drizzle and spread this mixture over the top piece of puffed pastry spreading like icing.

(Continued on Page 130)

(Continued from Page 129)

Then microwave semisweet chips and shortening in a mixing cup on power level three for approximately 1½ minutes. Remove and stir with a spoon. If not totally melted return for another ½ minute on power level three. Then with a wire whisk dipped into the chocolate, drizzle the mixture over the confectioner's icing leaving small strands of chocolate all over the top.

Refrigerate to chill and serve.

— Rich Allison

These chocolate eclairs may sound like a lot of work, but actually they are fairly easy. Using puffed pastry from the freezer section really simplifies the process.

APPLE ENCHILADAS

1 (21 oz.) can apple fruit filling
6 (8") flour tortillas
1 tsp. cinnamon
⅓ C. margarine or butter
½ C. sugar
½ C. firmly packed light brown sugar
½ C. water

Spoon fruit filling evenly down center of each tortilla. Sprinkle evenly with cinnamon. Roll up and place seam side down in a lightly greased 2 quart baking dish. Make certain that you only place one layer in a dish.

Bring margarine and next three ingredients to a boil in a medium saucepan. Reduce heat and simmer stirring constantly for 3 minutes.

Pour over enchiladas. Let stand 30 minutes. Then bake at 350° for 20 minutes. Makes 4-6 servings.

— Sandy Allison

SOFT SUGAR COOKIES

1 C. butter – do not substitute margarine
2 C. sugar
1 tsp. vanilla
1 tsp. almond extract
2 eggs
2 tsp. baking powder
1 tsp. baking soda
1 C. buttermilk
Approximately 6 C. flour – enough to make a soft dough.

Mix all together and roll out dough and cut into cookie shapes. Sprinkle extra sugar over cookie before and after baking.

Bake on an ungreased cookie sheet at 350° for 10 minutes.

Makes 5 dozen.

PINK HOLIDAY SALAD

1 lg. box cherry jello
1 (8 oz.) cream cheese or small Cool Whip
½ C. sugar
1 can crushed pineapple, drained
1 can evaporated milk
½ C. nuts

Put can of milk in freezer for 1 hour. Cook pineapple and sugar for 5 minutes. Dissolve the dry jello into the pineapple. Let stand until cool. Beat in cream cheese or cool whip.

Whip canned milk until stiff. Add to pineapple mixture. Add chopped nuts (reserve a few for garnish). Pour into serving bowl. Garnish with remaining chopped nuts.

In memory of
— Violet "Cass" Glass

RUSSIAN TEACAKES OR MEXICAN WEDDING CAKES

1 C. butter
½ C. sifted confectioner's sugar
1 tsp. vanilla
2¼ C. flour
¼ tsp. salt
¾ C. pecans, finely chopped

Mix butter, sugar and vanilla thoroughly. Add flour along with nuts and salt.

Chill dough at least 8 hours.

Heat oven to 400°. Roll dough into 1" balls. Place on ungreased baking sheet. (Cookies do not spread). Bake 10-12 minutes.

While still warm, roll in confectioner's sugar. Cool. Roll in sugar again.

Makes about 4 dozen.

In memory of
— Margie Binotto

FAUX TAGALONGS

1 lb. milk chocolate melting discs
2½ dz. Ritz crackers
2 C. (approx.) peanut butter

Spread top of cracker with peanut butter. Set aside.

Melt chocolate in microwave in large bowl. Dip crackers into melted chocolate (a large serving fork works best). Place on wax paper. After each cracker is dipped, cool slightly and re-dip. Put on wax paper until cooled. Store in sealed container.

Note: For Christmas use the snowflake shaped Ritz crackers.

— Kera Knisely

OATMEAL CINNAMON CHIP COOKIES

1½ C. soft butter or margarine
1 C. white sugar
2 tsp. vanilla
2 C. brown sugar firmly packed
2 eggs

Cream butter or margarine with sugars. Add eggs and vanilla.

Combine with:

2 C. flour
2 tsp. salt
1 tsp. baking soda

Batter can be mixed with electric mixer, but fold in 4 C. oatmeal (quick or old fashioned) and 1 bag (10 oz.) of Hershey's cinnamon chips.

Drop by round teaspoon on greased cookie sheet.

Bake at 350° for 10-12 minutes.

Watch closely, these brown quickly on the bottom.

— Chris Wilkins

BIA'S BRAZILIAN CANDY

1 can Eagle Brand sweetened condensed milk
2 tbsp. cocoa powder
1 tbsp. Butter or margarine
  (plus enough to grease hands with)
Chocolate or colored sprinkles

Mix condensed milk, cocoa powder and margarine in a large microwave safe bowl. Microwave 4 minutes, stirring half-way through. Refrigerate on a plate until well chilled. Grease hands with lots of butter. Roll into small balls. Roll the balls in the sprinkles. Place in tart papers.

— Kera Knisely

CARAMEL AND CHOCOLATE APPLES

4 medium to large tart apples - Stayman or some other tart apple. (Note: must not have wax on them. All Washington State apples have wax on them.)

1 bag (13 oz.) Kraft caramels.

Remove caramels from wrappers. Add 2 tbsp. water and microwave in a round bowl slightly larger than the apples. Microwave 2 minutes. Stir after one minute and thoroughly stir after 2 minutes until caramels are all melted.

Place Popsicle sticks in apples. Dip apples one at a time in the caramels and let excess drain off. Use a spoon to coat the tops of the apples if not completely covered. Place on wax papered tray.

In a food processor while caramels are melting, finely chop 2 C. salted cashews.

After dipping all four apples in caramel, roll the apples through the chopped nuts in a soup bowl. Use your hand to cover any areas not covered with nuts.

Place in a refrigerator to chill at least 15 minutes or until the caramel is set.

Melt 2 C. milk chocolate chips (preferable Ghirardelli) along with 2 tbsp. of Crisco shortening sticks in a microwave. Microwave for 1½ minutes on Power level 5 and stir. Then microwave another 1½ minutes on power level 5 and stir until all chocolate is smooth.

Dip the cooled caramel apples in the chocolate and use a spoon to cover the tops. Sprinkle chopped nuts over the chocolate.

Place back in the refrigerator until chocolate sets about 15 minutes.

Melt 1 C. white chocolate chips (preferably Ghirardelli) with 1 tbsp. of Crisco shortening sticks in a microwave for 1½ minutes on power level 5. Stir and then microwave another 1½ minutes on power level 5. Stir until chocolate is smooth.

Using a wire whisk, drizzle the white chocolate over each apple letting it run from the top of the apple to the bottom in streaks.

Add more crushed nuts.

If desired, grind 1 candy cane per apple and drizzle over the soft chocolate.

Chill until firm over night. Wrap in cellophane and tie with a ribbon.

— Rich Allison

PUMPKIN BARS

Mix Together:

4 eggs
1⅔ C. sugar
1 C. Crisco Oil
1 (16 oz). can pumpkin

Mix together and add to above mixture:

2 C. flour
2 tsp. baking powder
2 tsp. cinnamon
1 tsp. salt
1 tsp. baking soda

Place on an ungreased cookie sheet.
Bake at 350° for 20-25 minutes.

Icing:

3 oz. cream cheese
½ C. oleo
1 tsp. vanilla
2 C. confectioner's sugar

— Hona Crabtree

PEG'S WACKY CAKE

Sift Together:

3 C. flour
½ C. cocoa
3 tsp. baking soda
2 C. sugar
1 tsp. salt

Mix:

¾ C. oil
3 tbsp. vinegar
3 tsp. vanilla
2 C. cold water

Mix ¾ of the liquid to dry ingredients. Add remaining liquid and stir until mixed well.

Pour into an ungreased cake pan and bake at 350° for 35-45 minutes.

For Cupcakes:

Fill cupcake holder ⅔ full.
Bake at 350° for 12+ minutes.
Makes 24 cupcakes.

> In memory of
> — Peggy Allison

PEANUT BUTTER ICING

1½ C. powdered sugar
2 tbsp. margarine
2+ tbsp. peanut butter, to taste
1 tsp. vanilla

Add enough milk to spread. Serve on Wacky Cake.

For cupcakes:
Double icing recipe for cupcakes.

> In memory of
> — Peggy Allison

This is Rich's sister-in-law, Peg's famous chocolate cake with peanut butter icing. Peg is a great cook, but this cake is one of her best foods. One unusual note, this has no eggs in it.

CHOCOLATE WACKY CAKE
WITH WHITE CHOCOLATE MOUSSE

Bake Chocolate Wacky Cake as per directions using two round pans rather than oblong pan. Let cool.

White Chocolate Mousse:

4 eggs
4 egg yolks
1 tbsp. Amaretto
1 tsp. almond extract
½ tsp. vanilla
2 envelopes unflavored gelatin

Put eggs and yolks in a double boiler over a pan of simmering water.

Beat eggs with a mixer on medium until they are warmed through and until they coat the back of a wooden spoon. Remove from heat.

Add gelatin to Amaretto, almond extract and vanilla, mix well. Stir into egg mixture.

While eggs are warming on stove, take 1½ lb. white chocolate and melt in microwave. Microwave for 1 minute intervals at Power level 5 for approximately 3 intervals or minutes. Stir chocolate after each 1 minute of microwaving. When chocolate is totally melted, wire whisk chocolate into egg mixture and set aside.

In another bowl, whip 3 C. heavy whipping cream until stiff peaks form. After white chocolate mixture is totally cool, fold the whipped cream into the mixture.

Cover and chill the mousse until it sets up.

To assemble the cake:

Take one layer of cake and ice with mousse. Generously sprinkle shredded coconut over that layer of cake.

(Continued on Page 134)

CHOCOLATE WACKY CAKE
WITH WHITE CHOCOLATE MOUSSE

(Continued from Page 133)

Put other layer of cake on top of coconut. Finish icing cake with mousse.

Take slivered almonds and cover the sides of the mousse on the cake with almonds.

Shave chocolate on top of cake if desired.

Keep chilled in refrigerator.

— Rich Allison

The white chocolate mousse is the toughest part of making this cake. It takes a while until the white chocolate mousse is done and sets up for assembling the cake. However, the combination of all these ingredients make this a winner.

BIRD NESTS

½ C. butter
¼ C. brown sugar
1 egg yolk
1 C. flour

Form balls the size of a hickory nut. Dip in slightly beaten egg white and then in chopped pecan meats. Before baking, make a dent in the center of each cookie. Bake at 350° for 8 minutes. Cool. Make butter cream icing. Divide and make different colors with food coloring. Fill dents in cookies with frosting.

In memory of
— Grace Allison

PUMPKIN NUT JAR BREAD

⅔ C. Crisco shortening
⅔ C. water
2⅔ C. sugar
½ tsp. baking powder
1 tsp. cloves
1 tsp. cinnamon
½ C. chopped walnuts
4 eggs
2 C. pumpkin
3½ C. flour
1½ tsp. salt
½ tsp. allspice
2 tsp. baking soda

Mix ingredients. Wash 8 pint (wide mouth) canning jars. Lightly grease entire inside of each jar with Crisco shortening.

Fill jar ½ full with batter.

Clean and dry off top of jar carefully.

Place on cookie sheet.

Bake 325° for 45 minutes.

Turn off oven. Do not remove jars from oven yet.

Heat lids. Dry off.

Take one jar at a time from oven and seal like you do for canning. Jars will seal.

Both the pumpkin bread on this page and the apple bread on the next page make great gifts. Once they are baked in jars and sealed, they will keep for a period of time.

APPLE NUT JAR BREAD

3 C. chopped apples
2 eggs
2½ C. flour
¾ C. oil
2½ tsp. baking powder
½ tsp. salt
1 tsp. soda
2 C. sugar
2 tsp. cinnamon
1 tsp. vanilla
½ C. chopped walnuts

Mix ingredients. Wash 6 pint (wide mouth) canning jars. Lightly grease entire inside of each jar with Crisco shortening.

Fill jar ½ full with batter.

Clean and dry off top of jar carefully.

Place on cookie sheet.

Bake at 325° for 45 minutes.

Turn off oven. Do not remove jars from oven yet.

Heat lids. Dry off.

Take one jar at a time from oven and seal like you do for canning. Jars will seal.

ICE CREAM TOPPING

48 oz. marshmallow crème
¾ jar of 18 oz. peanut butter

Add boiling water and beat with mixer until smooth.

— Sandy Allison

> *This recipe came from a local ice cream shop and while very simple is very good. Just add boiling water and mix until you reach the desired consistency.*

DROP SAND TARTS

1½ C. granulated sugar
1 C. margarine, room temperature
2 eggs
2 C. un-sifted flour
½ tsp. vanilla
½ tsp. baking soda

Mix ingredients together and chill ½ hour. Drop by ½ tbsp. on cookie sheet and press down with floured glass. Sprinkle with sugar, cinnamon and chopped nuts. Chill dough before baking.

Bake at 370° until light brown, 10-12 minutes.

BLACK WALNUT COOKIES

2 C. brown sugar
1 C. butter
2 eggs
1 tbsp. baking soda
3 C. flour
1 C. black walnuts, chopped

Cream together sugar, butter, eggs and baking soda. Add flour and black walnuts. Blend thoroughly and make into 2 rectangle rolls. Chill over night in refrigerator. Slice very thin.

Bake at 350° for 10 minutes.

RAISIN FILLED COOKIES

5 C. sifted all-purpose flour
2 tsp. baking powder
1 tsp. baking soda
½ tsp. salt
1 C. shortening or 2 sticks margarine melted
2 C. granulated sugar
2 eggs
2 tbsp. vanilla butternut extract
1 C. commercial sour cream

Sift together flour, soda, baking powder and salt.

Mix shortening, sugar, eggs and vanilla until creamy.

Then mix in sour cream, then flour mixture a little at a time.

Refrigerate until easy to handle.

Preheat oven to 425°.

On lightly greased flour surface, roll dough to ¼" in thickness. Cut with a 3" round cutter. Place on ungreased cookie sheet.

Place a teaspoon or more of filling in center of each. Cover top with another piece of dough, seal edges and bake 8-10 minutes or until golden brown.

Raisin Filling

1½ C. seedless raisins
⅓ C. water
½ C. granulated sugar
1 tbsp. corn starch
Pinch of salt
1 tbsp. lemon juice

Cook slowly and cool.

> In memory of
> — Vivian Lingenfelter

LOUISE HILDEBAUGH'S CHOCOLATE CHIP COOKIES

2 C. butter flavored Crisco
1½ C. sugar
1½ C. brown sugar, firmly packed
2 tsp. vanilla

Cream together until smooth

Beat & Add:

4 eggs
4½ C. flour
2 tsp. baking soda
1½ tsp. salt
3 to 3½ C. chocolate chips

Make them right away. Do not refrigerate. Add ½ C. extra flour to each batch to prevent it from thinning out.

Bake at 350° for 8-10 minutes.
Makes 12 dozen.

> In memory of
> — Louise Hildebaugh

GRANDMA'S CREAM CHEESE COOKIES

1 (8 oz.) package of cream cheese
1 C. margarine
1 tsp. vanilla
3 C. sifted flour

Nut Mixture:

4 C. ground nuts
1½ C. milk
1 tsp. vanilla
⅓ C. sugar to taste

Leave cream cheese and margarine out until soft. Cream them together then add vanilla. Add flour slowly and mix well. Knead on board for a few minutes then put in refrigerator for at least 15 minutes or more. Roll out on board covered with powdered sugar. Cut dough into 2" squares and fill with nut mixture. Roll dough and mixture up from the triangle point. Bake 12-15 minutes in 400° oven.

> — Cindi Miller

CHOCOLATE PEANUT BUTTER PIE

1 (6 oz.) graham cracker pie crust
1 (14 oz.) chocolate sweetened condensed milk
¼ C. creamy peanut butter
1 (8 oz.) frozen non-dairy whipped topping, thawed (3½ C.)

1. In large bowl, combine sweetened condensed milk and peanut butter.
2. Fold in whipped topping.
3. Spoon into crust. Freeze 6 hours.
4. Garnish as desired. Freeze leftovers.

MACE CAKE

Preheat oven to 350°.

2 pkg. Crescent rolls
2 (8 oz.) blocks cream cheese
1 C. sugar
1 egg yolk (save the white)
1 tbsp. vanilla extract or almond extract

Unroll 1 package Crescent rolls.
Lay in 9"x13" ungreased pan.

Mix the next 4 ingredients with electric mixer. Spread on top of rolls. Lay second package of Crescent rolls on top of mixed spread.

Beat the saved egg white.
Spread on top of second layer of Crescent rolls.

Mix ½ C. sugar and 1 tbsp. cinnamon
Sprinkle all on top of beaten egg white.

Bake at 350° for 30 minutes.

— Kylee Burket

CHERRY WINKS

Sift:

2¼ C. flour
1 tsp. baking powder
½ tsp. baking soda
½ tsp. salt

Combine:

¾ C. margarine
1 C. white sugar
Blend in 2 eggs
2 tbsp. milk
2 tsp. vanilla – Cream well.

Blend in dry ingredients. Mix well and shape into balls.

Crush approximately 5 C. corn flakes. Roll each ball in corn flakes and top with ½ red maraschino cherry.

In memory of
— Margie Binotto
— Leota Noffsker

WALNUT SQUARES

1 egg, unbeaten
1 C. brown sugar, packed
1 tsp. vanilla
½ C. all purpose flour
¼ tsp. baking soda
¼ tsp. salt
1 C. walnuts, coarsely chopped

Grease an 8" square pan. Stir together the egg, brown sugar and vanilla. Quickly stir in the flour, baking soda and salt. Add walnuts.

Spread in pan and bake at 350° for 18-20 minutes.

Cookies should be soft in center when taken from the oven. Cool in pan. Do not over bake. Cut into 2" squares.

In memory of
— Louise Hidlebaugh

CINNAMON WALNUTS

2 C. walnuts
1 C. sugar
5 tbsp. water
1 tsp. cinnamon
½ tsp. salt
1½ tsp. vanilla

Heat walnuts in oven. Bring syrup to a boil. Add walnuts. (Cook to thicken)
Spread on cookie sheet until cool.

CREAM PUFF DESSERT

1 C. water
1 stick butter

Boil until butter melts.
Take off stove and add 1 C. flour, mix.
Add 4 eggs, one at a time, and mix until smooth

Butter 9"x13" pan and bake at 375° for 35 minutes, until golden brown – cool.

Mix:

2 boxes vanilla instant pudding
1 (8 oz.) cream cheese, softened
2½ C. milk
Spread over cooled crust.

Top with 1 container of Cool Whip.
Cherries and nuts on top are optional.

— Nancy Strawbridge

SNICKERDOODLE COFFEECAKE

½ C. (1 stick) butter
2 C. sugar
2 eggs, separated
¼ tsp. salt
2 tsp. baking powder
3 C. flour
1 C. milk
1 tsp. ground cinnamon
1 tbsp. powdered sugar

In large bowl, cream butter and sugar with electric mixer. Add egg yolks and salt. Beat well.

In separate bowl, sift baking powder into flour. Alternately add flour mixture and milk to egg mixture, beating well after each addition.

In separate bowl (not plastic), beat egg whites until light and frothy. Then fold them into batter.

Preheat oven to 350°.

Spread batter into greased 13"x9" pan. Sift cinnamon and powdered sugar over top. Bake in preheated oven 30 minutes or until toothpick inserted into center comes out clean. Remove from oven and let sit a few minutes before cutting.

Makes 20–24 servings.

— Sandy Allison

DUMP CAKE

Dump 1 large can crushed pineapples into an oblong cake pan.

Add 1 can blueberry or cherry pie filling and stir together.

Dump one box white cake mix over pineapple and fruit mixture.

Cut two sticks of margarine over top of cake mix in pieces and cover entire cake.

Place 1 C. walnuts over the top of the butter.

Bake at 350° for 1 hour.

> In memory of
> — Betty Howard

BANANAS FOSTER - SOUTHERN STYLE

¾ stick butter
¾ C. brown sugar

Heat in a skillet until mixture melts

Add:

1½ Shots dark rum
1½ Shots banana liquor
¾ C. orange juice

Let cook over medium heat until alcohol evaporates, about 3 minutes.

Season With:

½ tsp. cinnamon
½ tsp. nutmeg

Add:

½ C. shredded coconut
½ C. pecans, chopped
4 bananas, sliced in half lengthwise, and then cut in half.

Cook 3 minutes on low. Serve over French Vanilla ice cream! Serves 6.

> — Rich Allison

PEANUT BUTTER BALLS

1 C. butter or margarine
1 C. peanut butter
1 C. marshallow cream
1 tsp. vanilla
1 box confectionery sugar

Cream first four ingredients well. Gradually add confectionery sugar. For a creamier ball, don't add all the sugar.

Roll balls the size of a walnut. Dip balls into melted chocolate and drop onto wax paper. Refer to page 9 for directions on how to melt chocolate.

Makes about 80 to 90 balls.

> In memory of
> — Rhet Walter

BANANAS FOSTER

½ lb. butter, cubed
1¼ C. brown sugar, packed
8 firm, ripe bananas cut in half lengthwise
1 tsp. cinnamon
1 C. banana liqueur
1½ C. rum
1 qt. vanilla ice cream

In a sauté pan, large enough to fit the bananas, heat the butter and brown sugar for 3 to 5 minutes, stirring until the mixture becomes a smooth caramel.

Add the bananas, baste them with the sauce and sprinkle with cinnamon.

Carefully add liquors and heat well. If you want to flame the dessert, remove pan from the heat and, just before serving, ignite the liquors with a long kitchen match.

To Serve:

Scoop ice cream into 8 dishes. Top with banana slices and sauce.

> — Rich Allison

DESSERTS

MARGIE BINOTTO'S ICING

Cream Together:

½ C. margarine, soft, room temperature
½ C. Crisco shortening
1 C. sugar, granulated

Add:

½ C. warm water
½ tsp. vanilla
Blend with a mixer 10 minutes until smooth and sugar is all dissolved.

Does not have to be refrigerated.

MEXICAN DESSERT

1 pkg. flour tortillas (8")
½ C. melted butter
Cinnamon sugar
Whipped cream

Preheat oven to 350°. Place tortillas on a cooking sheet and brush with butter. Sprinkle with cinnamons sugar. Bake in oven for 8 minutes. Cut into 8 slices. Top with whipped cream.

Drizzle with honey.

— Kera Knisely

LEMON PUDDING DESSERT

Same recipe as chocolate pudding dessert from page 170 except:

Replace Layer 3 With:

3½ C. milk
2 sm. boxes lemon instant pudding

Layer 4:

Delete shaved chocolate

— Marianne Erhart

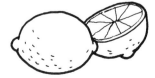

PEANUT DELIGHT

First Layer:

2 C. graham cracker crumbs
1 stick melted margarine
½ C. salted peanuts, chopped

Mix and place first layer into a 9"x13" pan. Put into freezer while preparing second layer.

Second Layer:

8 oz. cream cheese, room temperature
½ C. peanut butter
⅔ C. powdered sugar
2 C. Cool Whip

Cream all ingredients in second layer together and spread over crust.

Third Layer:

1 (3¾ oz.) pkg. chocolate instant pudding
1 (3¾ oz.) pkg. vanilla instant pudding
3 C. cold milk

Beat third layer ingredients together and place over second layer.

Spread balance of Cool Whip from container on top and shred chocolate bar on top.

Refrigerate.

— Marianne Erhart

HEATH BAR TOFFEE GRAHAMS

Layer graham crackers in a baking dish and top with Heath Bar bits from the cooking section. Bake in oven at 200° until melted. Remove from oven and top with milk chocolate bits. Place back in oven and melt.

Remove from oven and place slivered almonds on the melted chocolate. Let cool. Melt white chocolate in a microwave on power level 5 for several minutes maximum stirring every 30 seconds. Place in a plastic bag, cut small tip off one corner of the plastic bag and pipe chocolate over the cooled crackers in diagonal lines. Let cool.

— Barb Sadler

APPLE STRUDEL

⅓ C. sugar
2 tbsp. cornstarch
½ C. apple juice
5 C. sliced tart apples (about 2 lb. Granny Smith or Cortland)
⅓ C. light brown sugar, firmly packed
1 tsp. ground cinnamon
¼ tsp. ground nutmeg
⅓ C. raisins
⅓ C. walnuts, chopped
12 Phyllo pastry sheets from 1 lb. pkg. 16"x12" size – use about 8 oz.
¾ C. (1½ sticks) margarine, melted
¾ C. dry bread crumbs

Combine sugar, cornstarch and juice in small saucepan. Cook over medium heat stirring constantly until mixture thickens and boils.

Toss apples with brown sugar, cinnamon and nutmeg in bowl. Mix in juice mixture until apples are coated. Fold in raisins and nuts.

Unfold Phyllo dough and cover with damp towel to prevent drying out. Place clean towel on flat surface. Spray with cold water to dampen lightly. Place one sheet of Phyllo on towel, long side toward you.

Place another sheet overlapping 4" at top to make 20"x16" rectangle. Brush with margarine. Sprinkle with 2 tbsp. crumbs. Repeat with remaining Phyllo, margarine and crumbs. Do not sprinkle crumbs on top layer.

Spoon apple mixture in an even row across side of pastry near you, 2" in from edge. Using towel as an aid, roll dough over filling, fold ends in to enclose filling completely. Roll up like a jelly roll.

Preheat oven to 375° and line a large cookie sheet with heavy duty foil.

Ease roll onto cookie sheet, seam-side down.

Brush with melted margarine. Turn foil up ½" all around edge to catch spills.

Bake for 35 minutes until pastry is crisp and golden. Let cool 20 minutes and slide onto board. Sprinkle with confectioner's sugar.

— Sandy Allison

BUTTER SHORTBREAD

12 tbsp. unsalted butter, softened
½ C. sugar
1¾ C. flour
½ tsp. salt

In a heavy 2 quart saucepan, melt 6 tbsp. butter over low heat. Cook for 12 minutes. Stir until the butter is a rich, brown color in the bottom of the pan. It will have a nutty aroma. Take off the stove immediately.

Pour onto a plate and put in refrigerator to firm up to a softened butter consistency.

Preheat oven to 350°.

Mix in a bowl with a mixer at medium speed the sugar, the cooled brown butter and remaining 6 tbsp. softened butter.

Hand mix on low the flour and salt and add to the mixture until crumbs form. Do not overwork.

Pat crumbs into ungreased 9" round tart pan with removable bottom.

Bake 30-40 minutes. When golden brown remove from oven and cool. Cut into pieces and let in pan until cooled.

Cut into 16 wedges. Sprinkle with powdered sugar. You can also use cookie cutters to cut the dough. Just don't work the dough too much.

— Linda Paul

DESSERTS

SOUR CREAM COOKIES

1½ C. sugar
1 C. butter
1 C. sour cream
3 eggs
4 C. flour
1 tsp. baking soda
2 tsp. baking powder
½ tsp. salt
1 tsp. almond extract
1 tsp. vanilla

Cream butter, adding sugar gradually, then add eggs and mix well. Stir in sour cream and extract and vanilla. Sift the dry ingredients and add to the creamed mixture. Chill thoroughly. Roll out on lightly floured surface (rolling pin must be kept floured). Cut out desired shapes about ¼".

Bake at 350° for 11 minutes

Do not over bake. Cookies should not be brown. Frost as desired with butter cream frosting and decorate.

BUTTER CREAM FROSTING

½ C. butter
⅓ C. milk
4 C. powdered sugar
1 tsp. vanilla

Cream butter and half of sugar with mixer until light. Add milk, mixing until smooth. Add remaining sugar and vanilla. Add food coloring to make frosting for various holidays. Blend well.

SUSIE'S FAVORITE ICING

1 C. milk
5 tbsp. flour
½ C. butter, softened
½ C. shortening
1 tsp. vanilla

Combine milk and flour in a saucepan. Cook until thickened. Cover and refrigerate.

In a mixing bowl, beat butter, shortening, sugar and vanilla until creamy. Add chilled milk-flour mixture and beat for 10 minutes.

— Susie Dodson

FRESH PEACH COBBLER

½ stick butter or margarine
2 C. sugar, divided
¾ C. flour
2 tsp. baking powder
¾ C. milk
2 C. sliced peaches

Melt butter and pour in a 2 qt. baking dish.

Combine 1 C. sugar, flour and baking powder. Add milk, stir until mixed. Pour batter over butter in baking dish, do not stir. Combine peaches and remaining 1 C. of sugar mix. Spoon over batter. Do not stir.

Bake at 350° for 45 minutes to 1 hour.

EGG CUSTARD PIE

Make one 9" pie crust.

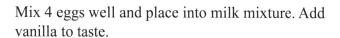

Take 2½ C. milk and heat on stove with ½ C. sugar and ¼ tsp. salt. Stir until it gets heated – do not boil.

Mix 4 eggs well and place into milk mixture. Add vanilla to taste.

Pour into crust and sprinkle with nutmeg. Bake at 400° until firm.

In memory of
— Leota Noffsker

PEANUT BUTTER CRUNCH

In a cold iron skillet greased with oleo, spread an 18 oz. jar of creamy Jiff. Set aside in refrigerator.

In a pot:

3 C. sugar, granulated
½ C. water
1 C. white syrup

Boil to 300°. Remove from heat. Let set until bubbles die down. Pour over peanut butter in skillet. Take a table knife and fold away from edge to center. Do not fold too fast. Do not beat or stir, just keep folding. The hot syrup melts the peanut butter and forms a ball. Cut into pieces with scissors. You have to work fast when cutting. (Works better with 2 people cutting).

BUTTER PECAN DESSERT

2 pkgs. Lorna Doone cookies, crushed
1 stick butter, melted

Mix and press into 9"x13" pan.

Blend:

2 sm. pkg. instant vanilla pudding
2 C. milk

Mix above and add 1 qt. softened butter pecan ice cream. Place on top of crust. Top with Cool Whip and grate 2 Heath Bars over top. Refrigerate.

— Marianne Erhart

SOCK IT TO ME CAKE

1 butter cake mix or yellow cake mix
½ C. sugar
¾ C. oil
4 eggs
1 C. pecans, chopped
1 tsp. vanilla
1 C. sour cream
½ C. brown sugar
1 tbsp. ground cinnamon

Mix together cake mix, sugar, oil, eggs, pecans and vanilla. Fold in sour cream. Pour half of batter into a thoroughly greased bundt pan.

Mix together brown sugar and cinnamon and sprinkle over batter in pan. Add remaining batter.

Bake at 350° for approximately 70 minutes or until toothpick inserted comes out clean.

Cool completely before removing from pan.

CHERRIES JUBILEE

1 lb. frozen pitted dark sweet cherries.

Thaw and reserve juice.

Add To Juice:

¼ C. Kirsch cherry brandy
¼ C. dry red wine

In A Saucepan:

4 tbsp. sugar, granulated
1 tbsp. cornstarch
Add 1 C. liquid
Mix with spatula

Add cherries and wire whisk, then use spatula to stir. Cook 4 minutes until thickened.
Add ¼ tsp. almond extract

Serve cherries over vanilla ice cream.

— Rich Allison

DESSERTS

GRANGER PIE

Take ½ pastry recipe previously shown for 9" pie crust.

Take:

1 C. dark Karo syrup
1 C. boiling water
1 tsp. baking soda

Do not cook on stove, just add boiling water to syrup and add soda. Mix and pour into pie crust and bake with topping on pie.

Crumb Topping:

1 C. flour
½ C. sugar
¼ C. butter
1 tsp. cinnamon

½ of this crumb recipe is enough topping for 2-4 pies.

Bake at 375° for 45 minutes.

In memory of
— Esther Burket

MONKEY BREAD

⅔ C. sugar
1 tbsp. cinnamon
Mix together

4 pkgs. refrigerated buttermilk biscuits cut into 4 pieces each.
1¼ C. fresh or frozen blueberries.
Rinse and drain.

Layer biscuits, berries, and biscuits, berries, etc. in baking dish.

Mix:

⅔ C. combined white and brown sugar
1¼ stick oleo
1 tsp. vanilla
1 tbsp. cinnamon
1 C. berries

Mix together. Place in saucepan. Bring to a boil and cool. Pour over top. Bake at 325° for approximately 65 minutes.

In memory of
— Louise Hidlebaugh

CHERRY PIE

Use basic vegetable oil pastry recipe on page 126. Form into pie shell.

Take 2 cans cherry pie filling and add a few drops of almond extract. Mix well. Pour into pastry shell. Add 2 tsp. of stick margarine in slices over top of pie filling.

Cover with top crust. Bake at 425° for 40-45 minutes until golden brown.

— Sandy Allison

MINI-CHEESECAKES

12 vanilla wafers
2 (8 oz.) packages cream cheese
½ C. sugar
1 tsp. vanilla
2 eggs

Line muffin tin with foil liners

Place one vanilla wafer in each liner.

Mix cream cheese, vanilla, and sugar on medium speed until well blended. Add eggs. Mix well. Pour over wafers, filling ¾ full.

Bake at 325° for 25 minutes.

Remove from pan when cool. Chill.

Top with cherry or blueberry pie filling.

Makes 12

— Sandy Allison

KITTY LITTER CAKE

Need 1 kitty litter pan and scoop.

1 yellow cake mix
1 chocolate cake mix
Bake according to directions

2 lb. bag vanilla crème cookies, blenderize leaving a little lumpy
1 lb. box vanilla instant pudding (6 oz.), mix as directed
Save ½ of the cookie crumbs and mix this with green food coloring for topping

Mix together 2 crumbled cakes and ½ of the cookie crumbs and vanilla pudding. Put in bottom of pan. Sprinkle with vanilla cookie crumbs then green cookie crumbs.

Cut 9 Tootsie Rolls and place on top

FLAN-ARUBA STYLE

1 C. sugar
1 C. water
8 eggs
14 oz. sweetened condensed milk
14 oz. milk
4 tbsp. vanilla

Step One:

Cook sugar and water in a metal pan that you can put in the oven. Cook on medium heat until mixture becomes caramelized and coats pan. Do not let it get too dark or it will burn. Remove from heat and let set until cooking stops.

Step Two:

Mix remaining ingredients in a blender. Pour mixture from blender into pan on top of caramelized mixture. Put oven proof lid on pan and place the pan in a water bath approximately two inches thick.

Bake at 350° for one hour.

Remove from water bath. Remove lid, let set ½ to ¾ hour to cool. Place pie plate over pan and invert over sink to prevent spillage.
Serve chilled.

Makes 1 serving

— Rich & Sandy Allison

PEANUTTY BROWNIE PIZZA

1 (19-21 oz.) pkg. brownie mix
1 (8 oz.) cream cheese, softened
½ C. brown sugar, packed
¼ C. creamy peanut butter
Chopped Reese's peanut butter cups
¼ C. peanuts, chopped
2 bananas, sliced
Chocolate syrup

Preheat oven to 375°. Prepare brownie mix according to package directions. Spread evenly on pizza pan. Bake 15-18 minutes until brownie is set.

Mix:

Cream cheese, brown sugar and peanut butter until smooth. Spread mixture over brownie crust to within ½" of crust.

Spread chopped candy, nuts and bananas over top Drizzle with chocolate syrup.

—Tammy Claycomb

Tammy Claycomb is known for her brownies. The key to making good, moist brownies is not to overbake them. Remove them from the oven while they have just set up and not baked until dry testing with a toothpick.

The cream cheese and peanut butter mixture and toppings give this a very rich taste.

DESSERTS

PUMPKIN CAKE

1st Layer

1 box Duncan Hines yellow cake mix, hold out 1 C. dry mix
1 stick melted butter
1 egg
Mix these 3 ingredients and press into a 9"x13" cake pan - you can either press it just on bottom or around sides

2nd Layer

1 (29 oz.) can pumpkin
3 eggs
½ C. brown sugar
1½ tsp. cinnamon
¾ C. canned milk
Mix together and pour over first layer

3rd Layer

1 C. saved cake mix
¼ C. oleo, do not melt
1 C. white sugar
Crumble these 3 ingredients and put over 2nd layer

Bake at 350° for 1 hour.

— Tammy Claycomb

APPLESAUCE CAKE "NO OIL"

2½ C. flour
2 C. sugar
¼ tsp. baking powder
1½ tsp. baking soda
1 tsp. salt
2 tsp. cinnamon
1 tsp. cloves
½ C. water
1½ C. applesauce (homemade is best)
2 eggs
½ C. chopped nuts, optional
¾ C. raisins, optional

Mix altogether and pour in 9"x13" pan.

Crumb Topping:

¼ C. flour
½ C. brown sugar
½ C. white sugar
½ stick margarine or 4 tbsp. softened
½ C. walnuts, chopped
Sprinkle cinnamon

Bake at 350° for 40–50 minutes.

— Jane Claycomb

PEACHES & CREAM DESSERT

¾ C. flour
1 tsp. baking powder
½ tsp. salt
1 pkg. vanilla pudding (not instant)
1 egg
½ C. milk
1 can sliced peaches
8 oz. cream cheese, softened
½ C. sugar
5-6 tbsp. peach juice
1 tbsp. sugar
½ tsp. cinnamon

Put flour, baking powder, salt, dry pudding, egg and milk into blender. Blend well. Pour into 10" pie pan. Put layer of peaches on top of mixture.

In blender mix cream cheese, ½ C. sugar and peach juice until creamy. Spread over the peaches, leaving about 1" from the edge of the pan.

Mix tbsp. sugar and ½ tsp. cinnamon together. Sprinkle on top.

Bake at 350° for 30 minutes.

In memory of
— Sally Bowser

TOM JONES FROZEN PEANUT BUTTER PIE

4 oz. cream cheese
1 C. confectioners' sugar
⅓ C. peanut butter
½ C. milk
1 (9 oz.) pkg. nondairy whipped topping
1 (9") piecrust, baked and cooled
¼ C. finely chopped peanuts

Whip cheese until soft and fluffy. Beat in sugar and peanut butter. Slowly add milk, blending thoroughly. Fold topping into mixture. Pour into baked pie shell. Sprinkle with chopped nuts. Freeze until firm and serve.

APPLE DUMPLINGS

Pastry for two-crust 9" pie
6 baking apples, pared and cored (3" in diameter)
3 tbsp. raisins
3 tbsp. chopped nuts
2½ C. brown sugar
1 ⅓ C. water

Heat oven to 425°. Prepare pastry. Gather into a ball. Roll ⅔ of pastry into 14" square on lightly floured cloth covered board; cut into 4 squares. Roll remaining pastry into 14"x7" rectangle; cut into 2 squares.

Place an apple on each square. Mix raisins and nuts. Fill each apple. Moisten corners of each pastry square. Bring opposite corners up over apple and pinch. Repeat with remaining corners. Pinch edges of pastry to seal. (We made this pastry on a hot day, and next time we will divide dough into thirds for easier handling). Place dumplings in an ungreased baking dish 9"x13"x2" Heat brown sugar and water to boiling. (We did this in the microwave). Carefully pour around dumplings. Bake, spooning or basting syrup over dumplings 2 or 3 times. Bake 40 minutes until crust is golden and apples are tender.

Serve warm with cream or sweetened whipped cream. Also good with cinnamon ice cream.

— Sandy Allison

BERRY PEACH APPLE PIE

Ingredients:

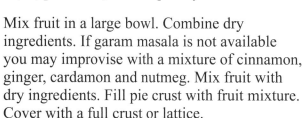

2 C. fresh peeled sliced peaches
1 C. peeled sliced baking apples
½ C. blackberries
½ C. blueberries
¾ C. sugar
½ C. flour
1 tsp. garam masala (a mixture of Indian spices)
2 (9") pie crusts, use recipe of your choice.

Mix fruit in a large bowl. Combine dry ingredients. If garam masala is not available you may improvise with a mixture of cinnamon, ginger, cardamon and nutmeg. Mix fruit with dry ingredients. Fill pie crust with fruit mixture. Cover with a full crust or lattice.

Bake at 425 for 15 minutes. Cover edges with foil. Bake additional 20 minutes. Cool slightly before serving.

— Sandy Allison

OATMEAL LACE COOKIES

1 C. flour
½ tsp. baking soda
1 C. sugar
1 C. oats
¼ C. cream
¼ C. corn syrup
1 C. melted butter
2 tbsp. vanilla extract

In a mixer with a paddle combine dry ingredients. In a separate bowl stir together wet ingredients then blend them into dry ingredients. Drop spoonfuls of batter, spaced far apart, onto nonstick sheet pans.

Bake at 350° for 5 to 8 minutes, or until golden brown.

Yield: 3 dozen

APPLE DAPPLE CAKE

3 eggs
2 C. sugar
1½ C. oil
3 C. flour
1 tsp. salt
1 tsp. baking soda
1 tsp. cinnamon
2 tsp. vanilla
1 C. pecans, chopped
3 C. apples, chopped

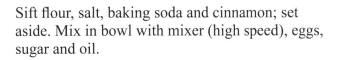

Sift flour, salt, baking soda and cinnamon; set aside. Mix in bowl with mixer (high speed), eggs, sugar and oil.

Add sifted flour mixture; mix for 2 minutes. Add vanilla, pecans and apples. Mix until blended. Pour into an oblong pan, greased and floured.

Bake at 350° for 1 hour.

TOPPING

¼ C. butter
¼ C. milk or cream
1 C. brown sugar

Boil for 4 minutes over medium heat. Pour over moderately cooled cake.

— Sue Johnson

FRUIT SALAD

½ lb. Acini Di Pepe, cooked and rinsed
1 lg. fruit cocktail, drain well
11 oz. can mandarin oranges, drain well
1 can pineapple tidbits, drain well

Save the juice from the fruit, heat and add ¾ C. sugar + 2 tbsp.

Beat 2 eggs and add to juice, cook to rolling boil. Mixture will be thin. Pour over fruit and Acini Di Pepe. Let stand over night. Add 8 to 12 oz. cool whip.

— Myrt McGee

TOADS

Layer 9"x13" pan with club crackers.

Melt together the following and boil 5 minutes:

1 stick oleo or butter
1 C. graham cracker crumbs
¾ C. brown sugar
½ C. white sugar
⅓ C. milk

Spread over bottom layer of cracker and layer again with crackers.

Melt Together:

⅔ C. crunchy or creamy peanut butter
1 C. chocolate chips (milk chocolate or semi-sweet)

Spread over top of crackers. Refrigerate overnight then cut in squares.

JENNY'S CHESS PIES

¾ C. raisins
1 C. water
¼ C. butter
1 C. sugar
3 egg yolks
1 heaping tbsp. flour
¾ C. milk
1 tsp. vanilla
¾ C. nuts, chopped
Favorite pie crust
Favorite meringue recipe

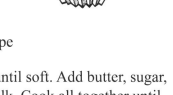

Cook raisins in water until soft. Add butter, sugar, egg yolks, flour and milk. Cook all together until thick. Add vanilla and nuts. Cool.

Line cupcake pans with your favorite pie crust. Bake crusts. Fill crusts and top with meringue.

Bake at 350° until brown.

In memory of
— Jenny Stombaugh

PEANUT BUTTER MELTAWAY CAKE

1 C. oleo
1 C. water
2 eggs, slightly beaten
¼ C. cocoa
½ C. buttermilk or canned milk

Combine and cook over medium heat until mixture starts to bubble. Take off heat and add:

2 C. sugar
1 tsp. baking soda
2 C. flour
1 tsp. vanilla

Beat with wire whisk or low speed on mixer until smooth. Put in greased jelly roll pan. Bake 20 minutes at 350°. Let cool and put in refrigerator until chilled.

Mix 1 C. peanut butter and 1 tsp. oil – spread on cooled cake. Refrigerate again until chilled.

Mix:

½ C. butter and 6 tbsp. buttermilk or canned milk and ¼ C. cocoa.

Heat until bubbly; remove from stove; add:

1 tsp. vanilla
1 box powdered sugar
Beat with a mixer until smooth and spread on cake.

7-UP CAKE

Cake:

1 pkg. yellow cake mix
1 pkg. French vanilla instant pudding
¾ C. oil
3 eggs
1 (12 oz.) can 7-Up
½ C. walnuts, chopped
½ C. coconut, shredded

Topping:

2 envelopes Dream Whip
1½ C. cold milk
1 pkg. French vanilla instant pudding

Prepare cake from first 5 ingredients.

Bake in oiled and floured 12"x9" pan @ 325° for 45 minutes. When cool – frost with the following topping:

Beat Dream Whip and cold milk until very stiff. Then add French vanilla instant pudding. Beat well. Spread on cake. Sprinkle with chopped nuts and coconut.

— Marianne Erhart

PUMPKIN PIE CAKE

1 box yellow cake mix (remove 1 C. and set aside)
1 stick margarine, melted
1 egg, beaten

Mix well. Press into a greased and floured 13"x9" pan.

In a separate bowl mix:

1 lg. (29 oz.) can Libby's pumpkin
3 eggs
½ C. sugar
⅔ C. (small can) evaporated milk
1½ tsp. cinnamon

Beat well and spread over cake mixture.

Take 1 C. reserved cake mix and add:

½ C. sugar
½ C. nuts, optional
½ stick (¼ C.) margarine

Crumble together and spread over pumpkin mixture.

Bake @ 350° for 55-60 minutes. Let cool. Refrigerate. Serve with whipped cream or ice cream.

In memory of
— Betty Howard

NUT ROLL

Make only in the winter - dough doesn't do well in hot weather!

1 C. total (½ C. salted butter + ½ C. Blue Bonnet margarine), melted and cooled.
4 egg yolks, beaten
1 C. canned milk

Take ¼ C. of canned milk (warmed) and add one small cake of yeast. Add 1 tsp. sugar. Cool.

Mix yeast, butter and remaining canned milk and egg yolks together. Then add 1 tsp. vanilla.

Take 4 C. flour; add 1 tsp. salt and 6 tbsp. sugar.

Mix very well using your hands for 15 minutes. If sticky add a little flour.

Makes 4 loaves. Divide into 4 balls; refrigerate covered overnight.

Nut Mixture

1 lb. ground walnuts, chopped by hand
1 jar Baker's apricot
½ C. sugar
½ tsp. cinnamon
1 tsp. vanilla

Moisten nut misture with canned milk to paste consistency. Roll out dough like a pie but not too thin. Spread nut mixture on dough and roll up.

Bake at 350° for 30-45 minutes on parchment paper on a cookie sheet. Bake 2-4 loaves together.

Take out of oven and brush tops with canned milk. Cool. – Enjoy!

— Helen Novak

Note: You can eliminate the apricot from the nut mixture and use all the other ingredients. Make it to a paste consistency.

PISTACHIO CHEESECAKE

2 C. flour
½ C. ground almonds
½ C. cold butter
6 (8 oz. each) pkgs. cream cheese
1 (14 oz.) can sweetened condensed milk
2 pkgs. instant pistachio pudding (3-4 oz. each)
5 eggs
Chocolate syrup (optional)
Whipped cream (optional)

In small bowl combine flour and almonds, cut in butter until crumbly. Press onto bottom and sides of greased 10" spring form pan.

Bake at 400° for 10 minutes.

Meanwhile in a large mixing bowl, beat cream cheese, milk and pudding mixes until smooth. Add eggs; beat on low speed just until combined. Pour over crust. Place pan on baking sheet.

Reduce heat to 350°.

Bake at 350° for 55-60 minutes, or until center is almost set.

Cool on wire rack for 10 minutes. Run knife around edge of pan. Cool 1 hour longer. Refrigerate over night. Remove sides of pan.

Drizzle with chocolate syrup and whipped cream.

— Pat Holland

Helen Novak's nut roll rates among one of the best we have ever eaten. It is moist and flavorful. The key is that this recipe must be made entirely by hand as noted in the recipe.

PEPPERMINT CHOCOLATE BARK

Use a cookie sheet and spread cashews one layer high. Microware 2 C. dark chocolate chips (Ghirardelli) + 2 tbsp. butter Crisco; stir.

Microwave for 1½ minutes at power 5 and stir, then 1½ minutes again at power 5 and stir.

When smooth add 4 drops peppermint oil.

Pour onto cookie sheet and slightly cool, but not hard.

Microwave 2 C. milk chocolate chips (Ghirardelli) + 2 tbsp. Crisco. Repeat microwave procedure. Do not add peppermint oil.

Microwave 3 C. white chocolate (Ghirardelli) + 3 tbsp. Crisco. Repeat microwave procedure. Stir until smooth. Add 10 drops peppermint oil. Pour on top.

Crush 6 candy canes in food processor and sprinkle over white chocolate. Chill until firm. Break up bark with large knife.

— Rich Allison

PINEAPPLE UPSIDE DOWN CAKE

1 (20 oz.) can pineapple slices in syrup
1 jar maraschino cherries
¼ C. butter
⅔ C. brown sugar, firmly packed
1 C. flour, unsifted
¾ C. sugar
1½ tsp. baking powder
½ tsp. salt
½ C. milk
¼ C. vegetable oil
1 large egg
¼ tsp. grated lemon peel
1 tbsp. lemon juice
1 tbsp. vanilla extract

Drain the pineapple reserving 2 tbsp. of the juice. Melt the butter in a 10" iron skillet. Stir in the brown sugar and reserved pineapple syrup, blending well. Remove from heat, arrange the pineapple slices in the skillet and place a maraschino cherry in the center of each pineapple slice.

Combine the flour, sugars, baking powder and salt in a large bowl. Add the milk and oil, then beat on high speed with an electric mixer for 2 minutes.

Add the egg, lemon rind, lemon juice and vanilla extract and beat for an additional 2 minutes.

Carefully pour the batter over the pineapple in the skillet spreading evenly.

Bake in a preheated over at 350° for 25 minutes or until cake tests done.

Remove from oven and cool on a wire rack for 5 minutes.

Place a serving plate upside down on the top of the skillet, and invert the skillet and plate. Be careful mixture may still be very hot in the bottom of skillet.

Best served warm.

— Susie Dodson

OATMEAL PIE

2 eggs, slightly beaten
1 C. sugar
½ C. milk
¾ C. Karo Syrup
½ stick butter, melted
¾ C. oatmeal, uncooked
1 tsp. vanilla
Dash salt
½ pkg. coconut

Mix together and put in an unbaked pie shell. Bake at 350° until brown.

In memory of
— Donna Burket

FRUIT SALAD

1 (11 oz.) can mandarin oranges
1 (20 oz.) can pineapple chunks
1 (16 oz.) can peach slices
3 bananas
2 red apples
Fresh blueberries (optional)

Fruit Sauce:

1 (3¾ oz.) box instant vanilla pudding
1 C. milk
⅓ C. orange juice (concentrate)
¾ C. sour cream (do not dilute)

Drain all fruit (save juice). Chop unpeeled apples, peach slices and mix all fruit together.

To Make Sauce: Combine dry pudding with milk. Add all juices and sour cream. Beat with wire whisk until smooth. Mix fruit into sauce with wooden spoon. Stir well. Cover and chill.

— Myrt McGee

NEW YORK DELI STYLE CHEESECAKE

Crust:

Combine 1 C. sifted flour
¼ C. sugar
1 tsp. grated French's lemon peel
Cut in ½ C. butter till crumbly

Thoroughly add:

1 egg yolk, slightly beaten
1 tsp. vanilla

Line bottom of 10" spring pan with crust. Pat down till thin. Bake at 400° for 10 minutes until golden yellow. Cool.

Put ring around pan and clamp shut. Put remaining crust around crack where pan fastens together and around bottom edge of pan.

Cheese Filling:

Cream together a little at a time the following ingredients until all is mixed well:

5 (8 oz. packages) pkgs. Philadelphia Cream Cheese
1¾ C. sugar
3 heaping tbsp. flour
¾ tsp. lemon peel, grated
4 tbsp. lemon juice
½ tsp. salt
5 medium eggs or 1 C. eggs
2 egg yolks
½ C. sour cream
1 tsp. vanilla

When above is mixed with mixer, place in blender till smooth.

Take ½ C. heavy whipping cream. Beat until foamy. Gently add to mix. Put in pan. Bake at 500° for 10 minutes till crust on crack of pan is golden. Open oven door and cool down to 250°. Bake 1½ hours longer, sometimes up to 2 hours if center is thin and shakes when you move the pan. Cool and refrigerate.

In memory of
— Louise Hidlebaugh

This recipe is really a New York Delistyle Cheesecake. This cheesecake is very rich as you can see by 7 eggs, five package of cream cheese, sour cream and whipping cream plus the other extras. Forget the calories, forget the cholesterol and try this. It is outstanding! This takes a long time to make so plan ahead.

PEANUT BUTTER BROWNIE
MIDGET CUPCAKE

1 box Duncan Hines brownie mix; follow directions for cake-like brownies.

Pour batter into midget size cupcake paper holders and fill ⅔ full. Push one Reese's miniature peanut butter cup down until batter comes up over the top. If it doesn't, pour more batter on top.

Bake at 350° for 15 minutes or more until done. One batch makes 2½ dozen.

— Sandy Allison

These peanut butter brownie cupcakes are very tasty and are great for a tailgate.

SNICKERDOODLES

½ C. margarine – room temperature
½ C. Crisco shortening
1½ C. sugar
2 med. eggs
2¾ C. Gold Medal flour
2 tsp. cream of tartar
1 tsp. baking soda
¼ tsp. salt

Whip sugar and room temperature margarine until fluffy. Add eggs and Crisco shortening and mix thoroughly.

Blend flour (do not add additional flour) cream of tartar, soda and salt. Stir in shortening mixture.

Shape dough in 1" balls. Roll in a mixture of 2 tbsp. sugar and 2 tsp. cinnamon. Place 2" apart on ungreased baking sheet.

Bake 8-10 minutes at 400°. These cookies puff up first and then flatten out. Don't make more than 2 batches at one time; it's too much to mix.
Let set approximately 2 minutes before removing from cookie sheet.

One batch equals 5 dozen.

— Sandy Allison

This is one of Sandy's signature cookies. She has been baking them for years. They are easy to make and their cinnamon and sugar coating make them flavorful.

COCONUT CRUMB
CHERRY PIE

½ C. flour
¼ C. sugar
¼ C. margarine, melted
1 C. coconut
1 unbaked 9" pastry shell
1 (21 oz) can cherry pie filling

Combine first three ingredients. Add coconut and stir until mixture is crumbly. Set aside.

Bake pastry shell at 450° for 5 minutes.

Cook pie filling in sauce pan over medium heat until hot. Pour into pastry shell.

Sprinkle coconut mixture over filling.

Bake at 375° for 25 minutes or until top is lightly browned.

— Sandy Allison

OREO ICE CREAM CAKE

Take 1 (20 oz.) pkg. Oreo Cookies and grind fine in a food processor

Put in bowl and add 1 stick melted margarine. Mix well and pat into bottom of oblong cake pan. Slice ½ gallon French Vanilla ice cream into slices and place on top of Oreo mixture.

Grind additional Oreos and place on top of ice cream. Place and store in freezer.

— Donna Claar

RAISIN SQUARES

1¼ lb. raisins
1 C. sugar
1½ tbsp. flour
1½ C. water

Cook until thickened and cool in refrigerator. This is the filling.

For the dough, mix:

1 lb. brown sugar
3 eggs
1 C. margarine
1 tsp. baking soda
4 C. flour

Use an 11¾"x18" cookie sheet. Spread filling over this. Take other half of dough and spread over top. Very difficult to do! Spread thin as it does puff up. Press edges together.

Bake at 375° until golden brown. Cut into squares while it is still hot.

Make sure you spread under layer of dough thin, but also be careful when you pour filling on top as not to push the filling down through the dough layer.

In memory of
— Donna Burket

ROBERT REDFORD CAKE

1 C. flour
1 C. finely chopped pecans or walnuts
1 C. oleo softened

Mix above together until crumb like. Press mixture into a greased 13"x9" pan. Bake at 350° for 15 minutes until golden brown. Cool.

1 (8 oz.) pkg. cream cheese, softened
1 C. granulated sugar
1 (8 oz.) frozen non-dairy whipped topping, thawed

Beat cream cheese with sugar until smooth. Fold in ½ of whipped topping. Spread mixture over cooled crust.

2 (3.4 oz.) boxes instant vanilla pudding
2 (3.4 oz.) boxes instant chocolate pudding
3 C. cold milk

Combine pudding mixes with milk until smooth and thickened. Spread over cream cheese layer.

Spread remaining whipped topping over top. Cover and refrigerate overnight.

In memory of
— Grace Allison

This recipe goes back to the early 1970's when Grace Allison got this from a friend on a visit to Michigan. Thirty plus years later, it is still a good dessert.

FROZEN PEANUT BUTTER PIE

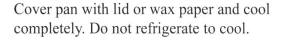

4 oz. cream cheese
1 C. confectioner's sugar
⅓ C. peanut butter
½ C. milk
1 (8 oz.) pkg. non-dairy whipped topping
1 (9") pie crust, baked and cooled
¼ C. finely chopped peanuts

Whip cream cheese until soft and fluffy. Beat in sugar and peanut butter. Slowly add milk, blending thoroughly. Fold whipped topping into mix.

Pour into baked pie crust. Sprinkle with chopped peanuts. Freeze until firm and serve. Store in freezer.

— Rich Allison

FRUIT TART

Pie crust mix for 2 crusts.

3 tbsp. granulated sugar
1 C. powdered sugar
2 (5 oz.) jars Kraft cream cheese with pineapple
⅓ C. finely chopped pecans
1 tbsp. cornstarch
1 C. unsweetened pineapple juice
¾ C. fresh fruit – strawberries, kiwi, bananas, peaches, papaya, blueberries and pineapple chunks.

Roll pie crust onto cookie sheet (10"x15" small size). Do not grease pan. Prick with fork. Bake at 425° until golden brown – approximately 8-10 minutes. Cool.

In saucepan stir sugar and cornstarch together. Add pineapple juice. Cook and stir until bubbly — then cook two more minutes on medium heat.

Cover pan with lid or wax paper and cool completely. Do not refrigerate to cool.

In mixing bowl, combine cheese, pulverized sugar and pecans.

To assemble, spread cheese mixture over pie crust. Then arrange fruit. Spoon pineapple glaze over fruit.

Chill 2-6 hours.

You can mix everything one day ahead but only assemble six hours before serving – it gets soggy!

— Pam Bowser Knisely

> *This fruit tart of Pam Knisely's looks like one direct from a bakery. It is rich in fruit flavor and cream cheese.*

PUMPKIN PIE

2 C. pumpkin
3 eggs
2½ C. milk
3 tbsp. flour
1 C. sugar or more to taste
1 tsp. salt
1 tsp. cinnamon

Mix above ingredients. Put in 2 (9") pie crusts.

Sprinkle tops with a little cinnamon. Don't use too much or they will look black when baked.

Bake at 450° for 10 minutes; then 350° for 40 minutes.

In memory of
— Esther Burket

OLD SOUTHERN PECAN PIE

⅔ C. sugar

3 eggs

1 C. dark corn syrup

⅓ C. melted butter or margarine

⅛ tsp. salt

1 tsp. vanilla

1 C. pecan halves

1 (9") unbaked pastry

Preheat oven to 350°. Beat eggs thoroughly with sugar, corn syrup and melted butter. Add salt, vanilla and pecans. Pour into pastry shell.

Place in oven and bake for 50-60 minutes at 350° or until knife inserted one quarter of way into the center comes out clean.

Cool.

— Shirley Knisley

NUT CUPS

Nut Cups:

1 stick oleo

1 C. flour

1 (3 oz.) pkg. cream cheese

Mix dough and divide into four equal parts. Make six balls from each part. Form cups by pressing dough balls into baking tins. Wet fingers with water to make it easier to shape in the tins.

Filling:

1 tbsp. melted butter

1 egg

¾ C. light brown sugar

1 tsp. vanilla

Beat with a fork and put 1 tsp. into each pastry cup. Chop 1 C. walnuts or pecans and put nuts on top of filling.

Bake at 350° for 25-30 minutes.

One batch makes 1 dozen.

— Connie Burket

NO BAKE CHEESECAKE

2 C. graham cracker crumbs

½ C. butter, melted

1 pkg. lemon jello

⅓ C. pineapple juice

⅓ C. boiling water

6 oz. cream cheese, softened

½ C. sugar

1 tsp. vanilla

1 can milk, well chilled (put in freezer at least 2 hours ahead of time, but do not freeze).

1 can crushed pineapple, well drained.

Mix jello with boiling water. Add pineapple juice. Let cool.

Combine graham cracker crumbs and melted butter. Put into bottom of 13"x9" pan.

Whip cream cheese. Add lemon jello mixture, sugar and vanilla. When well blended add pineapple. In large bowl whip the can of milk until fluffy. Fold the jello mixture into the whipped milk. Pour into the graham cracker crust. Chill well before serving.

In memory of
— Sally Bowser

This no-bake cheesecake of Sally Bowsers has been a favorite of people for many years.

PEANUT BUTTER PIE

1 baked pie crust shell

Mix the following:

1½ C. confectionery sugar
2 lg. tbsp. peanut butter

Make into crumbs with a fork. Put most of crumbs in pie shell and save a little for the top of the pie.

Take 2 boxes of vanilla instant pudding and make according to package directions. Place pudding on top of crumbs in shell.

Top with Cool Whip and place remaining crumbs on top of pie.

In memory of
— Jean Replogle

OLD WORLD APPLE PIE

1½ C. all purpose flour
6 tbsp. (¾ stick) unsalted margarine
Cut into pieces
2 tbsp. well-chilled vegetable shortening
¼ tsp. salt
3-4 tbsp. ice water

Combine all ingredients but water in a chilled large bowl. Blend until mixture resembles coarse meal. Add 3 tbsp. ice water and mix until dough holds together,adding another tbsp. of water if necessary.

Use a deep dish pan. Form dough and fit into a pie pan. Prick with a fork and bake at 350° for 10 minutes.

Combine:

2½ C. Macintosh apples – peeled, cored and sliced.
1 C. firmly packed brown sugar
¼ C. cornstarch
3 tbsp. dark rum
1 tsp. cinnamon

Combine above ingredients in a large bowl and mix well. Spoon into pie shell.

Combine:

1 C. brown sugar, firmly packed
¾ C. pecans, chopped
½ C. rolled oats
½ C. all purpose flour
½ C. (1 stick) butter, melted

Mix well in a large bowl. Mixture will be crumbly. Sprinkle over apple mixture. Bake at 350° for about 50 minutes until top is golden brown and juices are bubbling.

Serve warm.

— Sandy Allison

LEMON BARS

1 C. margarine
2 C. powdered sugar
2 C. all purpose flour
4 tsp. lemon juice
Rind of 2 lemons, grated, about 3 tsp.
4 eggs, well beaten
2 C. sugar
1 tsp. baking powder
4 tbsp. all purpose flour
1 C. shredded coconut, optional

Mix margarine, powdered sugar and flour. Spread batter in a small size (10"x15") cookie sheet that has been sprayed with Pam.

Bake at 350° for 15 minutes until tan colored. Cool. Mix remaining ingredients and pour over crust. Bake at 350° for 25 minutes.

DESSERTS

PAWLEY'S ISLAND PIE

2 lg. eggs
1 C. sugar
½ C. flour
1 tsp. vanilla
1 stick unsalted butter
1 C. walnuts, chopped
1 C. chocolate chips
1 (10") pie shell

Melt butter; add to other ingredients in order listed. Pour into unbaked pie shell and bake at 350° for approximately 30 minutes.

— Sandy Allison

This is a very rich chocolate chip and walnut pie. When we first had this in Pawley's Island, SC, we asked for the recipe. When the restaurant closed several years later, the recipe arrived in our mailbox!

SPICE CAKE

3 C. cake flour
2 C. sugar
2 eggs
1 C. Crisco Shortening
1½ C. buttermilk
1 heaping tsp. baking soda
1 tsp. cinnamon
1 tsp. nutmeg
½ tsp. baking powder

Dissolve baking soda in buttermilk. Add baking powder to flour and then mix all ingredients together.

Bake at 350° for 20 minutes in two 8" round layer cake pans. Do not use a bundt pan.

If you don't have buttermilk, mix 1 tbsp. lemon juice or white vinegar per C. of milk.

In memory of
— Evelyn Dodson

CARROT CAKE AND FROSTING

2 C. sugar
1 C. Mazola Oil
4 eggs
3 C. grated carrots
½ C. walnuts, chopped
½ C. pineapple, chopped and drained
½ C. coconut, shredded
¼ C. pineapple juice
2 C. flour
2 tsp. baking soda
2 tsp. cinnamon
2 tsp. baking powder
1 tsp. salt

Cream sugar and oil. Add unbeaten eggs one at a time beating well after each addition. Sift together dry ingredients and add along with remaining ingredients.

Bake in an ungreased 9"x13" pan at 350° for 40 minutes. You can also bake in a greased bundt pan for 55 minutes. Makes about 30 cupcakes. Bake 15-20 minutes. Cool cake in refrigerator before icing.

Use Cream Cheese frosting.

— Sandy Allison

CREAM CHEESE FROSTING

4 C. or 1 lb. powdered sugar
4 oz. cream cheese, room temperature
¼ C. soft butter or margarine
1 tsp. vanilla
3 tbsp. buttermilk

Combine all ingredients and beat with an electric mixer until creamy.

Double recipe if you are icing a layer cake.

— Sandy Allison

PINACOLADA COCONUT CAKE

Duncan Hines Butter Recipe Golden Cake Mix
⅔ C. water
½ C. margarine
3 eggs

Mix according to directions on back of cake mix. Also add: ¾ C. coconut to batter and pour into a greased bundt pan.

Bake at 375° for 40-50 minutes.

Cool and take out of bundt pan. Take a fork and poke holes all over the cake.

Pour approximately ½ can Coco Lopez over it all. Ice with Cool Whip and sprinkle coconut all over it

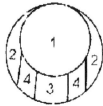

In memory of
— Jean Replogle

EASTER BUNNY CAKE

Traditionally made every Easter!

Bake Pinacolada Coconut Cakes -Double recipe
Makes 4 (9") round cakes
Bake at 375° for 25+ minutes

Cut cakes into bunny shapes.
Use extra pieces for Easter eggs.

Pour Coco Lopez over cake. Ice with cool whip and cover with coconut.

Dye coconut different colors and decorate. Decorate with licorice and jelly beans.

— Sandy Allison

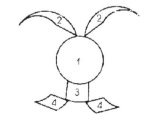

These are the famous peanut butter eggs that were always made in large quantities like 50 lb. per Easter. They were then decorated with icing and given away.

EASTER EGGS

4 lb. powdered sugar
1 lb. margarine, room temperature
1 C. milk
1 pt. peanut butter

Mix above together and shape into eggs. Place in refrigerator to chill.

Later, in a double boiler, melt a mixture of half milk chocolate and half semi-sweet chocolate with a small amount of paraffin. Do not let the heat get too hot or chocolate will get too hot and be ruined. Chocolate can also be melted in a microwave. Dip eggs in chocolate and cool in refrigerator.

Coconut or maraschino can be substituted for peanut butter.

In memory of
— Grace Allison

This Easter Bunny cake has been a tradition every Easter for 30 years. The rich pina colada cake and the Cool Whip icing along with all the decorations make it a treat for kids. We have placed a copy of the diagram for cutting the cake to make it easier to assemble. Also Sandy normally makes an extra cake and cuts them into small "egg shaped pieces" and also decorates them. That way each kid can take an egg home with them.

DOUBLE GINGER MOLASSES COOKIES

½ C. butter, no substitute
¾ C. light brown sugar
¼ C. dark molasses
1 egg white
1 tbsp. fresh ginger, grated
1 tsp. ground ginger
¼ tsp. cloves
½ tsp. cinnamon
¼ tsp. salt

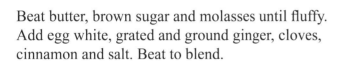

Beat butter, brown sugar and molasses until fluffy. Add egg white, grated and ground ginger, cloves, cinnamon and salt. Beat to blend.

Combine 2½ C. flour and 1½ tsp. baking soda. Add to butter mixture. Beat on low speed until combined. (Mixture may be refrigerated for up to five days).

Preheat oven to 375°. Place ¼ C. sugar in bowl. Drop dough no bigger than the size of a marble in the sugar and toss to coat.

Place 1½" apart on ungreased cookie sheets. Bake 7 minutes. Yields 2½ dozen. Note: 1 lb. fresh ginger makes 4 batches of cookies.

— Alma Juram

PEANUT BUTTER CANDY

3 C. white sugar
1⅓ C. white Karo syrup

Using a candy thermometer, boil this together until mixture reaches 290°. Spread 2 pints peanut butter in a buttered oblong pan.

Pour hot syrup over peanut butter. Stir quickly with spoon.

Pour out of pan. While hot cut with scissors in small pieces.

In memory of
— Donna Burket

NUT ROLL ICE BOX COOKIES

12 C. flour
2 tsp. baking powder
1 tsp. salt
1 tsp. baking soda
1 tbsp. sugar
1 lg. (2 oz.) cake of yeast
2 lb. Crisco
24 oz. canned milk - Carnation 12 oz. cans
3 eggs
2 tsp. vanilla

Sift flour, baking powder, baking soda, salt and sugar.

Crumble yeast and add to flour mixture. Add Crisco and mix well.

Beat 3 eggs and vanilla well. Add this and milk to the flour mixture. Mix real well.

Divide dough into 4 long pieces and put in cake pans.

In the morning cut dough into desired pieces. Roll dough in a handful of sugar. Use filling mixture below and roll up as nut rolls.

Filling:
5 C. nuts, ground fine
2 C. sugar
2 tbsp. oleo or butter

Bake at 325° for 14 minutes until golden brown or at 350° for 10-12 minutes. Adjust your time and temperature after baking the first batch.

You may substitute a jar of Baker's Apricot Filling for the nut filling.

— Irma Chovanec

APPLE NUT CAKE

1 C. walnuts, chopped
2 C. flour
2 C. sugar
2 tsp. cinnamon
1 tsp. nutmeg
½ tsp. cloves
1 tsp. salt
2 tsp. baking soda
2 eggs
½ C. cooking oil
1 (20 oz.) can apple pie filling
1½ tsp. vanilla

Mix dry ingredients together. Add eggs, oil, apple pie filling and vanilla; mix thoroughly.

Bake in a 10" greased tube pan at 350° for one hour.

Do not remove from the pan until completely cooled.

— Shirley Knisely

MINT CHOCOLATE CHIP COOKIES

¾ C. butter (1½ sticks)
1½ C. brown sugar
2 tbsp. water
12 oz. chocolate chips
2 eggs
2½ C. flour
1¼ tsp. baking soda
½ tsp. salt
3 (4.67 oz.) box Andes Crème de Menthe Candies

In a 2 quart saucepan over low heat, cook butter, brown sugar and water until melted.

Add chocolate chips. Heat until partially melted. Remove from heat and stir until chocolate is completely melted.

Pour this mixture into a large mixing bowl and let stand for 10 minutes.

With mixer at low speed add eggs to the slightly cooled mixture. Keep speed on low and add dry ingredients. Make sure batter is completely mixed.

Grease cookie sheet. Drop dough 2" apart on cookie sheet.

Bake at 350° for 12-13 minutes. Remove from heat immediately.

Place one mint on top of each cookie. After a few seconds swirl the mint with your finger.

Cool and remove from cookie sheet.

One batch makes six dozen.

— Kathy Crilly

STRAWBERRY COOKIES

1 lb. ground walnuts – grind in blender
1 lb. coconut, chopped
1 can Eagle Brand milk

Mix together adding milk last. Form into small balls shaped like strawberries.

Put 2 small pkgs. dry strawberry Jello in a bowl and roll each cookie in the Jello. Place green stems on them. Stems may be purchased at specialty food stores. Refrigerate.

In memory of
— Margie Binotto

These mint chocolate chip cookies are always a favorite at holidays and weddings. They are very easy to make.

DESSERTS

ANGEL FOOD CAKE

1 C. cake flour
¾ C. plus 2 tbsp. sugar
12 egg whites – must be room temp.
1½ tsp. cream of tartar
¼ tsp. salt
¾ C. sugar
6 egg yolks – must be room temp
1½ tsp. vanilla
½ tsp. almond extract

Mix flour and ¾ C. plus 2 tbsp. sugar.

In a separate bowl, beat egg whites then add cream of tartar and salt. Add ¾ C. sugar (¼ at a time) to the egg white mixture.

In another bowl, beat 6 egg yolks to a lemony texture with a mixer.

Add vanilla and almond extract to egg white mixture folding in gently.

Take cake flour and sugar mixture and blend this into the meringue mixture – gently folding. Take ½ of this mixture and mix into egg yolks.

Take ungreased angel food cake pan and layer yellow and white batter.

Take a knife and swirl mixture. Bake immediately so egg white and egg yolk mixture doesn't separate.

Bake at 375° for 40 minutes.

Turn upside down and cool. Do not remove from pan until cooled!

— Joy Dodson

PEANUT BUTTER COOKIES

½ C. Parkay margarine spread
½ C. peanut butter
½ C. white sugar
½ C. brown sugar
1 medium egg, well beaten
1¼ C. flour
¾ tsp. baking soda
½ tsp. baking powder
¼ tsp. salt

Use a mixer and cream margarine and peanut butter. Add sugar gradually and cream mixture.

Add egg to mixture. Sift flour and add to cream mixture. Add soda, baking powder and salt to mixture; mix.

If using spread margarine, not stick margarine, cookie stays firmer and you don't have to add more flour. Use greased cookie sheets.

Chill dough. Form into balls and press with a fork.

Bake at 350° for 10-12 minutes.

Makes 2 dozen cookies.

Note: These cookies are softer when baked on air bake cookie sheets for 11 minutes.

— Sandy Allison

These are Sandy's famous peanut butter cookies that everyone loves. These also are always at holiday events and weddings. They are very easy to make.

MACAROON ALMOND COOKIES

2 lb. almond paste
12 oz. powdered sugar
12 oz. granulated sugar
8 oz. egg whites

Break up almond paste by putting in a blender. Then place the almond paste and sugar in a bowl and mix with a mixer until fine.

Gradually add egg whites, using a mixer until a smooth paste is obtained. Use a blender to make it a smooth paste.

Line a sheet tray with parchment paper. Place mix in a pastry bag with a round tip. Pipe out even balls. Press the tips down with a moist towel or wet hand, or drop about 1 tsp. of dough on parchment paper and flatten down with wet fingers. Use a plastic quart size freezer bag as a pastry bag. Make approximately the size of a nickel.

Bake at 325° for 15 minutes. Makes approx. 12 dozen. When cookies are cooled use a wetted sharp knife to take off parchment paper.

These macaroon cookies originally came from a famous Pittsburgh business club. They are expensive to make because of the almond paste, but they are worth it!

BROWNIE CAKE

Boil:

½ C. Crisco Shortening
1 stick oleo
4 tbsp. cocoa
1 C. water

Mix dry ingredients:

2 C. sugar
2 C. flour
¼ tsp. salt
1 tsp. baking soda
1 tsp. cinnamon

Pour liquid mixture over dry ingredients and mix in ½ C. sour milk (½ tbsp. white vinegar or lemon juice + ½ C. milk), 2 eggs and 1 tsp. vanilla.

Pour into a greased jelly roll pan (large deep cookie sheet).

Bake at 350° for 30 minutes.

Frosting:

1 stick oleo
6 tbsp. milk
4 tbsp. cocoa

Melt and bring to a boil.

Add:

1 box powdered sugar (1 lb.)
1 tsp. vanilla
¾ C. nuts

— Shirley Knisely

DESSERTS

HOMEMADE ICE CREAM

5 tbsp. cornstarch
5 tbsp. flour
5 C. whole milk (2% can be used)
3 C. sugar
5 whole eggs
1 (13 oz.) can evaporated milk
2 tbsp. vanilla
2 C. whole milk

Warm 5 C. milk on stove over medium heat. Add enough milk to the flour and cornstarch for it to mix together. Then add this to the milk mixture. Stir constantly until flour taste is gone in mixture. Bring to a boil, but be careful not to burn it.

Beat eggs and sugar until frothy.

Pour hot milk, cornstarch and flour mixture through a sieve and into ice cream can. Be sure that mixture is not too hot to add egg and sugar mixture. If necessary, let it cool slightly. Then add sugar and egg mixture.

To the freezer add 2 tbsp. vanilla – more or less to suit your taste. You may add more sugar to taste. Make the flavor with sugar and vanilla sweet enough, because when you freeze the ice cream, part of the sugar/vanilla flavor freezes out of it.

Add two more C. of milk plus 1 can evaporated milk.

For various flavors do the following:

Vanilla:

Add a vanilla bean to the milk mixture when cooking it.

Chocolate:

Add ½ C. plus of cocoa to the cornstarch/flour mixture.

Teaberry:

Omit vanilla. Only add 1 C. sugar instead of 3 C. and dissolve approximately 28 oz. + Brach's Wintergreen Lozenges and a little water over medium heat. No vanilla!

For all flavors, add enough milk to the freezer to make it only ⅔ full.

Freeze in a 6 qt. freezer for ½ to ¾ hour until freezer almost stalls out.

In memory of
— Esther Burket
— Vivian Lingenfelter

This is truly a home made ice cream recipe that has been handed down from generation to generation in the Burket family.

PIZZELLES

12 lg. eggs
3½ C. sugar
2 C. melted margarine
6 C. flour
1 tsp. salt

To the melted margarine add flavorings – either:
1 tsp. pure anise oil-one drop added at a time (ANISE FLAVOR IS THE BEST)
or
4 tsp. vanilla

Beat eggs well, add sugar gradually and beat. Then add melted margarine and beat until blended smoothly.

Add flour and salt, a little at a time, mix well.

Chill dough overnight to enhance flavor. Bake in pizzelle iron according to instructions. Let pizzelle iron get hot first then spray with Pam.

— Sandy Allison

BANANA CAKE

⅔ C. butter
1½ C. sugar
2 eggs
2½ C. cake flour
1¼ C. ripe bananas, mashed
1 tsp. baking soda
½ tsp. baking powder
¼ C. sour milk or buttermilk
1 tsp. vanilla

Cream together butter, sugar and eggs until fluffy. Sift flour with baking soda and baking powder. Mix bananas, vanilla and sour milk together. Add banana mixture and flour mixture alternately to butter mixture.

Pour batter into two 8" size round cake pans. Bake at 350° for 25-30 minutes.

Icing for Banana Cake:

½ C. mashed bananas
½ tsp. lemon juice
½ C. butter, room temperature
1 lb. powdered sugar

Mix together and make certain cake is completely cooked before icing.

Double the recipe for icing a layer cake.

In memory of
— Evelyn Dodson

Buckeyes have been a favorite of many tailgate parties for years. The rich peanut butter center and chocolate confection are also a favorite at weddings.

BUCKEYES

2 C. powdered sugar
1½ C. creamy peanut butter
½ C. (1 stick) <u>unsalted</u> butter, room temperature
1 tsp. vanilla extract

1 lb. milk chocolate, semi-sweet chips or milk chocolate wafers.

Mix first four ingredients in large bowl to blend. Cover and refrigerate at least four hours or overnight.

Form peanut butter mixture into ¾" diameter balls. Arrange on a baking sheet. Freeze one hour.

Line additional baking sheets with waxed paper.

Melt chocolate in top of double boiler over barely simmering water stirring until smooth. Remove from water.

You can also melt the chocolate in the microwave on half power.

Remove ⅓ of peanut butter balls from freezer. Pierce one with a toothpick and dip into chocolate, coating ¾ of ball. Let excess chocolate drip off into the pan.

Arrange chocolate side down on waxed paper sheets. Repeat with remaining peanut butter balls. Refrigerate until chocolate is firm. Serve well chilled.

Milk chocolate chips are the best to use.

Chocolate will lose its dipping consistency if overheated. If this occurs, add 2 tsp. hydrogenated vegetable shortening per 14 oz. candy melts.

— Sandy Allison

BAKED APPLES WITH
CHOCOLATE PUDDING SAUCE

2-3 cooking apples, seeded, peeled and halved.
Butter
White sugar
1 box (3⅝ oz.) Jello Chocolate pudding-to be cooked, not instant.

Seed and peel apples. Drop ½ tsp. butter into each apple half and sprinkle with white sugar.
Bake at 350° until cooked soft.

Cook pudding per directions on box.

After pudding and apples are done, pour pudding over apples and serve.

In memory of
— Esther Burket

HEAVENLY PUDDING

1 (20 oz.) can crushed pineapple with juice
½ C. sugar
3 oz. strawberry Jello powder – don't add water
8 oz. canned milk
8 oz. Philadelphia Cream Cheese, softened
Chopped nuts, optional

Take can of pineapple with juice and add sugar. Cook. Bring to a boil for 5 minutes. Add strawberry Jello powder. Chill mixture.

Whip canned milk and cream cheese. Blend into Jello/pineapple mixture. Add nuts. Place mixture in refrigerator to cool and gel.

In memory of
— Esther Burket
— Vivian Lingenfelter

APPLE COBBLER

4 C. thinly sliced apples
¾ C. chopped walnuts
1½ C. sugar
1 tsp. cinnamon
1 egg
1 C. melted butter
½ C. milk
1 C. sifted flour
1 tsp. baking powder
¼ tsp. salt
Whipped cream or vanilla ice cream

Place apples in 2 qt. buttered casserole. Mix: ½ C. sugar, cinnamon and ½ C. walnuts. Sprinkle over apples. Beat egg; add milk and butter. Add flour, baking powder and salt to 1 C. sugar and then add to egg mixture.

Stir until smooth. Pour over apples. Sprinkle with ¼ C. nuts.

Bake at 350° for 55 minutes. Serve with whipped cream and a little cinnamon or ice cream if desired.

Serves 8-10.

—Jean Stefanski

KEY LIME PIE

4 egg yolks
1 can sweetened condensed milk
½ C. lime juice = juice of 3 limes

Beat all together and pour into 8-9" graham cracker crust or baked and cooled regular crust.

Do not bake mixture.

Refrigerate overnight. Top with whipped cream and strawberries.

Must double recipe for 9" pie pan.

Do not place into crust until ready to serve or it will get soggy.

— Sandy Allison

MISSISSIPPI FUDGE CAKE

2 sticks melted margarine
3 eggs
⅓ C. cocoa
1 small (3½ oz.) can coconut
1½ C. flour
2 C. sugar
Marshmallows

Mix all ingredients except marshmallows thoroughly and place in ungreased, floured 13"x9" pan.

Bake at 350° for 30 minutes. Cake will be soft when taken from oven. Cover top with marshmallows. Keep from sides of pan. Place in oven to melt or soften.

Cool and then cover with icing.

Icing:

½ C. margarine
⅓ C. cocoa
1 box powdered sugar
1 tsp. vanilla
⅓ C. Pet evaporated milk
Pecans to taste
— Pam Hildebaugh
In memory of
— Louise Hildebaugh

ITALIAN BISCOTTI

3 eggs
6 oz. Orville Redenbacher's Popcorn Oil
1 (1 oz.) bottle of butter flavoring
1 stick margarine
1 C. sugar
1 tsp. vanilla (Anise can be substituted for vanilla)
3+ C. flour
2 tsp. baking powder

Mix all together. Place in refrigerator for about one hour to make it easier to roll. Roll into small logs. Use more flour if necessary to make batter stiffer. Place on greased cookie sheet.

Do not let it set.

Bake at 350° for 25 minutes or until lightly browned.

Cut on an angle after slightly cooled with a serrated knife. Set oven to 500° and place cut pieces on cookie sheet. Toast them until they are a little more brown.

In memory of
— Margie Binotto

GOB CAKE

Cake:

1 box chocolate cake mix
¼ C. salad oil
1 (3 oz.) pkg. instant chocolate pudding mix
4 eggs
1½ C. milk

Mix together and pour equal amounts in 2 greased 9"x13" pans. Bake at 350° for 20 minutes.

Filling:

5 tbsp. flour
1 C. milk
1 C. confectioner's sugar
½ C. margarine
½ C. shortening
¼ tsp. salt
1 tsp. vanilla

Cook flour and milk until thick, cool. Add rest of ingredients. Beat until fluffy and spread between layers.

— Edith Weyant

> *Edith Weyant of Bedford, PA makes a gob cake that we all fight to take home. Excellent!*

DESSERTS

SOUR CREAM COFFEE CAKE

Filling:

6 tbsp. margarine
2 tsp. cinnamon
1 C. walnuts, chopped
1 C. light brown sugar
Mix all with fork to crumbly mixture.

Cake:

½ C. Crisco
¾ C. sugar
Beat together

Add:

3 eggs
1 tsp. vanilla
2 C. flour
1 tsp. baking soda
1 tsp. baking powder
¼ tsp. salt
½ pt. sour cream

Add flour mixture and sour cream, alternately, ending with flour.

Grease angel food cake pan. Take ½ batter, then half of filling and pat it down. Then add the rest of the batter and top with filling.

Bake at 350° for 50-55 minutes.

In place of cinnamon and brown sugar filling, place a can of blueberry filling or apple slices in the center of cake.

Then make the above filling mixture, but only a half recipe for the topping.

In memory of
— Betty Howard

This is a great coffeecake recipe with lots of flavor.

APPLE CAKE

2 C. sugar
⅔ C. shortening
2 eggs
3 C. flour
1 tsp. cinnamon
2 tsp. baking soda
2 tsp. salt
2 tsp. vanilla
4 C. chopped apples

Mix as any cake. Moisture will come from topping.

1 C. nuts, chopped

Place batter in oblong pan. Put chopped nuts on top of batter and cover with topping.

Topping:

⅔ C. brown sugar
4 tbsp. flour

Bake at 350° for 45 minutes.

In memory of
— Virgie McDonald

CHESS PIE

1 C. sugar
½ C. shortening
¼ tsp. salt
½ tsp. vanilla
3 eggs
1 C. nuts, chopped
½ C. raisins
½ C. dates

Cream sugar and shortening until light and fluffy. Add salt, vanilla and one egg at a time; beating well after each one. Stir in nuts, raisins and dates. Pour into a 9" pie shell.

Bake at 350° for 40-45 minutes.

In memory of
— Sally "Nan" Lingenfelter

PUMPKIN LOG

3 eggs
⅔ C. canned pumpkin
1 C. sugar
1 tsp. baking soda
1 tsp. cinnamon
¾ C. flour
1 C. walnuts, chopped (optional)

Grease 10"x15" (small size) cookie sheet. Place waxed paper over pan; grease again.

Mix above ingredients, pour onto prepared cookie sheet. Bake at 375° for 15 minutes.

Turn into well sugared towel or pastry cloth. Roll like a jelly roll – towel and all. Let cool completely about 1 hour. Unroll and spread with filling. Re-roll and refrigerate.

Filling:

2 tbsp. margarine
¾ tsp. vanilla
8 oz. cream cheese (not fat free)
1 C. powdered sugar

— Christine Bulger

> *This pumpkin log dessert is very rich and full of flavor. This is always made in the fall and for holidays.*

PEANUT BLOSSOMS

Master cookie mix:
Use 3 of the 4 C. made from this recipe.

2 C. flour
½+ C. sugar
½ C. brown sugar
1 tsp. salt
¼ + ⅛ tsp. baking soda
¾ C. Crisco Shortening

Thoroughly combine above ingredients with pastry blender. Take 3 C. of the 4 C. of above recipe and add to it:

¼ C. brown sugar
1 tsp. vanilla
2 eggs
½ C. chunky or smooth peanut butter

Mix all together. Roll into small balls - walnut size and place on a greased baking sheet. Bake at 375° for 8-10 minutes. Remove and place chocolate Hershey Kiss* on top. Return to oven for 2 more minutes. Air baked cookie pans work best for baking these cookies.

*Use regular Hershey kisses only!

— Sandy Allison

APPLE FRITTERS

1½ C. flour
¼ C. sugar
⅛ tsp. salt
2 tsp. baking powder
½ C. milk
2 eggs
3 or 4 apples, pared and cored

Sift flour, sugar, salt and baking powder together in bowl and set aside. Put milk, eggs and apples in blender. Cover and run on low speed just until apples go through blades once.

Stir apple mixture into dry ingredients just until batter is smooth.

Drop by teaspoon into deep fryer. Fry until brown. Drain on paper towel. Sprinkle with powdered sugar.

In memory of
— Donna Burket

CHOCOLATE PUDDING DESSERT

Spray 9"x13" pan with Pam

Layer one:

1 stick margarine
1 C. flour
1 C. walnuts, chopped
⅓ C. powdered sugar
Mix above ingredients and press into pan. Make crust real thin. Bake at 325° for 20 minutes. Let cool.

Layer two:

1 C. powdered sugar
1 (8 oz.) pkg. cream cheese
1 C. Cool Whip
1 tsp. vanilla

Mix above and pour over layer one.

Layer three:

1 (3¾ oz.) pkg. chocolate instant pudding
1 (3¾ oz.) pkg. vanilla instant pudding
3 C. cold milk

Beat above ingredients together and place over layer two.

Layer four:

1 small container Cool Whip
1 Hershey's Chocolate Bar, shaved
½ C. nuts, chopped

For layer four, pour Cool Whip on top of layer three, add shaved chocolate and top with chopped nuts.

Refrigerate.

— Marianne Erhart

RICE PUDDING

1 C. un-cooked rice
½ C. raisins, optional
¾ C. sugar
Milk
1 egg
2 tbsp. cornstarch

Cook rice and raisins together according to rice directions. Drain and rinse.

Mix sugar, milk, egg and cornstarch together. Add to rice mixture; add additional milk if not enough liquid.

Cook on medium heat until hot and thickened. Add vanilla if desired for extra flavor.

In memory of
— Esther Burket

TOLL HOUSE PIE

2 eggs, room temperature
⅔ C. flour
½ C. sugar
½ C. brown sugar
1½ sticks, softened margarine/butter
1 C. walnuts – ¼" pieces
6 oz. Nestle's Chocolate Chips
Unbaked 9" pie shell

1. Beat eggs at high speed with mixer for 3 minutes. Add flour, sugar, brown sugar and beat for 3 more minutes.

2. Add softened margarine and beat 3 more minutes at high speed.

3. Stir in walnuts and 4 oz. of the chips.

4. Spread batter evenly in pie shell. Top with other 2 oz. chips.

5. Bake at 350° for 55-60 minutes.

— Rich Allison

DATE AND NUT PINWHEELS

4 C. flour
1 tsp. baking soda
1 tsp. salt
1 C. shortening (½ butter and ½ Crisco)
2 C. brown sugar
1 tbsp. lemon juice
1 tsp. vanilla
2 eggs

1. Sift flour, baking soda and salt three times. Then measure 4 C.

2. Cream shortening. Add sugar gradually.

3. Add eggs one at a time, beating well. Add lemon juice and vanilla. Gradually add dry ingredients blending well.

4. Divide dough into two portions. Roll each portion to thickness of ½" and spread with date filling. Roll like a jelly roll. Place in refrigerator overnight.

5. When ready to bake, cut thin slices from the roll and place on greased baking sheet.

Bake at 400° for 10 minutes.

Date filling:

1 lb. dates
1 C. water
1 C. sugar
2 tbsp. lemon juice
½ C. nuts, chopped

Cook chopped dates, water and sugar slowly until dates are soft. Remove from heat and beat until smooth. Add lemon juice and nuts. Cool before spreading on dough.

Note: You can freeze the rolls of cookie dough and bake later. Wrap in wax paper.

In memory of
— Leota Noffsker

BUTTER NUT TWISTS

4 C. flour
2 sticks oleo
4 egg yolks
1 lg. cake yeast
½ tsp. salt
⅓ C. sugar
1 C. sour cream

Mix above and let raise over night.

Roll ¼ dough out in rectangle shape as if to roll a nut roll using 1 tbsp. sugar and 1 tbsp. flour.

Spread ½ rolled out dough with nut filling – fold over other half of dough. Pat lightly and spread ½ dough again. Fold over and pat lightly.

It should look like a nut roll. With a pizza cutter, cut ½" strips. Roll in sugar, twist and put on lightly greased cookie sheet.

Bake at 350° for about 12-13 minutes or until golden brown. Yields about 12 dozen.

Nut filling:

1 C. coconut
2 lb. nuts, ground
3 tbsp. melted butter
1 tsp. vanilla
1½ C. sugar
Pinch of salt
1 C. heated milk (add enough to spread filling easy).

— Sandy Allison

These nut twists are a take-off on nut rolls. They have good flavor and are a little time consuming, but they are very good.

DESSERTS

FAMOUS BLACK BOTTOM PIE

1 graham cracker pie shell.
2 C. milk – heated in double boiler until hot.

Mix together:

1¼ tbsp. cornstarch
½ C. sugar

Add to hot milk – 4 egg yolks
slightly beaten. Stir into milk mixture.

Take ½ the above cooked mixture and add 1½ oz.
melted chocolate.

Take the other ½ of cooked mixture and add 1
tbsp. gelatin melted in ¼ C. cold water. Cool and
add to:

4 egg whites
½ C. sugar
Pinch of cream of tartar

Beat the egg whites, sugar and tartar until stiff.
Add ½ oz. melted chocolate.

Put first part in bottom of pie shell and second
half on top. Refrigerate.

Top with whipped cream before serving.

In memory of
— Gladys Dodson

IMPOSSIBLE PIE

½ C. Bisquick
4 eggs
2 C. milk
1 C. sugar
¼ C. margarine
1 tsp. vanilla
½ C. coconut

Put in blender and mix well. Pour into greased
pan. Sprinkle cinnamon on top of mixture.

Bake at 350° for 45-50 minutes.

— Sandy Allison

LADY FINGERS

1 lb. oleo
3 C. flour
2 tbsp. sugar
2 egg yolks, beaten
1¼ C. water

Mix flour and sugar. Cut in one stick oleo. Add
yolks and water and mix as for pie crust. Roll into
circle and fold four ways. Refrigerate 1 hour.

Roll out again and spread another stick of oleo.
Repeat this until all the margarine is used.

One hour after last spreading, separate dough into
five sections. Take one section and work it cutting
it into 9" length strips and wind loosely around
clothes pin.

Bake at 400° for 10-12 minutes. Cool 2 minutes
and take off top of pin.

Filling:

1 C. milk
4 tbsp. flour

Cook until thick and <u>cool</u>.

½ lb. oleo
2 C. powdered sugar
6 tbsp. marshmallow whip
1 tsp. vanilla

Mix with milk and flour mixture and fill pastry
using pastry bag. Refrigerate.

— Connie Burket

PUDDING CREAM PIE

Beat 1 (8 oz.) cream cheese at room temperature, ¼ C.sugar and a dash salt. Beat above together until soft.

Then gradually add: 2 small instant puddings - any flavor with a total of 1⅓ C. milk, alternating pudding and milk and add 1 tsp. vanilla at the end.

After cream mixture is mixed well, pour into a bought pie crust, graham cracker crust, nilla, chocolate or shortbread crust or make your own. Put Cool Whip on top for topping. Chill and serve.

— Karen Fincham

CREAM PUFFS

1 C. water
½ C. butter or margarine
⅛ tsp. salt
1 C. flour
4 eggs

Combine water, butter and salt. Bring to a boil. Add flour all at once. Reduce heat to low and stir rapidly over heat until mixture forms a ball and follows spoon around.

Cool pan slightly. Beat in eggs, one at a time. Beat well until smooth. Drop by teaspoon on ungreased sheet. Bake at 400° for 20-25 minutes. Split tops open when they come out of the oven.

When cooled, fill with any kind of pudding or ice cream. Also, you can fill with any type of chicken, ham, pimento, cheese or turkey salad.

— Karen Fincham

FRUIT DIP

Beat 1 (8 oz.) cream cheese at room temperature until soft. Then add and blend in: ½ C. brown sugar, ¼ C. white sugar and 1 tsp. vanilla. Fold in (8 oz.) Cool Whip and one (8 oz.) bag Heath Bar toffee chips. Chill and serve with fresh fruit as a dip.

— Karen Fincham

POTATO CHIP COOKIES

1 C. shortening (½ margarine, ½ Crisco)
1 C. brown sugar
1 C. white sugar
1 C. crushed potato chips
2 eggs
2 C. flour
1 tsp. baking soda
1 tsp. vanilla
¾ C. walnuts, chopped

Cream shortening, sugar and eggs until creamy. Add remaining ingredients and mix well.

Drop by spoonful on lightly greased cookie sheet. Let in ball. Do not flatten.

Bake at 350° for 12 minutes.

In memory of
— Margie Binotto

WHITE CHOCOLATE CHIP COOKIES

1 C. oil
1 C. margarine (2 sticks)
1 C. brown sugar
1 C. white sugar
1 egg

Beat above ingredients well.

12 oz. chocolate chips
½ bag (6-8 oz.) small Hershey kisses, chopped
(6 kisses=1 oz.)
10 oz. Hershey white chocolate chips
3½ C. flour
1 tsp. baking soda
1 tsp. cream of tartar
½ tsp. salt
1 tsp. vanilla
1 C. nuts, chopped

Mix all ingredients. Drop by teaspoon on ungreased cookie sheet.

Bake at 350° for 12 minutes.

— Ernie McMillen

DESSERTS

CHOC-AU-LAIT (WHITE)

1 C. dark brown sugar
1 C. butter

Boil hard – about 3 minutes

12 oz. grated white chocolate
1 C. pecans, chopped
Regular soda crackers

Spray Pam on large cookie sheet. Line with white soda crackers. Pour sugar mixture over crackers. Bake at 400° for 4 minutes. Remove – very hot.

Spread grated white chocolate and then nuts on top. If possible press nuts into chocolate. Put in freezer immediately for about 30 minutes. Break into pieces. May store in tin.

— Jan Brisky
— Marie Horwat

WHITE CHOCOLATE POPCORN

Pop one package of Orville Redenbacher Gourmet Popping Corn – 1 lb. size per instructions on package. Salt lightly.

Melt 6 oz. white chocolate bits in microwave on power level 5 until melted. Mix together. Can add candy sprinkles for color and for Christmas.

— Cathy Cook
— Hildi Wisniewski

ORANGE CREAMSICLE SALAD

2 boxes tapioca (cooking type)
2 boxes orange Jello
3 C. water
2 cans mandarin oranges
8 oz. Cool Whip

Bring water to a boil with tapioca and Jello. Boil a few minutes and stir while boiling. Take off stove until it cooks. Add oranges and cool whip. Let cool and refrigerate.

— Joan Leach

MARINA NOODLE PINEAPPLE DESSERT

1 lb. box Rosmarino – 30 Noodles by Vimco, cooked according to box directions.

1 (20 oz.) can crushed pineapple, drained (save juice).
1 (10 oz.) jar Maraschino cherries, drained (save juice).
1 (11 oz.) can Mandarin oranges, drained (save juice).

Add together all juices from fruit and:

¾ C. sugar
1 tbsp. flour
2 beaten eggs

Cook until thick. Pour sauce over fruit and noodles. Chill overnight. Add 9 oz. container Cool Whip and serve.

In memory of
— Louise Hidlebaugh

ORANGE SLICE BARS

½ C. margarine, melted
2 C. brown sugar, packed
4 eggs, beaten
2 C. flour
1 lb. candy orange slices, chopped
1 C. pecans, chopped
1 C. powdered sugar

Combine margarine and brown sugar. Stir in eggs and mix well. Add flour, chopped orange slices and pecans. Stir until well blended.

Pour batter in well greased 15"x10"x1" jelly roll pan. Bake at 350° for 25 minutes. Cool 15 minutes in pan.

Cut into 2"x2" squares. Remove from pan. Cut into diagonals and roll in powdered sugar.

In memory of
— Betty Nutter

CARROT CAKE

4 eggs
2 tsp. baking soda
1 tsp. baking powder
2 C. flour
1 C. sugar, granulated
1 C. brown sugar, packed
1¼ C. oil
2 tsp. cinnamon
1 tsp. salt
3 jars baby food carrots (2nd step jar)

Cream sugar and oil. Add unbeaten eggs one at a time. Add the dry ingredients and mix well. Pour into ungreased 9"x13" baking pan.

Bake at 350° for 40 minutes.

— Pat Holland

CREAM CHEESE ICING

1 (8 oz.) cream cheese
2 tbsp. butter or margarine
2 C. powdered sugar
1 tsp. vanilla

Combine all ingredients and beat with electric mixer until creamy.

— Pat Holland

Donna Burket's peanut butter fudge recipe was very good. This cooked recipe takes some time to make. The key to making this is cooking to a soft ball and then beating the mixture for at least five minutes until smooth and creamy.

CHOCOLATE ÉCLAIR CAKE

1 large and 1 small pkg. vanilla instant pudding
5 C. milk
1 (8 oz.) pkg. Cool Whip
1 box graham crackers

Topping:

¼ C. milk
⅓ C. cocoa
⅛ tsp. salt
1 tsp. butter
Vanilla to taste

Mix pudding and milk. Fold in Cool Whip and beat well.

Spray 9"x13" dish. Place a layer of graham crackers. Spread half the pudding mixture, then crackers, pudding, etc.

Topping:

Cook all topping ingredients except butter and vanilla. Boil 1 minute. Remove from heat, and then add vanilla and butter. Mix well. Cool and spread over cake and refrigerate.

— Marianne Erhart

PEANUT BUTTER FUDGE

4½ C. granulated sugar
1 C. milk
Pinch of salt
4 tbsp. white Karo syrup

Boil above ingredients until it forms a soft ball.

Remove from heat and add:

¼ lb. butter or oleo
1 pt. jar marshmallow cream
1 lb. peanut butter

Beat about 5 minutes. Pour into a large buttered pan. Makes approximately 4½ lb.

In memory of
— Donna Burket

DESSERTS

CHERRY NUT DESSERT

36 Ritz crackers, crushed
1 C. walnuts, chopped
3 egg whites, beaten
1 C. sugar
½ tsp. baking powder

Mix all together and spread in a greased long pan. Bake at 350° for 15 minutes. Watch very close. Cool.

Whip 8 oz. cream cheese, softened
12 oz. Cool Whip
1 can crushed pineapple, juice and all
1 jar Maraschino cherries cut up
Mix all together. Put on top of crust and refrigerate.

In memory of
— Louise Hidlebaugh

CHOCOLATE CHIP COOKIES

2¼ C. flour
1 tsp. baking soda
1 tsp. salt
Combine above ingredients.

1 C. Parkay margarine soft spread
¾ C. granulated sugar
¾ C. brown sugar, firmly packed

Beat and whip the margarine, granulated sugar and brown sugar. Add and blend:

1 tsp. vanilla
2 eggs

Add flour mixture to creamy mixture and mix well.

Stir in 12 oz. package Nestle's Semi-Sweet Chocolate Morsels. Drop by well rounded half teaspoonfuls onto ungreased cookie sheet.

Bake at 375° for 10-12 minutes.
Makes 100 – 2" cookies.

— Sandy Allison

RUM CAKE AND TOPPING

Batter:

1 pkg. Butter Recipe Cake Mix
1 lg. (6 oz.) vanilla instant pudding
½ C. Crisco Oil
½ C. light rum
½ C. water
1 C. broken pecans + handful
4 eggs

Sauce:

1 C. sugar
½ C. water
½ C. rum
½ C. butter

Put the handful of pecans in the bottom of a greased bundt pan. Blend together cake ingredients. Beat 4 minutes at medium speed. Bake at 350° for 50 minutes.

For rum sauce, put ingredients in a large saucepan and bring to a boil. Boil 6 minutes. Glaze bottom of hot cake. Let set five minutes and turn out cake and glaze lightly.

— Marianne Erhart

MILLION DOLLAR FUDGE

2 (12 oz.) bags chocolate chips
1 lg. Hershey Bar
1 can evaporated milk
1 (7 oz.) jar Kraft Marshmallow Cream
Walnuts, chopped
4½ C. sugar

Cook milk and sugar for 5 minutes.

Pour over chocolate chips, Hershey bar, marshmallow cream and nuts. Mix well.

In memory of
— Donna Burket

PEANUT BUTTER BALLS

2 sticks oleo, soft
1 C. crunchy peanut butter
2 C. graham cracker crumbs
1 lb. confectionery sugar
1 C. coconut
¼ tsp. salt

Mix together with a spoon and form into balls. Melt either chocolate, butterscotch or peanut butter morsels in a double boiler.

Dip balls in melted chocolate and place in refrigerator to cool.

In memory of
— Patty Walter

CARAMEL POPCORN

8 qts. popcorn, popped

Cook together until melted:

2 C. brown sugar
2 sticks oleo
½ C. dark Karo syrup
½ tsp. salt

After melted add ½ tsp. baking soda

Pour over popped corn and coat well. Then put popcorn out on two cookie sheets.

Bake 1 hour at 140° or warm.

Stir loose every 10-15 minutes.

In memory of
— Donna Burket

This caramel popcorn was always a favorite of everyone. This was a tradition to make every Christmas.

HEATH BAR COOKIES

56 saltine crackers
1 C. butter
1 C. brown sugar
¼ tsp. baking soda
12 oz. Hershey's milk chocolate bits
1 C. nuts, chopped

Line a cookie sheet with foil and spray with Pam. Lay saltine crackers to cover cookie sheet. Melt butter over medium heat and then add brown sugar. Bring to a boil and boil for 1 minute only.

Remove from heat and add baking soda. Pour mixture over crackers and spread with a spatula so all crackers are covered.

Bake no longer than 10 minutes at 375°. Remove from oven and sprinkle with chocolate bits. Spread to cover crackers. Sprinkle with chopped nuts. Let cool overnight or until set.

In memory of
— Margie Binotto

CARAMEL ICING

10 tbsp. milk
10 tbsp. brown sugar
4 tbsp. butter

Combine and boil 3 minutes. Let cool.

Add:

½ C. nuts
½ C. coconut
Stir and spread on any cake

In memory of
— Grace Allison

DESSERTS

FRUIT CAKE

¼-½ lb. citron, chopped
1 lb. or 6 boxes candied mixed fruit, chopped
2 lb. cherries, sliced in half
2 lb. pineapple, sliced
¼ lb. candied lemon or orange peel, slivered
1 lb. pitted dates
1 C. walnuts, chopped
1 C. almonds, blanched
1 C. pecans

Combine above ingredients in a large container and pour in 6 oz. molasses, brandy and rum over fruit and nuts. Soak for several days covered tightly. Stir frequently.

Flour and set aside the following:

1 (15 oz.) box currants
2 (15 oz.) boxes raisins

Sift and set aside:

5-6 C. flour
1½ tsp. cream of tartar
½ tsp. mace
1 tbsp. cinnamon
½ tsp. salt
A little nutmeg, ground cloves and all spice.

Cream together:

1 pt. buttermilk
½ lb. butter (do not substitute)
1 dozen eggs
2 C. sugar
2 tsp. baking soda

Add flour mixture to above

Then add:

Beer mug of Sweet Ruby Port Wine
1 C. total grape/orange juice
Small amount of rum
Add fruit

Fill pans ¾ full with batter after you spray pans with Pam and line. Place a pan of water in oven bottom to steam bake the fruitcakes.

Bake at 275° for 2½ hours for a loaf pan or 4 hours for a tube pan.

After they are baked, wrap in cheesecloth and sprinkle with rum and whiskey everyday for several weeks.

Keep fresh in Tupperware or airtight container. Can be frozen.

Recipe makes 4 large loaf pans plus 4 small loaf pans.

— Joy Dodson

HUMMING BIRD CAKE

2 C. sugar
2 C. flour
1 tsp. salt
1⅓ C. Crisco oil
1 (8 oz.) can crushed pineapple, drained
2 bananas, diced
1½ tsp. vanilla
3 eggs
1 tsp. cinnamon
1 tsp. baking soda
¾ C. nuts, finely chopped

Mix together but do not beat. Bake in greased and floured tube or bundt pan at 350° for one hour.

Do not frost this cake. Freezes well.

In memory of
— Donna Burket

The Very Best Recipes of Rich & Sandy Allison

VANILLA BUTTER NUT POUND CAKE

Use an angel food cake pan for this cake.

½ C. Crisco
2 sticks margarine, softened
3 C. sugar
¼ tsp. salt

Cream above ingredients carefully until all sugar is blended well.

Add one at a time – 5 eggs.

3 C. flour
1 C. canned milk

Add flour and canned milk alternating, ending with flour. Blend in 2 tbsp. vanilla butter nut flavoring.

1 C. nuts, chopped
1 (10 oz.) jar Maraschino cherries, chopped and drained

Chop walnuts and slice cherries in half. Drain off all juice on a paper towel. Fold walnuts and cherries into batter.

Spray Pam in tube pan and then flour pan.

Bake at 325° starting in a cold oven. Do not preheat oven. Bake for 1 hour and 45 minutes. Do not open oven door or cake will fall.

In memory of
— Margie Binotto

FRUIT BARS

1 C. butter (no substitutes)
1½ C. sugar
4 eggs
2 C. flour
1 tsp. vanilla
1 tsp. orange, lemon, or almond extract

Cream butter and sugar. Add eggs, flour and extract. Pour into a greased 15½"x10½" cookie sheet. Smooth batter.

Add 1 can of cherry, apple or blueberry pie filling on top of batter. Do not add more than one can!

Bake at 350° for 25 minutes. Slightly before finished baking, mark it off in squares. Sprinkle with powdered sugar after baking.

— Kathy Crilly

POTATO CANDY

½ C. mashed potatoes
2½ lb. powdered sugar
1 tsp. vanilla

Mix above on a board covered with powdered sugar. Mix until mixture is dough-like.

Roll out into round circles approximately ¼" thick. Spread peanut butter over dough with a knife. Roll up jelly roll style and refrigerate until firm. Slice into pieces.

In memory of
— Grace Allison

This is an old, old family recipe that has been handed down through the years from generation to generation. It is very sweet from all the confectioner or powdered sugar in the recipe, but the peanut butter helps to override that sweetness.

DESSERTS

COOKIE KILLERS

Bake Pillsbury Chocolate Chip Cookies from dairy section – slice into ¾" pieces until lightly brown as directions.

Place cookie in a bowl, scoop French vanilla ice cream on top, top with hot fudge or hot butterscotch and walnuts. Top with whipped cream and cherries.

— Rich Allison

PEPPERMINT CREAMS

Empty a small can of Eagle Brand condensed sweetened milk or ½ of a large can into a bowl. Gradually mix in 1 lb. confectionery sugar.

Add peppermint essence (flavoring) to taste and a few drops of green food coloring. Work evenly through mixture.

Roll the mixture out to ¼" thickness and cut into small round pieces. Leave in a cool place to set.

Dip the peppermint creams into 6 oz. of melted plain chocolate coating one half of each sweet only.

Makes 1½ lb. of peppermint creams.

— Margaret Jeffries

PEANUT BUTTER FUDGE SAUCE

½ C. sugar
1 C. water
16 oz. can Hershey's syrup
12 oz. jar peanut butter
7 oz. jar marshmallow cream

Make syrup of sugar and water. Shake in jar until sugar is dissolved.

Combine chocolate syrup, peanut butter and marshmallow cream. Add sugar syrup until you reach desired consistency. Beat with mixer. Refrigerate.

In memory of
— Bonnie Dilling

OATMEAL CAKE

1 C. Quick Oats
1½ C. hot water
Mix and let stand while making the next part.

1 C. brown sugar
1 C. white sugar
½ C. shortening
2 eggs
1½ C. flour
1 tsp. vanilla
1 tsp. baking soda
1 tsp. cinnamon
½ tsp. salt

Cream shortening, sugars and eggs. Add dry ingredients and oatmeal. Mix well. Bake at 350° for 40 minutes in a 9"x13" pan.

Icing for Cake:

¾ C. coconut
¾ C. nuts
¾ C. brown sugar
1 stick oleo
6 tbsp. cream or canned milk

Bring to a boil on stove until sugar is dissolved.

In memory of
— Belvadean Mowery

CORN FLAKE YUMMIES

1 C. sugar
1 C. corn syrup
¼ C. oleo
1 tsp. vanilla

Bring this all to a boil and boil for 1 minute. Then add 1 C. peanut butter and mix well. Then add 6 C. of corn flakes and mix well.

Spoon mixture out onto foil and let cool.

In memory of
— Peggy Allison

A&P SPANISH BAR CAKE

4 C. water
2 C. raisins
1 C. shortening
2 C. sugar
2 tsp. baking soda
4 C. flour
1 tsp. ground cloves
1 tsp. cinnamon
1 tsp. allspice
½ tsp. salt
1 C. walnuts, chopped (optional)
2 eggs, beaten

Add:

Water to raisins and simmer for 10 minutes. Add shortening and allow to cool. Sift together spices, flour, salt, sugar and baking soda. Add cooled raisin mixture and blend well. Add beaten eggs and nuts and stir well. Place into a 9"x13" pan and bake in a preheated 350° oven for 35 minutes, or until tester comes out clean. It can also be baked in a jelly roll pan for 25 minutes.

Frost when cool!

Frosting:

⅓ C. shortening
3 C. powdered sugar
3 tbsp. milk or cream
1½ tsp. vanilla

Beat till smooth and creamy.

FLUFF

1 (8 oz.) Cool Whip
1 (8 oz.) cream cheese
1 small can sweetened condensed milk
1 can your favorite pie filling (apple, blueberry, peach, cherry, etc.)
1 can crushed pineapple, drained

Blend with mixer. Refrigerate until chilled.

— Laurie Diehl

CHERRY FRUIT CAKE

1½ C. sifted all-purpose flour
1½ C. sugar
1 tsp. baking powder
1 tsp. salt
2 (7½ oz. ea.) pkgs. pitted dates
1 lb. diced candied pineapple
2 (16 oz.) jars red Maraschino cherries, drained
18 oz. (about 5½ C.) pecan halves
6 eggs
⅓ C. dark rum
½ C. light corn syrup

Grease two 9"x5"x3" loaf pans and line with foil allowing a 2" overhang and grease again.

Sift flour, sugar, baking powder and salt into a very large mixing bowl. Add fruits and pecans; toss until coated.

Beat eggs and rum thoroughly. Pour over fruit mixture. Mix until combined. Turn mixture into prepared loaf pans pressing frequently with a metal spatula to pack tightly.

Bake at 300° for 1¾ hours or until toothpick comes out clean.

Allow cake loaves to cool in pan 15 minutes. Then remove from pan and tear off foil. Brush loaves with corn syrup while still warm. Cool before serving.

In memory of
— Donna Burket

CREAMSICLES

Prep Time: 1 Hour
Yield: 10 Servings

Sorbet:

1 C. water
½ C. sugar
2 C. tangerine juice
¼ C. fresh lemon juice

Ice Cream:

1½ C. milk
⅔ C. sugar
4 egg yolks
½ C. sour cream

Equipment:

An ice water bath
An ice cream machine

10 small clear decorative glasses, for serving.

Sorbet: Place a bowl or 2 sheet pans in the freezer to chill. Combine the water and sugar in a saucepan and bring to a boil. Whisk the juices together in another bowl. Let cool slightly, and then whisk half the syrup into the juices and taste. Slowly add more syrup, tasting frequently. The mixture should taste definitely tart and sweet; you might not use all the syrup. Freeze in an ice cream machine, then transfer to the frozen bowl and keep frozen.

Ice Cream: Combine the milk with ⅓ C. of the sugar in a saucepan and heat just to a boil. Immediately remove from the heat. Whisk the egg yolks with the remaining 1⅓ C. sugar until well combined. Whisk a few tablespoons of the hot milk mixture into the egg mixture, then pour back into the saucepan with the remaining milk mixture.

Cook over medium heat, stirring constantly with a wooden spoon. At 160° the mixture will give off a puff of steam. When the mixture reaches 180° it will be thickened and creamy, like eggnog. Test it by dipping a wooden spoon into the mixture.

Run your finger down the back of the spoon. If the stripe remains clean, the mixture is ready; if the edges blur, the mixture is not quite thick enough yet. When it is ready, quickly remove it from the heat. Strain the mixture into a bowl and place it in the ice bath to cool. Let cool, stirring often. When cold, whisk in the sour cream and freeze in an ice cream machine. When frozen, use a small ice cream scoop to make walnut-sized balls and freeze solid again.

To assemble, let the sorbet soften slightly. With a larger ice cream scoop, dig out flat gobs of sorbet and pack it around the ice cream balls, covering completely. Freeze for 30 minutes.

PEANUT BUTTER SQUARES WITH CHOCOLATE TOPPING

1⅓ C. sugar
1⅓ C. white Karo syrup

Bring sugar and Karo to a boil.

When boiling add:

2½ C. peanut butter

Spray a big mixing bowl with Pam. Have ready 8 C. of Special K cereal. Stir sugar and peanut butter mixture into Special K.

Butter a long (9"x13") cake pan. Press this mixture into pan.

Take a small Corning dish and spray with Pam. Put in 2 C. chocolate bits and 2 C. butterscotch bits. Microwave; stirring constantly. Beat and whip with a mixer until creamy.

Pour over other mixture and spread with a knife. Put in refrigerator uncovered for 25 minutes. Take out and cut, then put back in refrigerator for 20 minutes.

One batch makes 6 dozen.

In memory of
— Louise Hidlebaugh

CINNAMON RAISIN NUT BREAD PUDDING

One pound loaf cinnamon raisin bread
8 tbsp. (one stick) unsalted butter, melted
6 eggs
4 C. whole milk
1 C. granulated sugar
½ C. raisins
½ to 1 C. walnuts, chopped
1 tbsp. vanilla extract
1½ tsp. cinnamon

Preheat oven to 375°. Cut bread into one inch squares, spread on a baking sheet and toast in preheated oven until light brown approx., 8 minutes. Pack toasted bread into 2½ qt. baking dish or into 8 one C. ramekins and drizzle with melted butter.

In medium bowl whisk together eggs, milk and sugar until sugar is dissolved. Add walnuts, raisins, vanilla and cinnamon. Pour custard over bread and leave to soak for ten minutes.

Reduce oven temp. to 350°. Bake pudding in preheated oven until slightly puffed and firm, approx. 45 minutes. Cool slightly and serve warm with vanilla sauce. Serves 8.

VANILLA SAUCE

1 C. heavy cream
¼ C. granulated sugar
2 egg yolks
1½ tsp. flour
1½ tsp. vanilla
⅛ tsp. salt
1 medium scoop of vanilla ice cream

In a small saucepan, combine cream and sugar and bring to a boil, stirring to dissolve sugar. In a small bowl whisk together egg yolks, flour, vanilla and salt until smooth and pale yellow.

Pour a little of the hot cream into the yolk mixture, whisking rapidly until smooth, then pour all of the yolk mixture back into the pan of cream. Cook over very low heat (do not boil), stirring constantly with a wooden spoon, until cream has thickened slightly. Remove from heat, stir in scoop of ice cream until melted and strain sauce through a fine sieve. Serve warm or at room temperature. Makes 1½ C. Make several batches for the bread pudding.

— Sandy Allison

TRIPLE CHOCOLATE FUDGE CAKE

1 chocolate cake mix
1 (3 oz.) box instant chocolate pudding mix.

Directions:

Follow directions on cake box for water and eggs. If mix calls for oil, use ¼ C. mayonnaise and ¼ C. oil and add dry pudding mix with cake mix.

Pour into 3 (8") cake pans that have been buttered and dusted with cocoa. Bake according to directions on the box.

Chocolate Mousse

1 (3 oz.) box instant chocolate pudding mix
1 C. milk
1 tsp. instant coffee
¾ tub of 8 oz. of Cool Whip

Directions:

Mix pudding, coffee and milk with mixer. Fold in Cool Whip and chill mousse. When cake is cool, spread mousse between layers and on top of cake and chill.

Chocolate Glaze

1½ C. chocolate chips
1 tbsp. clear corn syrup
¼ C. butter

Melt until mixture is shiny. If too thick, add a little milk and drizzle glaze over cake. Don't put too much glaze on cake since the glaze is very rich.

— Karen Bilger

DESSERTS

LARGE PEARL TAPIOCA

½ C. pearl tapioca
2 C. water
½ tsp. salt
2 C. milk
½ C. sugar
2 eggs, beaten
1 tsp. vanilla

Soak tapioca in water overnight. Add salt and cook 30 minutes stirring constantly. Add milk and sugar and cook 15 minutes frequently stirring. Add mixture a little at a time to beaten eggs and then add vanilla.

In memory of
— Donna Burket

POPCORN BALLS

½ C. water
2 C. sugar
1 C. syrup

Boil above together until mixture spins a fine thread or soft ball. Then add a pinch of soda.

Mix syrup mixture with popcorn continuing to add popcorn until consistency to form popcorn balls. Coconut may be added if desired.

In memory of
— Donna Burket

RASPBERRY SAUCE

1 pint fresh or frozen raspberries
4 tbsp. sugar
1 tsp. fresh lemon juice

Place in a blender and puree mixture. Taste for sweetness and adjust by adding more sugar or lemon juice to taste.

Strain to remove seeds, stirring to get sauce through strainer. Refrigerate. Serve on ice cream and other desserts.

— Rich Allison

ICE BOX PUDDING CAKE

1 lg. box vanilla pudding
1 lg. box chocolate pudding
2 sm. boxes butterscotch pudding
1 box graham crackers

Do not use instant pudding.

Line 13"x9" pan with graham crackers.

1st Layer:
Cook butterscotch pudding and put in dish on top of graham crackers. While pudding is till hot smooth out and put another layer of graham crackers.

2nd Layer:
Cook chocolate pudding and put on top of graham crackers. Put another layer of graham crackers on top.

3rd Layer:
Cook vanilla pudding and put on top of graham crackers.

Topping:
Top with cherries, nuts or both.

Put in refrigerator until pudding cools before cutting. Enjoy!

— Pat Holland

PEANUT BUTTER MELT-AWAY FUDGE

1 lb. white chocolate discs
1 lb. milk chocolate discs

Melt one at a time (can use microwave). Then pour together.
Add 8 oz. jar smooth peanut butter
Mix well.
Pour in 9"x13" cake pan.
Refrigerate until sets up.
Cut into squares.

— Beccie Weyant

PERFECT CHOCOLATE CAKE

Cake:

1 C. un-sifted unsweetened cocoa
2 C. boiling water
2¾ C. sifted all-purpose flour
2 tsp. baking soda
½ tsp. salt
½ tsp. baking powder
1 C. margarine, softened
2½ C. granulated sugar
4 eggs
1½ tsp. vanilla extract

Chocolate Cake Frosting:

1 (6 oz.) pkg. semisweet chocolate pieces
½ C. light cream
1 C. margarine
2½ C. un-sifted confectioner's sugar

Filling:

1 C. heavy cream, chilled
¼ C. un-sifted confectioner's sugar
1 tsp. vanilla extract

In medium bowl, combine cocoa with boiling water, mixing with a wire whisk until smooth. Cool completely. Stir flour with soda, salt and baking powder. Preheat oven to 350°.

Grease well and lightly flour three (3) 9"x1½" layer cake pans. In a large bowl with an electric mixer at high speed beat margarine, sugar, eggs and vanilla scrapping bowl occasionally. Beat until light – about five minutes.

At low speed, beat in flour mixture (in fourths) alternately with cocoa mixture (in thirds) beginning and ending with flour mixture. Do not over beat.

Divide evenly into pans by measuring out 2½ C. batter for each cake pan. Smooth tops and bake 25-30 minutes or until surface springs back when gently pressed with a fingertip.

Cool in pans for 10 minutes. Carefully loosen sides with a spatula and remove from pans and cool on racks.

Frosting:

In medium saucepan, combine chocolate pieces, cream and margarine. Stir over medium heat until smooth. Remove from heat. With wire whisk, blend in 2½ C. confectioner's sugar. Put mixture in a bowl and set over ice and beat until it holds its shape.

Filling:

Whip cream with sugar and vanilla. Refrigerate.

To assemble cake:

On plate, place a layer, top side down. Spread with half the cream filling. Place second layer top side down and spread with rest of cream filling. Place third layer top side up.

To frost with spatula, frost sides first covering whipped cream. Use rest of frosting on top swirling decoratively.

Refrigerate at least one hour before serving. To cut use a thin edged sharp knife with a sawing motion.

Serves 10-12. Follow directions exactly – no substitutions! Excellent if made a day ahead and refrigerated for more flavor.

— Marianne Erhart

This is another chocolate cake that was always very good and very moist. As noted, make in advance and it develops more flavor.

DESSERTS

SUGAR COOKIES AND ICING

Cream together:

½ C. butter
1 C. sugar
Blend in: 1 large egg

Sift together and add to mixture:

2-2¼ C. all purpose flour
2 tsp. baking powder
½ tsp. salt
½ tsp. vanilla

Divide dough in two parts. Chill 1-2 hours so it will be easy to handle. Roll dough, one part at a time to ⅛" thickness and cut with cookie cutters dipped in flour to avoid sticking. Keep other part of dough chilled until ready to roll.

Transfer to a cookie sheet and bake in a preheated oven at 375° for 8-10 minutes. Frost with glaze icing. Makes approximately 2 dozen cookies.

CONFECTIONER'S SUGAR-WATER GLAZE ICING

Blend 1 C. sifted confectioner's sugar and 5-6 tsp. water. Add food coloring.

Brush glaze over cookies while still warm.

— Linda Berkhimer

> *These sugar cookies are great to make, and have the kid's help decorate them with various colors of icing.*

JELLO CAKE

1 pkg. white cake mix
1 sm. pkg. cherry Jello

Mix and bake cake as directed. Cool 20-25 minutes.

Dissolve Jello in ¾ C. hot water. Add ½ C. cold water.

Poke holes in cake ½" apart. Pour Jello into holes. Refrigerate while making topping.

Topping:

1 envelope Dream Whip
1 sm. vanilla instant pudding
1½ C. cold milk
1 tsp. vanilla

In chilled bowl, blend and whip topping as directed on envelope. Add pudding, vanilla and milk. Frost cake and keep in refrigerator.

— Aimee Schultz

DIRT PIE

1 C. milk
1 pkg. Jello chocolate instant pudding
3½ C. Cool Whip
20 Oreo cookies, crumbled up
1½ C. granola chunks, peanuts, etc.
1 pkg. graham cracker pie crust

Pour milk into bowl and add pudding. Beat 1-2 minutes. Let stand 5 minutes.

Fold in whipped topping. Stir in 1 C. of cookies and granola. Spoon into pie crust. Sprinkle top with remaining cookies.

Freeze until firm.

— Aimee Schultz

CRÈME FRITE
Fried Cream

Beat Together:

3 egg yolks
¼ C. sugar
1 tbsp. dark rum
Pinch of salt

Mix 5 tbsp. cornstarch with 3 tbsp. milk and stir into egg mixture. Add 2 C. light cream, ½" stick of cinnamon and cook until thick and smooth. Remove cinnamon stick and pour into buttered pan that has been covered with crushed vanilla wafers and ground almonds. Cover with crumbs and almonds also. Chill. Cut into diamonds and recoat with crumbs.

At time of serving – fry lightly and quickly in butter.

Serve – Passing favorite liquors for topping or flamed!

— Traci Aviles

CHESS CAKE

1 box yellow Duncan Hines cake mix
1 stick margarine, soft
1 C. pecans, chopped

Mix all together and press into a large glass cake dish (9"x13") including up the sides.

Cream:

1 (8 oz.) cream cheese
2 eggs
1 tsp. almond flavoring
1 box confectioner's sugar (4 C.)

Pour this mixture over crust and bake at 325° for 40 minutes. Do not over bake. Cool and refrigerate until it sets up. Freezes well.

In memory of
— Peggy Allison

GINGERBREAD

½ C. Crisco Shortening
½ C. sugar
1 egg
2½ C. sifted flour
1½ tsp. baking soda
1 tsp. cinnamon
1 tsp. ginger
½ tsp. cloves
½ tsp. salt
1 C. Brer Rabbit Molasses
1 C. hot water

Melt shortening in 3 or 4 quart saucepan over low heat. Remove from heat. Let cool.

Add sugar and eggs and beat well. Sift together flour, baking soda, salt and spices.

Combine molasses and water. Add alternately with flour to first mixture. Pour in greased waxed paper lined 9"x9"x2" pan.

Bake at 350° for 50-60 minutes. Cool 5 minutes. Remove from pan.

Cover with white frosting and sprinkle with coconut.

— Louise Noffsker

PECAN GRAHAMS

40 split graham crackers
2 sticks butter
½ C. white sugar (Splenda can be substituted)
1 tsp. Vanilla
1 C. chopped pecans
small container milk chocolate frosting, softened

Spread the graham crackers on a 15"x10" cookie sheet. Boil butter and sugar for 2 minutes, stirring constantly. Remove from heat, stir in vanilla and pecans. Spread mixture over crackers, bake in 350° oven for 10 minutes. Transfer crackers to clean cookie sheet. Drizzle with chocolate frosting softened in microwave. Refrigerate. Can be frozen.

— Janie DeBlasio

PUMPKIN BARS

4 eggs
1½ C. sugar
1 C. oil
16 oz. can pumpkin

Beat above ingredients until fluffy.

Add:

2 C. flour
2 tsp. baking powder
1 tsp. cinnamon
1 tsp. salt
1 tsp. baking soda

Spread mixture into lightly greased jelly roll pan.

Bake at 350° for 25-30 minutes.

Cool and frost.

— Kim Decker

FROSTING

3 oz. cream cheese
½ C. margarine
1 tsp. vanilla
2 C. powdered sugar, sifted

Recipe can be doubled for 9"x13" pan.

— Kim Decker

PEACH COBBLER

6 tbsp. butter
1 C. flour
1 C. sugar (granulated)
3 tsp. baking powder
¾ C. milk
1 (28 oz.) can sliced peaches or fresh or frozen, or any other fruit.
1½ tsp. vanilla
¾ C. brown sugar

Melt butter in a deep casserole dish. Mix flour, ½ of the granulated sugar, baking powder and milk. Spread peaches over butter, then spread flour mixture over peaches.

Do not stir. Sprinkle with vanilla and brown sugar.

Bake at 350° for 30 minutes. Sprinkle with remaining granulated sugar and return to oven until golden brown.

— Sandy Allison

PEACH FLAMBE

6 tbsp. sugar
6 tbsp. butter
Juice of 1 orange
Peel of half of a lemon
Peel of half of an orange
6 tbsp. Cointreau or other orange liqueur
10 peaches
Brandy

Caramelize sugar until medium gold in color. Add butter, orange and lemon peels, orange juice and orange liqueur. Simmer a few minutes. Peel the peaches and cut into eighths. Add peaches to the sugar mixture and simmer again for a few minutes.

Add Brandy and ignite.
Serve over ice cream.

— Sandy Allison

CARAMEL CORN

1 C. sugar
⅓ C. water
⅓ C. light Karo syrup
⅓ C. margarine

Bring to a boil and cook until it reads "hard crack stage" on a candy thermometer.

Remove from heat.

Add:

1 tsp. vanilla
Red or green food coloring

Butter hands and use 3 qts. air popped popcorn and form popcorn balls or pour mixture over popcorn and stir. Serve loosely not forming into balls.

— Ira Claycomb

QUICK CREAM CHEESE BROWNIES

1 pkg. brownie mix for 13"x9" pan
Water oil and eggs as called for on fudge-like directions.
8 oz. cream cheese, softened
⅓ C. sugar
1 egg
Chocolate icing

Preheat oven to 350°. Grease bottom of 13"x9" pan. Make brownie batter according to directions for fudge-like brownies. Pour into pan.

Beat cream cheese until smooth. Beat in sugar until blended. Beat in vanilla and egg just until blended. Pour mixture over brownie batter. Cut through batter several times with knife for marbled effect.

Bake 35-40 minutes or until cream cheese mixture is lightly browned. Cool. Frost with your favorite chocolate icing.

— Pam Bowser Knisely

PINEAPPLE COOKIES

½ C. shortening
2 C. flour
1 tsp. baking powder
¾ C. crushed pineapple, drained
1 tsp. vanilla
1 C. brown sugar
1 tsp. baking soda
1 egg
¼ C. nuts, if desired

In bowl, combine flour, baking powder and baking soda.

Cream shortening, brown sugar, eggs and vanilla. Add pineapple. Mix in flour mixture. Add nuts if desired.

Drop spoonfuls onto cookie sheet.

Bake at 375° for 6-8 minutes or until brown.

Makes 2½ dozen.

In memory of
— Edna Bowser

HEAVENLY HASH

1 C. dry rice
1 C. sugar
1 can pineapple tidbits
1 (8 oz.) Cool Whip

Cook rice per directions on box until no liquid is left in pan.

Cool. Preferably overnight.

Fluff with fork. Add drained pineapple and sugar. Stir in Cool Whip. Can garnish with pineapple pieces or maraschino cherries.

Refrigerate until ready to serve.

— Dot Corley

DESERTS

BUTTER NUT CRUNCH TOFFEE

About 40 Saltine crackers
1 C. butter, not margarine
1 C. brown sugar
12 oz. chocolate chips
1 C. crushed nuts

Place crackers (do not overlap) on a foil lined cookie sheet. Melt butter in a saucepan; add brown sugar and boil for 3 minutes exactly, stirring constantly. Pour mixture over crackers, spreading all over the tops.

Bake at 400° for 5 minutes. Take out of oven and sprinkle with chocolate chips. After 2 minutes spread chocolate chips over top with back of spoon. Sprinkle crushed nuts evenly over the top. Cool in refrigerator for at least 2 hours. Cut with a sharp knife in long rows and then cut into pieces. Clean up is a snap because of the aluminum foil.

CHOCOLATE PEANUT SWEETIES

1 C. peanut butter*
½ C. butter, softened (no substitutes)
3 C. confectioner's sugar
5 dozen miniature pretzel twists (about 3 C.)
1½ C. milk chocolate chips
1 tbsp. vegetable oil

In a mixing bowl, beat peanut butter and butter until smooth. Beat in confectioners' sugar until combined. Shape into 1" balls; press one on each pretzel. Place on waxed paper-lined baking sheets. Refrigerate until peanut butter mixture is firm, about 1 hour. In a microwave-safe bowl or heavy saucepan, melt chocolate chips and oil. Dip the peanut butter ball into chocolate. Return to baking sheet, pretzel side down. Refrigerate for at least 30 minutes before serving. Store in refrigerator.

Yield: 5 dozen.

*Reduced fat or generic brand peanut butter is not recommended for use in this recipe.

APPLE CRISP

3 med. apples
½ C. flour
½ C. margarine or butter
¾ C. brown sugar
¾ C. Quick Oats

Cut apples into quarters. Peel and core. Slice into thin slices and put into lightly greased round pie pan.

Mix oats, sugar and flour. Add butter and stir until you have a crumbly mixture. Pour over apples.

Bake 350° for 35 minutes.

Serves 6 people.

In memory of
— Sally Lingenfelter

POUND CAKE WITH WHITE CHOCOLATE, ICE CREAM AND FROZEN FRUIT

1 pound cake cut into 1" small cubes
2 lb. frozen mixed berries and fruit such as raspberries, strawberries, peaches, etc

White Chocolate Sauce:

1¼ lb. white chocolate cut into small pieces
2 tbsp. vanilla
2½ C. heavy cream

French vanilla ice cream

Take berries out of the freezer when you begin to melt the chocolate so they partially thaw.

Microwave chocolate, cream and vanilla on power level 5 stirring every 30-45 seconds. Mixture should be melted and blended in about three minutes total.

In small serving bowls, place servings of pound cake, topped with ice cream. Top with berries and ladle melted white chocolate mixture over berries.

— Sandy Allison

COCONUT BALLS

2 pkgs. vanilla or coconut instant pudding
½ C. milk
1 bag coconut
¼ lb. oleo
1 tsp. vanilla or coconut flavoring
1 lb. confectioners sugar

Melt oleo and add dry pudding. Stir until well blended. Add milk and blend well.

Shape into balls and dip in melted chocolate.

In memory of
— Peggy Allison

BAKED PINEAPPLE

1 stick oleo
1½ C. sugar
3 eggs
½ C. milk
2 lg. (1 lb. 4 oz.) cans crushed pineapple
4 C. bread cubes

Mix eggs, milk, pineapple and bread cubes together. Then cream oleo, sugar and add to the mixture.

Place in a baking dish and bake at 350° for 1 hour.

In memory of
— Peggy Allison

TEA CAKES

Cream:
¼ C. butter
1 C. sugar
1 C. milk
2 eggs
2 C. flour
3 tsp. baking powder
Pinch of salt
1½ tsp. lemon extract

Put mixture in cupcake pans. Bake at 375° for 20 minutes.

In memory of
— Peggy Allison

BREAD PUDDING

2 C. bread cubes
2 C. milk
2 tbsp. butter
Dash of salt
Dash of cinnamon
¼ C. sugar
2 eggs
½ tsp. vanilla

Put bread in a greased quart baking dish.

Put milk, butter and sugar in saucepan and heat just to melt butter while stirring.

Beat eggs slightly, add salt and cinnamon. Stir into warm milk and add vanilla. Pour over bread. Set baking dish in hot water and bake at 350° for 1 hour.

In memory of
— Peggy Allison

BROWN SUGAR CHEWS

1 egg
1 C. brown sugar, packed
1 tsp. vanilla
½ C. flour, sifted
¼ tsp. salt
¼ tsp. baking soda
1 C. walnuts, coarsely chopped

Mix together egg, brown sugar and the vanilla. Add sifted flour with salt and baking soda. Add walnuts. Bake in 8" square pan.

Bake at 350° for 18-20 minutes.

Cookies should be soft when taken from the oven. Cut into squares. Makes 25

In memory of
— Sally "Nan" Lingenfelter

DESSERTS

SORBET

3 C. water
1 C. sugar

Cook until mixture comes to a boil. Remove from heat and let cool.

Take any one of the three flavors below and add to the cooled sugar mixture. Place in ice cream freezer and freez according to ice cream makers directions – about 30 minutes. Remove from ice cream freezer and place in an airtight container. Put in freezer to continue setting up. Will make about 1 gallon.

RASPBERRY:

3 C. raspberry puree
3 tbsp. almond extract

ORANGE:

6 C. orange juice
2 tsp. orange rind, grated

PINA COLADA:

6 C. Pina Colada mix

CITRUS SORBET
LIME, LEMON OR ORANGE

1 C. water
1 C. sugar

Place in pan and bring to a boil. Boil for one minute. Remove from heat and let cool.

Grate the zest (outside peel, but not the white part) of a lime, lemon or orange, whichever you are using until you have 1 tsp.

Squeeze juice from 4 limes, lemons or oranges whichever you are using. Strain to remove seeds. Place this juice, the zest and the sugar syrup in a measuring cup and add enough water to make 3½ C. Chill in refrigerator for about 1 hour.

Freeze according to manufacturers directions as listed above. Makes about 1 quart.

STRAWBERRIES
DIPPED IN CHOCOLATE

Take 1 quart strawberries with stems and prewash if desired and let totally dry.

Melt 12 oz. white chocolate and 2 tbsp. Crisco Oil in microwave on power 3. Stir every 30 seconds until chocolate is melted. It should take about 2-3 minutes to melt the chocolate. Wire whisk the chocolate to make it smooth.

Dip the strawberries in the white chocolate by holding the strawberries by the stem portion. Dip the strawberry until almost completely immersed in the white chocolate. Place on sheets of waxed paper on a cookie sheet. Allow to cool. You can speed the cooling process by placing in the refrigerator for a few minutes.

Repeat the process by melting 12 oz. milk chocolate and 2 tbsp. Crisco Oil and microwaving as above directions for white chocolate.

Dip the cooled strawberries in milk chocolate at an angle immersing about ¾ into the chocolate. Place the strawberries onto waxed paper on a cookie sheet and let cool.

Refrigerate to store but do not seal them in a container or the chocolate will draw moisture and fall off the strawberries.

— Sandy Allison

BREADS

Cooking from the Farm to the City

The Very Best

Recipes

of

Rich & Sandy Allison

and Their

Family and Friends

WHITE BREAD

Dissolve ½ cake household yeast in ½ C. warm water
3½ C. warm water
⅓ C. sugar
2 tbsp. salt
½ C. lard or shortening
11 to 12 C. Robin Hood Flour

Combine liquid, sugar and salt. Then add shortening and yeast mixture with 4 C. flour and beat with mixer until smooth.

Then mix more flour until dough leaves the side of the bowl. Turn out on floured board and knead dough until it becomes smooth and elastic, about ½ hour.

Do not put all flour in at one time, because you must have flour to work in while you knead the dough to keep it from sticking.

Put in a greased bowl and let raise for 1 hour; then punch down and let raise until doubled.

Divide the dough into pans. This will make four loaves. Leave the rough side up and grease with shortening or lard. Let raise until the pans are filled and about 3" above the top of the pans.

Bake at 350° for 45 minutes. When done, grease with shortening or lard.

FRENCH BREAD

2 C. very warm water
1 package dry yeast
1 tbsp. sugar
2 tsp. salt
5¾ C. sifted flour
1 egg white, unbeaten

Measure water into warmed bowl. Sprinkle yeast over water. Stir until dissolved. Add sugar, salt and 3 C. flour. Stir to mix; then beat until smooth and shiny.

Stir in 2½ C. more of flour and sprinkle remaining ¼ C. on board. Turn dough out onto board and knead until satiny smooth, about 5 minutes.

Shape into smooth ball. Rub bowl lightly with shortening. Press the top of ball into bowl; then turn dough over. Cover with waxed paper and a clean towel.

Let raise until doubled, about one hour. Punch dough down, divide in half and shape each into a ball.

Cover and let rest 5 minutes. Rub a little shortening on palms of hands and roll each ball under the hands to for a long, slender loaf.

Start rolling at center and gently work hands toward end of loaf. Place loaves on greased baking sheet 4" apart. Cut diagonal slices 1½" apart on top of each loaf. Cover and let raise until double, about 1 hour.

Bake at 425° for 30 to 35 minutes. Remove from oven. Brush with egg whites and return to oven for 2 minutes. Remove from baking sheet and cool on rack.

BANANA NUT BREAD

1 stick margarine
1 C. sugar
2 eggs
2 lg. ripe bananas
2 C. flour
1 tsp. baking soda
½ tsp. salt
½ C. walnuts

Cream sugar and margarine well. Add eggs and bananas. Beat well again. Add rest of ingredients, beating well.

Put in greased and floured loaf pan. Let set ½ hour in pan. Bake at 340° about 1 hour.

Test with a toothpick when baked one hour.

For muffins, bake 30 minutes.

— Sandy Allison

ZUCCHINI BREAD

3 eggs
2 C. sugar
1 C. oil
2 C. peeled zucchini; put in blender and liquefy
3 tsp. vanilla
3 C. flour
1¼ tsp. salt
1 tsp. baking soda
¼ tsp. baking powder
1 tsp. cinnamon

Mix above ingredients together and add ½ C. coconut and ½ C. walnuts.

Bake in a greased bread pan at 325° one hour or less depending on size of loaf pan.

Recipe makes 2 loaves or a bundt pan.

For muffins, bake 30 minutes. One batch makes 2 dozen.

— Sandy Allison

PINCH ME CINNAMON ROLLS

Grease bundt pan real well.

Thaw two loaves of frozen bread.

Mix together:

1¾ C. brown sugar
1½ C. white sugar
Cinnamon to taste

In a separate bowl, melt ½ lb. butter or margarine.

Sprinkle some of the cinnamon/sugar mixture in the bottom of a bundt pan. After bread has thawed, pull pieces of bread apart (smaller than the size of a walnut). Dip each piece in the butter and then roll in the sugar/cinnamon mixture. Place in bundt pan.

Mix remainder of butter/cinnamon sugar mixture together. Allow rolls to finish rising in the pan. Then pour mixture over it.

Bake at 350° for ½ hour.

Let sit for 5 minutes. Then turn upside down onto aluminum foil. Leave bundt pan on top of rolls for a couple of minutes until all syrup runs off.

Pour water into empty bundt pan afterward for easy cleaning.

In memory of
— Grace Allison

Note: You can add ½ can evaporated milk to the mixture after placing rolls in pan and prior to adding cinnamon and sugar on top. The milk will give the cinnamon rolls extra moisture.

— Roger Knisely

These are very similar to "sticky buns" except that the dough does not need rolled out which is more time consuming.

BREADS

YEAST-RAISED GARLIC PUFFS

½ C. warm whole milk
1 pkg. active dry yeast
1 tbsp. sugar
2 C. all-purpose flour, + about ½ C. for the board
2 tbsp. butter, melted
1 lg. egg, at room temperature
1 tbsp. garlic powder
½ tsp. salt
Oil for deep frying, about 1 qt.
*Homemade Garlic Salt (recipe follows)

Heat milk until warm, about 110°. Transfer milk to a large, warmed mixing bowl and sprinkle dry yeast over the surface. Sprinkle sugar over the yeast. Let mixture stand 5 minutes until creamy.

Meanwhile, place 2 C. flour, garlic powder and salt in a medium bowl and stir to combine.

Add egg and melted butter to the yeast mixture. Stir in 1 C. flour mixture. Beat with wooden spoon until a smooth batter is formed.

Beat in remaining 1 C. flour. Turn dough out onto a lightly floured surface and knead by hand until smooth and elastic, about 5 minutes, working in (about) ¼ C. flour as necessary.

Wash the large bowl and spray it with nonstick baking spray. Transfer the dough to the bowl, cover with plastic wrap or a damp towel and let stand in warm place until dough is doubled in bulk, about 45 minutes.

Turn out dough onto a lightly floured working surface. Divide the dough into 4 portions. Roll each portion into a "snake" about 10" long. Cut into 10 pieces. Place pieces on lightly floured baking sheet. When all the pieces are cut, let them rest 15 minutes until slightly puffy. (If you want bigger puffs, cut each snake into 8 pieces).

Meanwhile, heat oil to 360°. Oil should be at least 2" deep. Deep fry garlic balls, several at a time, until golden brown on all sides. Use a slotted spoon and a chopstick to assist twirling them in the hot oil.

Drain on paper towels. Sprinkle with homemade garlic salt. As you work, keep puffs warm in a 200° oven, then serve at once. Makes 32 to 40 balls about the size of a doughnut hole or small golf ball. Allow about 4 to 6 balls to a serving. Leftovers re-heat well in a toaster oven in just a few minutes.

Note: Homemade Garlic Salt

Place 1 tbsp. kosher salt and 1 tbsp. garlic powder into a mortar, using the pestle, crush the mixture moderately fine. If you have a spice grinder (aka, extra electric coffee bean grinder) use that, pulsing the mixture).

HONEY PECAN BUTTER

1 lb. butter
¼ C. + 2½ tbsp. light brown sugar
2 tsp. vanilla extract
½ C. + 4 tbsp. roasted pecans
5½ tbsp. honey

Whip butter until softened, add remaining ingredients one at a time and continue to mix. Refrigerate to store. Let sit out at room temperature prior to serving.

This butter is great on any bread!!

SOUR DOUGH BREAD

Initial Starter:

Mix one package dry yeast with ½ C. warm water. Add ¾ C. sugar, 1 C. warm water, and 3 tbsp. instant potato flakes. Let set all day; refrigerate in plastic container or glass jar covered with plastic wrap. Punch holes in plastic wrap so started can get air, (it grows). In 3 to 5 days, feed with the following: ¾ C. sugar, 3 tbsp. instant potato flakes and 1 C. warm water. Stir well. Let stand out of refrigerator for at least 8 to 12 hours. Take out 1 C. for making bread and return remainder to refrigerator. Don't wait more than five days without feeding. If not making bread, give a cup to a friend before returning to refrigerator.

Bread:

6 C. bread flour
¼ C. sugar
1 tbsp. salt
1 C. starter
½ C. corn or canola oil
1½ C. warm water

Mix all ingredients in large bowl. Pat top with oil, cover lightly with foil and let rise for 8-12 hours. Push down and knead a little. Divide into 3 parts. Knead each part 12-15 times on floured board. Put into greased loaf pans. Brush top with oil and cover with oiled wax paper and two towels. Let rise for 8-12 hours. Place on lowest rack to ensure browning on bottom.

Bake at 350° for 30 minutes.

Let set in pans for about five minutes. Remove from pans; brush tops with melted butter and cool on racks.

— Sandy Allison

BEER BREAD

1 (12 oz.) can Coor's Beer, warm
3 C. self rising flour
5 tsp. sugar
4 tsp. butter, softened

Combine beer, flour and sugar in large bowl. Mix well. Pour 2 tsp. melted butter on dough. Don't stir butter into mixture. Turn into two greased 5"x9" loaf pans.

Bake at 350° for 1 hour or until golden brown. Remove from pan and brush tops with 2 tsp. butter.

— Rich Allison

CORN FRITTERS

1 C. flour
1 tsp. salt
½ tsp. pepper
2 eggs
½ C. milk
1 tsp. butter, melted
1 tsp. baking powder
2 C. corn

Add beaten egg yolks and milk to dry ingredients. Add butter to corn. Add to mixture. Fold in beaten egg whites.

Drop by tsp. into deep fryer. Fry until light brown. Drain on paper towel.

In memory of
— Leota Noffsker

BREADS

PUMPKIN BREAD

4 eggs, beaten

Add:

3 C. sugar
1½ tsp. salt
1 C. oil
1 tsp. nutmeg
1 tsp. cinnamon
⅔ C. water
2 C. pumpkin
3½ C. flour
2 tsp. baking soda

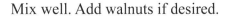

Mix well. Add walnuts if desired.

Bake at 350° for 1 hour.

Makes 3 loaves.

— Margaret Langham

WALNUT RAISIN AND CARROT LOAF

2 C. flour
3 tsp. baking powder
1 tsp. salt
¾ C. sugar
⅔ C. oil
2 eggs, large
1 ⅓ C. carrots, finely grated
2 tsp. lemon peel
1 C. walnuts
⅔ C. raisins

Mix well. Add raisins and nuts and mix by hand.

Pour into a well greased 9"x5"x2¾"pan. Sprinkle with nuts. Let stand 10 minutes.

Bake at 350° for 1 hours.

Remove from oven and let stand 10 minutes. Then turn upside down.

— Sally Weyant

APPLE SAUCE NUT BREAD

¼ C. shortening
¾ C. sugar
1 egg
2 C. flour
3 tsp. baking powder
1 tsp. salt
½ tsp. baking soda
½ tsp. cinnamon
1 C. applesauce
1 C. nuts

Mix well. Add nuts and applesauce last.

Bake at 350° for 50-60 minutes. Makes 1 large loaf or 2 small loaves.

— Sally Weyant

BANANA NUT BREAD

1 stick margarine
1 C. sugar
2 eggs
2 bananas, very ripe
2 C. flour
1 tsp. baking soda
½ tsp. salt
¼ C. English walnuts
¼ C. black walnuts

Cream sugar and margarine well. Add eggs and bananas. Beat well again. Add rest of ingredients, beating well. Put in a greased and floured loaf pan.

Garnish top with whole nuts and cherries. Let set ½ hour in pan.

Bake at 340° about 1½ hours. Test with a toothpick when baked 1 hour.

— Zoe Fickes

CANNING

Cooking from the Farm to the City

The Very Best
Recipes
of

Rich & Sandy Allison

and Their
Family and Friends

CANNING

STEP-BY-STEP INSTRUCTIONS FOR HOME CANNING

1. Select quality ingredients at their peak of freshness; prepare them according to a tested recipe. Assemble jars, lids, bands and canning equipment. Check all items to ensure they are in good working condition.

2. Process acid foods in a boiling water canner. Acid foods include: jellies, jams, preserves, marmalade and other soft spreads, fruits, tomatoes (with added acid), pickles, relishes and chutneys.

3. Process low-acid foods in a steam pressure canner. Low-acid foods include: vegetables, meats, poultry, seafood and combination recipes (with acid and low-acid ingredients).

4. Wash jars, lids, and bands in hot, soapy water. Rinse well. Dry bands and set aside. Heat jars and lids in hot water (180° F), keeping them hot until used. Do not boil lids. (For recipes requiring less than 10 minutes processing, sterilize jars by boiling them for 10 minutes. At elevations higher than 1,000 feet above sea level, add 1 minute for each, 1,000 foot increase).

5. Fill hot jar with prepared recipe. Leave recommended headspace: ¼" for fruit juices, pickles and soft spreads; ½" for fruits and tomatoes; 1" for vegetables, meats, poultry and seafood.

6. Remove air bubbles by sliding a non-metallic spatula between the jar and food to release trapped air. Repeat procedure 2 to 3 times around jar.

7. Wipe rim and threads of jar with a clean, damp cloth. Center heated lid on jar with sealing compound next to glass. Screw band down evenly and firmly until a point of resistance is met – fingertip tight.

8. Place jar in canner. Repeat procedure for filling jars until the canner is full. Process filled jars following the method and processing time indicated by a tested recipe.

9. When processing time is complete, cool canner according to manufacturer's instructions. Remove jars from canner; set them upright on a towel to cool. Bands should not be retightened. Let jars cool 12 to 24 hours.

10. After jars are cool, test for a seal by pressing the center of the lid. If the lid does not flex up and down, the lid is sealed. Remove bands. Wipe jars and lids with a clean, damp cloth. Label and store jars in a cool, dry, dark place.

FIRE ROASTED SALSA FOR CANNING

Take a metal pan that can be put under the broiler and place the following in it – skin side up:

9 tbsp. minced garlic cloves
¼ bushel plum tomatoes, cores removed and quartered.
16 medium onions quartered
10 jalapeno peppers seeded and cut in two
8 sweet red peppers quartered
8 green peppers quartered

Arrange in pan with skin side up. Drizzle with olive oil. Place under broiler and let skins get slightly charred. This will take approximately 7 minutes per pan.

Remove from pan and put through food processor and coarsely chop.

Meanwhile, while mixture is in oven, take a very large container and add the following:

5 (28 oz.) cans Fuhrman's crushed tomatoes
32 oz. can tomato juice
5 bunches green onions – chopped including some of the tops.
7 tbsp. salt
4 tbsp. black pepper
5½ tbsp. cumin
1¾ C. lime juice (8 limes)
1 lg. bunch cilantro, finely chopped
5 small cans diced green chilies

To this mixture add the items which were put through the food processor.

Bring mixture to a boil like spaghetti sauce. Pour in jars and seal.

Makes 28-30 pints.

— Rich Allison

SPAGHETTI SAUCE

½ bushel tomatoes washed and quartered. Run through processing machine to remove skins and seeds.

3 large onions
3 green peppers
2 heaping tsp. oregano
1 heaping tsp. basil
Garlic powder to taste

Place onions, peppers and spices in blender with a small amount of water and liquefy.

Take tomatoes, onion mixture and add:

2 C. sugar
¼ C. salt
1 tsp. celery salt
1 C. Crisco oil

Boil until thickness desired. Add 2 large cans tomato paste. Stir constantly, because it will stick on bottom of pan.

Place sauce in jars and place lids on to seal.

One bushel of tomatoes will make approximately 12 quarts of sauce.

In memory of
— Grace Allison

This spaghetti sauce recipe came from an elderly Italian lady in Altoona, PA when Grace Allison was selling produce door to door with her father. She began making this for our family over 50 years ago.

SPICY SPAGHETTI MARINARA SAUCE

Follow recipe from page 201 and add:

2 hot red peppers to the blender mixture.

1 additional tbsp. oregano
1 additional tbsp. basil

Season heavily with garlic powder.

— Rich Allison

CANNING PEACHES

Wash peaches and peel. Remove seeds. Slice peaches and fill jars ¾ full.

Make a syrup of approximately 6 C. sugar and enough hot water to sweeten it and dissolve sugar.

Pour syrup into jars, but do not fill completely to the top.

Seal and place in a canner and bring to a boil. Boil 10 minutes. Take off stove and let set to seal.

Yields: 18 to 21 quarts per bushel.

In memory of
— Esther Burket
— Vivian Lingenfelter

These peaches are canned in a heavy syrup that makes them very sweet. They are great to use with other fruits to make fruit salad.

GRAPE JELLY

Wash and clean one quart of grapes. Place in a large pan and cook over medium heat with 1 quart of sugar. Mash the grapes down while cooking.

When mixture comes to a rapid, bubbly boil, boil another 15 minutes.

Put mixture through a strainer to eliminate seeds and pulp.

Keep jelly hot and bubbly while putting in jars so they seal. If they don't seal, freeze them.

One batch makes 7 jelly jars.

In memory of
— Vivian Lingenfelter

STRAWBERRY JAM

Take 4 C. cleaned strawberries and 4 C. sugar. Bring to a boil and mash up berries while cooking. Boil 12 minutes.

Pour into containers and freeze.
One batch makes 7 jelly containers.

In memory of
— Esther Burket
— Vivian Lingenfelter

Both the grape and strawberry jelly can be made anytime during the year from grapes or strawberries that were previously frozen.

CORN RELISH

20 ears corn
6 green peppers
6 red peppers
4 large onions
1 large head cabbage
4-5 stalks celery
4 large carrots
4 C. sugar
5 C. vinegar
1 C. water
2 tbsp. dry mustard
2 tbsp. celery seeds
1 tbsp. turmeric
2 tbsp. salt

Cut corn off cob. Chop all ingredients. Cook 20 minutes after it starts to boil. Seal in pint jars.

In memory of
— Donna Burket

MOM'S RED BEETS

½ bushel red beets

Wash and cook until tender. Do not cut into the beets, just scrub them clean. Cook until soft. If you cut into them, they will "bleed".

Drain juice. Let beets cool. Cut tops and bottoms off and remove skin. Cut into quarters and add the following:

2 qt. water
2 qt. vinegar (dark)
8 C. brown sugar
4 tbsp. salt

Bring to a boil. Remove from heat.

Jar and seal. Makes 15 quarts.

— Rich Allison

CANNED PEARS

Wash pears. Peel and remove core. Fill jars that have been washed. Optional: Place 2 teaberry lozenges in bottom of jar.

Make syrup of approximately 6 C. of sugar and enough hot water to sweeten it and dissolve sugar.

Pour sugar mixture into filled jars, but not completely to the top.

Boil lids in a pan of water and thoroughly dry lids. Wipe rim of jars clean and place lids on top.

Place jars in a canner and cover with water. Boil 10 minutes. Take off stove and wait for them to seal before moving.

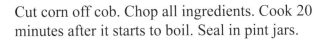

In memory of
— Esther Burket
— Vivian Lingenfelter

JALAPENO PEPPER JELLY

3-5 fresh jalapeno peppers, stemmed and seeded
4 medium sized bell peppers
1 C. white vinegar
2 pouches (3 oz. ea.) liquid fruit pectin
5 C. sugar

Grind jalapenos and bell peppers. Combine peppers and their juices, vinegar and sugar in a 6 quart or larger pot. Bring to a slow boil and boil for 10 minutes.

Remove from heat and stir in pectin. Add green food coloring. Return to heat and bring to a boil rapidly for one minute.

Remove from heat and skim foam. Ladle into hot jars leaving ⅛" space.

Makes 5 half pints.

Spread on snack crackers with cream cheese.

— Sandy Allison

CANNING 14 DAY PICKLES

4 gallons cucumbers, whole and small

Cover whole cucumbers with one gallon of cold salted water. Add enough salt until you can float an egg to the top of the water. Pour over cukes. Repeat for four gallons of brine solution.

Stir mixture each day from day 1 through day 6.

On the seventh day, wash cucumbers and cover with boiling water.

On the eighth day, slice cucumbers and cover with boiling water and a box of powdered alum.

On the ninth day, drain and cover with boiling water.

On the tenth day, make a syrup of:

1 box cinnamon sticks
1 box whole cloves
1 box celery seed
24 C. sugar
2 qt. dark vinegar

Heat syrup to a boil daily from the **tenth to the fourteenth day** and pour over cucumbers.

On the fourteenth day, pack pickles in jars and pour hot boiling juice down over pickles.

Take the cinnamon sticks; break in half and place ½ stick in each jar along with a couple cloves. Make certain they are on top of the pickles and not down with them.

Seal jars.

Note: During first couple of days when they are soaking in salt solution, mold and foam may develop on top of water.

In memory of
— Vivian Lingenfelter

OLD-FASHIONED SCRAPPLE

1 lb. boneless cooked pork, chopped
1 C. cornmeal
1 (14½ oz.) can chicken broth
¼ tsp. dried thyme
¼ tsp. salt
½ C. all-purpose flour
¼ tsp. pepper
About 3 tbsp. cooking oil

In a large saucepan combine pork, cornmeal, chicken broth, thyme and salt. Bring to a boil, stirring often. Reduce heat and simmer about two minutes or till mixture is very thick, stirring constantly.

Line an 8"x8"x2" baking pan or 9"x5"x3" loaf pan with waxed paper, letting paper extend 3 to 4 inches above top of pan. Spoon pork mixture into pan. Cover and chill in the refrigerator 4 hours or overnight.

Un-mold, and cut scrapple into squares. Combine flour and pepper; dust squares with flour mixture.

In large skillet, brown scrapple on both sides in a small amount of hot oil. (Add more oil, if necessary.)

Makes 12 servings.

— Rich Allison

> *This is the scrapple recipe that was used 50-75 years ago.*

HELL'S BUTTER

36 banana peppers – remove seeds from 30 and leave seeds in 6.
Grind peppers.

1 qt. yellow mustard
1 qt. white vinegar
Mix together – Bring to a boil

Add:

1⅔ C. water
1⅔ C. flour
Mix well.

Boil for 3-5 minutes
Jar and seal.

Serve by pouring over a block of softened cream cheese. Spread on crackers.

— Teri (Ellenberger) Coffman

SPAGHETTI SAUCE

Place ½ C. vegetable oil in a sauce pot.

In blender place:

¼ large onion
3 cloves garlic, peeled
1 tsp. salt
1 tsp. pepper
1 bay leaf
2 tsp. basil

Add enough water to process to liquid.

Add:

1 (18 oz.) can tomato paste
3 (18 oz.) cans water

Bring to a boil. Cook 5 minutes. Add ⅛ tsp. baking soda and continue to stir.

Cook at least ½ hour more and add meat if desired.

In memory of
— Sue Rotella

DILLY BEANS

6-8 C. green beans
1 tsp. cayenne pepper
4 cloves garlic
2½ C. water
2½ C. vinegar
¼ C. salt
4 heads fresh dill

Pack beans lengthwise into 4 hot pint jars. Allow ¼" head space to each jar. Add ¼ tsp. cayenne pepper, 1 garlic clove and 1 head dill.

In saucepan, combine water, vinegar and salt. Bring to a boil. Pour boiling mixture over beans in jars. Allow ¼" head space. Seal jars by placing in a pan of boiling water covering top of jars. Boil 10 minutes.

— Sandy Allison

CANNING

PICKLED RED BEETS

5+ C. water
1+ C. dark vinegar
1 C. brown sugar
1 tsp. salt

Cook scrubbed beets with tops and tails on until tender. Cool. Peel and slice. Cut into wedges or leave whole.

Combine beets with above mixture and bring to a boil. Put in jars and place in boiling water for 7 minutes.

In memory of
— Vivian Lingenfelter

CANNED STEWED TOMATOES

Place washed tomatoes in a dishpan. Boil water and pour over tomatoes to scald them. Peel off skins.

Fill jars with tomatoes. Pack jars full. Squeeze tomatoes in jar. Add no water! The tomatoes will make their own juice.

Add ½ tsp. salt per pint jar or 1 tsp. per quart, or add 1 tsp. sugar for each pint jar or 2 tsp. per quart jar.

Place lids on jars. Boil for 8-10 minutes. Take out of water and let seal.

In memory of
— Esther Burket

DRYING CORN

Cook corn on cob then cut it off.

Place corn on cookie sheets and bake at 200° turning quite frequently. Don't dry it too hot or it will brown but not dry out.

Dry until all kernels are hard and dry. Then place on cookie sheets on table and let dry for several more days.

Corn can then be stored in a jar or plastic bag or frozen.

In memory of
— Donna Burket

CANNED OX HEART CHERRIES

Wash cherries thoroughly. Let seeds in cherries.

Fill jars with cherries. Make a syrup of 2 C. water and 1 C. sugar, per jar. Heat on stove until sugar dissolves. There is no need to boil, just dissolve sugar.

Fill jars with syrup. Seal with lids. Place jars in a canner and bring to a boil. Boil for 8 minutes. Take jars out of canner and let seal.

In memory of
— Esther Burket

CANNING PLUMS

Gather plums. Wash and remove seeds. Fill jars. Dissolve a syrup of 1 C. sugar to 1 C. water. Heat to dissolve sugar. Do not boil. Fill jars with syrup. Seal with lids. Place jars in a canner and bring to a boil. Boil for 10 minutes. Take jars out of canner and let seal.

In memory of
— Vivian Lingenfelter

BREAD AND BUTTER PICKLES

25-30 medium pickles
8 lg. onions
2 green peppers
½ C. salt
5 C. vinegar
5 C. sugar
2 tbsp. mustard seed
1 tsp. turmeric
½ tsp. cloves

Wash and cut pickles thin. Add chopped onions, peppers and salt. Let stand 3 hours and then drain.

Put vinegar, sugar and spices in a large pot. Bring to a boil. Add drained pickles. Heat but don't boil. Jar and seal.

In memory of
— Esther Burket

BREAD AND BUTTER PICKLES

3 qts. sliced pickles
3 onions
½ C. salt
3 C. vinegar
1 C. water
3 C. brown or white sugar
Lump powdered alum
½ tbsp. celery seed
1 red pepper
1 tsp. cinnamon
½ tsp. ginger
2 tbsp. mustard seed
2 tsp. turmeric

Mix sliced onions, cucumbers and salt. Let stand three hours. Drain.

Boil water, vinegar, sugar and seasoning for 3 minutes. Add onions and cucumbers and simmer 10-20 minutes. Don't boil. Pack into jars and seal.

In memory of
— Leota Noffsker

APPLE BUTTER MADE IN THE OVEN

18 C. apple sauce
8 C. sugar
1 C. vinegar
2 tsp. cinnamon
1 tsp. ground cloves
1 tsp. allspice

Mix all in a large roaster and put in oven. Bake at 300° for 4-5 hours stirring every ½ hour.

In memory of
— Grace Allison

PICKLED WATERMELON RIND

10 C. watermelon rind
4 C. sugar
2 C. Heinz white vinegar
6 cinnamon sticks
2 tbsp. whole allspice
2 tbsp. cloves

Peel, cut rind in 1" cubes. Soak rind overnight in 2 quarts of water and 6 tbsp. salt. Drain. Cook tender in fresh water and drain.

In a large pan, heat to boiling sugar and vinegar. Tie cinnamon, allspice and cloves in a cheesecloth bag. Add with the rinds to the syrup and simmer 45 minutes until transparent.

Pack rind into jars and cover with boiling syrup to ⅛" of top. Seal jars. Rind can be colored green or red for the holidays. Makes 6 half pints.

— Sandy Allison

MINCE MEAT

24 qts. cherries
20 lb. sugar
2 boxes allspice
2 boxes cloves
2 bushel apples, diced
2½ gal. apple butter
1 lg. box cinnamon
4 lb. raisins
3 gallon wine
5 qt. grape juice
1 pt. brandy
10 lb. beef, cooked and ground

Mix well and jar. Makes approximately 82 quarts. Will keep for several weeks in refrigerator.

In memory of
— Grace Allison

SPICED CUCUMBER RINGS

7 lb. cucumbers, extra large — peeled and seeds removed.

1 C. pickling lime (get at Agway)

Peel and seed pickles and weigh out 7 lb. Soak in 1 C. pickling lime and 1 gallon water for 24 hours. Wash and soak in water 3 hours.

1 oz. red food coloring
1 C. dark vinegar
1 tbsp. alum

Mix 1 C. vinegar, 1 oz. red food coloring and 1 tbsp. alum and water to cover. Pour over cucumbers and simmer 2 hours. Pour off.

10 C. sugar
2 C. dark vinegar
1 lb. red hot cinnamon candies
8 cinnamon sticks
2 C. water

Bring to a boil, sugar, vinegar, red hots, cinnamon sticks and water.

Pour over cucumbers. Let stand 24 hours. Pour off liquid and bring to a boil again. Pour over

cucumbers. Let stand another 24 hours. Pour off. Bring to a boil and pour over cucumbers in jar and seal.

Makes approximately 11 pints.

In memory of
— Louise Hildebaugh

APPLE BUTTER BOIL

1 barrel cider
3 bushel apples, sliced (snitz)
100 lb. sugar
1 lg. box cinnamon
1 lg. box allspice

In a large copper kettle boil the cider, but keep 9 gallon for later. Boil the cider down until there is enough room for the apple snitz.

Wash sliced apples and add to the cider until all the apples are in the kettle. Then add the remaining 9 gallon of cider.

Continue boiling until you can put ½ of 25 lb. bag of sugar in at a time, until you have all the sugar added.

Continue boiling until it begins getting thick and a small amount in a dish will have a "scum" or begin setting up. Add the spices.

This apple butter must be stirred continually. This will make approximately 25 gallons and will take all day to make in a copper kettle.

Find an experienced person to help you with this!

In memory of
— Grace Allison
— Wilma Black Smith

Applebutter boiling began at 5 am, and it would take all day to complete or about a 12 hour day.

ZUCCHINI PICKLES

6 medium white onions, sliced
4 qts. zucchini, sliced (we use half zucchini and half yellow squash for added color).
1 green pepper, sliced in strips
1 red pepper, sliced in strips
⅓ C. salt
2 trays ice cubes
3 C. white vinegar
4 C. sugar
1½ tsp. turmeric
1½ tsp. celery seed
2 tbsp. mustard seed

Slice onions, zucchini and peppers. Layer with salt and ice cubes in large stock pot, ending with ice cubes. Let stand three hours, adding more ice partway through if most of the initial ice seems to have melted.

Meanwhile, wash 8 pint-size canning jars. About 20 minutes before the end of the three hour sitting time for the vegetables, place the jars on a cookie sheet and place in cool oven. Turn oven on to 250°. Remove from oven when ready to ladle pickles into them.

Boil canning jar lids.

Drain ice water from vegetables. Combine vinegar, sugar, turmeric, celery seed and mustard seed. Pour mixture over sliced vegetables. Heat just to boiling.

Fill hot jars with hot pickles and brine. Put on hot lids. Jars will seal themselves.

Makes 8 pints.

CHOW CHOW

6 qts. green tomatoes, chopped
3/8 C. salt

Mix tomatoes and salt. Let stand overnight. Drain well. (about 3 hours)

Mix with following vegetables-chopped:

6 green peppers
6 red peppers
1 med. head cabbage
1 lg. stalk celery
10 onions

Add:

5 C. vinegar
5 C. sugar
1 tbsp. salt
1 tsp. tumeric
3 tbsp. mixed pickle spice

Stir over medium heat until boiling. Boil 15 minutes. Jar and seal.

— Becky Eckard

CHRISTMAS RELISH

4 lg. yellow peppers or 16 carrots
4 green peppers
4 red peppers
1½ stalks celery
8 sm. onions
2 C. vinegar
2 C. sugar
1 tbsp. salt

Chop vegetables. Add to vinegar, sugar and salt mix in pot. Boil for 30 minutes. Put into canning jars. Cold pack for 30 minutes.

— Gwen Feathers

HOT PEPPERS WITH SAUERKRAUT

Top and seed hot peppers.
Stuff with sauerkraut.

Fill Jars:

Use wide mouth quarts and get 8-10 peppers per jar.

Brine:

1 pt. water
1 pt. white vinegar
1 C. sugar
¼ tsp. salt

Boil the above for 1 minute. This covers 3 quarts. Put 4 buds of garlic in each jar.

Process 15 to 20 minutes.

— Nancy Musselman

HOT BANANA PEPPERS IN BBQ SAUCE

Sauce:

1 (8 oz.) can tomato paste
1 tbsp. salt
1 (24 oz.) bottle ketchup
2 C. cider vinegar
2¼ C. sugar
1 pint canola or corn oil
4-8 garlic cloves, sliced thin

Boil 10 minutes. Cut and add hot banana peppers – about 8 pints. Cook an additional 1-3 minutes. Jar and seal while hot. Do not cold pack.

— Karen Fincham

MEATBALLS IN BBQ SAUCE

Put browned or cooked meatballs in a crockpot. Add 1 quart of peppers in BBQ sauce from the above recipe to the crockpot. Then take another 1 quart of peppers in BBQ sauce, and place in blender and grind to a puree. Add this to the crockpot.

Cook until meatballs are done.

— Karen Fincham

GARLIC PEPPER JELLY

1½ C. garlic, minced
1½ C. hot peppers, minced
14 C. white vinegar
24 C. sugar

½ C. pectin per 3 C. juice.

Heat garlic, peppers and vinegar. Measure liquid. Add pectin.

Bring to a rolling boil, stirring constantly.

Add sugar (have it pre-measured). Bring to a full rolling boil again. Boil 1 minute, stirring constantly. Remove from heat and put in jars. Process 10 minutes.

— Nancy Musselman

GARLIC JELLY

30 jelly jars
3 C. garlic, minced
14 C. white vinegar
24 C. sugar

½ C. pectin per 3 C. juice.

— Nancy Musselman

GREEN PEPPERS

1¼ peck sweet bell peppers
1-14 peck hot Italian peppers

Slice and remove seeds. Wear rubber gloves. Drop peppers into boiling mixture (recipe below). Process bell peppers first, they take a little longer to cook. Cook about 10-15 minutes.

Boiling Mixture:

2 C. sugar
4 C. olive oil
4 C. dark vinegar
4 C. ketchup

Bring to a boil.
You will get 5 pints canned.
Use any leftover sauce in chili dishes.

In memory of
— Louise Hidlebaugh

PICKLED PEPPERS

2 qts. vinegar
2 qts. water
½ C. salt
1 pkg. sweet and low sweetener

Bring liquid to a boil.

Wash and clean peppers and cut into pieces lengthwise. Put peppers in jars. Add 1 tsp. dry mustard on top of the peppers in each jar.

Pour the hot liquid over the peppers and seal the jars.

— Donna Claar

STRAWBERRY PINEAPPLE JAM

4 C. strawberries
7 C. sugar
1 (20 oz.) can crushed pineapple with juice

Boil all together for 30 minutes. Then remove from stove. Add 1 large box (6 oz.) strawberry jello. Put in containers. Let cool until the next day and freeze.

— Margaret Langham

END OF GARDEN RELISH

3 C. cucumbers, sliced
2 C. green peppers, chopped
3 C. cabbage, chopped
3 C. onions, chopped
3 C. green tomatoes, diced
3 C. carrots, chopped
3 C. string beans, chopped
3 C. celery, chopped
3 C. cauliflower, chopped
6 tbsp. mustard seed
6 tbsp. tumeric
6 C. sugar
3 tbsp. celery seed
6 C. vinegar
6 tbsp. garlic powder or more to taste

Soak cucumbers, peppers, cabbage, onions and tomatoes in salt water overnight. Salt water mixture should be ½ C. salt to 2 qts. water. Drain in morning.

Cook carrots, string beans and cauliflower until tender and drain.

Mix all vegetables, seasoning, sugar and vinegar, etc. Cook 10 minutes.

Jar and seal. Makes 10 pints.

In memory of
— Grace Allison
— Mary Dively

GARDEN RELISH

1 peck red sweet peppers
1 peck green peppers
1 peck ripe tomatoes
½ peck onions

2 tbsp. whole spice
3 C. vinegar
4 C. sugar

Peel tomatoes and cut into quarters. Cut peppers and onions. Scald onions. Drain. Add all together with ½ C. salt. Let come to a boil. Jar while hot.

In memory of
— Grace Allison
— Georgia Bridges

CANNING

CORN SALAD

1 dz. large ears corn
1 head cabbage
4 lg. red peppers
4 lg. onions
2 stalks celery
2 C. cider vinegar
4 C. sugar

Finely chop above vegetables. Add vinegar to taste and sugar to sweeten. Add one 20 oz. jar yellow prepared mustard and 2 tbsp. salt to taste.

Cook 20 minutes. 2 batches makes 24 pints.

In memory of
— Grace Allison
— Ellen Musselman Black

FRESH HORSERADISH

Dig up fresh horseradish roots. Scrub clean. Place roots in a blender with a small amount of water.

Blend until horseradish is finely chopped. Be careful of strong horseradish smell when opening blender. Add a small amount of white vinegar to thin to a spreading consistency. Jar and place in refrigerator.

— Rich Allison

BEAN SALAD

1 head cauliflower, cut up
2 C. lima beans
2 C. yellow beans
2 C. green beans
2 C. carrots, diced
2 C. celery, diced

Cook the above until almost soft. Drain.

3 red peppers, finely chopped

2 onions, finely chopped
Soak in salt water while above mixture is cooking. Drain and wash 1 can red kidney beans.

Mix:
3½ C. vinegar
3½ C. sugar
1½ tsp. tumeric
1 tsp. dry mustard

Put this in a large pan along with all vegetables and bring to a boil. Boil 8 minutes. Jar and seal. Makes 7 pints.

In memory of
— Grace Allison

CANNING GREEN/YELLOW BEANS

Clean beans breaking off both ends.
Break beans in small pieces.

Rinse beans twice. Fill jars with beans. Add ½ tsp. salt on top of beans and fill with warm water.

Seal jars and place in a canner. Once the water starts to boil, boil for 2 hours. Take out of canner and let seal.

In memory of
— Esther Burket

TOMATOES, GREEN PEPPERS AND ONIONS

4 gal. tomatoes, scalded, skins removed and cut into quarters
2 lb. green peppers, cut up
1½ C. chopped onion

Cook above ingredients. Add salt. Season heavily with garlic powder and Italian seasoning to taste.

Boil until everything is cooked soft. Jar and seal.

In memory of
— Donna Burket

CURE MEAT IN A BARREL

Put enough water in barrel to cover meat. Add enough salt until an egg floats to the top.

Add:

1 box salt petre
1 box red pepper
½ gal. molasses
4 tbsp. baking soda

Place meat in brine. Let hams in brine in a cool area for 6 weeks and bacon for 4 weeks. This is enough brine to cure meat from 2 hogs.

In memory of
— Grace Allison

MEAT CURE FOR TABLE

7½ lb. salt
2 lb. brown sugar
2% salt petre
2% red pepper
4% black pepper

Make a juice with warm water and above and put on meat. Keep meat in a cool area and let meat lay with above for 10 days.

This cures 500 lb. of meat.

In memory of
— Chester & Esther Burket

RED BEET JELLY

3½ C. fresh beet juice, not salted
½ C. lemon juice
1 box Sure Jell

Mix lemon, beet juice and Sure Jell together and bring to a boil.

Add 6 C. sugar and boil 2-3 minutes. Put in jars and seal.

In memory of
— Donna Burket

HOT PEPPER BUTTER

1 qt. yellow mustard
4 C. sugar
1 qt. vinegar
30-40 hot peppers

Clean peppers. Do not remove seed. Blend peppers using vinegar as liquid. Bring to a boil. Turn down heat and add 1½ C. flour and 1½ C. water. Keep stirring until it gets thick. Put in warm 8 ounce jelly jars with warm lids. Makes 15-16 (8 oz.) jars.

— Bill & Audrey Aungst

STUFFED PICKLED PEPPERS

Liquid Mixture:

4 C. sugar
2 C. vinegar
1 C. water
1 tsp. salt

Use jingle bell peppers. Cut small hole in the top of pepper and clean out. Shred cabbage and sprinkle with salt and celery seed. Mix well and stuff into peppers. Put peppers in pint jars and pour in liquid mixture. Place in canner and boil 15 minutes.

Makes 6-7 pints. Note: 1 large head of cabbage makes enough for 9-10 pint jars of peppers.

— Bill & Audrey Aungst

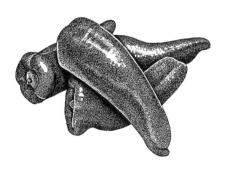

COUNTRY FIXIN'S

Remedies From Days Gone By

Have you ever wondered what your grandmother did when little Johnny came home with the flu? Or what the popular treatment of sore throats was before cough drops came along? Thankfully modern medicine makes most ailments and sicknesses quite endurable for us, but here's a little peek into the past, when things weren't always so easy, or pleasant.

Bleeding – Apply a mixture of flour and salt and wrap with a cloth or common paper. Or press cobwebs and brown sugar over the cut.

Blisters – Boil the bark from an oak tree in a small amount of water and apply directly to blisters.

Chapped Hands or Lips – Apply castor oil often to area. Rubbing hands regularly in sheep's wool will work too.

Chills and Cramps – Mix ginger and pepper in very hot water and drink.

Colds and Flu – Drink a mixture of cinnamon, sage and bay leaves, and add a little lemon juice. Drink warm. Drink hot ginger tea freely. Take a dose of quinine every six hours.

Cough – Make a tea of wild cherry bark and mix with honey.

Cuts and Scratches – Rub with a sliced clove of garlic or apply raw honey.

Diarrhea – Brown a little flour over the fire, add two tsp. of vinegar and one tsp. of salt, mix and drink. Do not eat fruit.

Earache – A piece of cotton sprinkled with pepper and moistened with oil or fat will give almost instant relief. Place a small piece of garlic in ear.

Headache – Inhale fumes of boiling vinegar.

Hiccups – Eat a tablespoon of peanut butter.

Insect Bites – Apply common mud, a slice of onion, garlic juice, lemon juice, baking soda, tobacco or honey.

Poisoning – Give a strong emetic of warm water, mustard and salt mixed. Cause vomiting by swallowing a small piece of soap or tobacco.

Ringworms – Apply kerosene to the area three times each day until ring and redness disappears.

Scalds – Relieve instantly by using common baking soda applied thickly to wet rags and then placed on scalded area.

Sore Throat – Apply fat bacon or pork to outside of throat and hold in place by tying a rag around it. Keep in place until soreness is gone. Hold a small piece of garlic in mouth for several minutes.

Sunburn – Apply butter or buttermilk to the sore area.

Toothache – Mix warm vinegar and salt, hold in mouth until pain ceases. For cavities, plug with cotton doused with pepper and ginger.

Well, what do you think? Are you more thankful now for that bottle of Aspirin in your medicine cabinet? I know I sure am!!!

HOMEMADE SOAP

5½ pts. water
4½ pts. melted grease
2 tbsp. borax

Mix above in water.

Add one can of lye. Sprinkle over top and stir in for 20 minutes.

In memory of
— Grace Allison

DRINKS

Cooking from the Farm
to the City

The Very Best
Recipes
of
Rich & Sandy Allison
and Their
Family and Friends

WINE

1 qt. red concord grapes rinsed in cold water, squeezed and smashed.
1 gallon water
2½ lb. sugar

Mix well and set in open container and cover with screen for 8-10 days.

Strain with colander and then put in container (water jugs or gallon jugs).

Put balloon on as a rubber stopper (put 2 pin holes in balloon). When balloon lays down flat, (about 2 weeks) strain again and bottle. Let stand another week.

— Rich Allison

ROCKET FUEL

1 Shot rum
1 Shot Southern Comfort
1 Shot dry gin
1 Shot vodka
1 Shot ginger brandy
1 Shot peach brandy
1 Shot triple sec
1 Shot apricot brandy
1 Shot amaretto
1 Shot sloe gin
1 Shot wild cherry vodka

— Beccie Weyant

IRISH CREAM

1 can evaporated milk
1 can Eagle Brand milk
½ tsp. chocolate flavoring
½ tsp. coconut flavoring
1 tsp. vanilla
2½ C. blended whiskey

Blend well.

CIDER

1 gallon pasteurized apple cider
1½ C. sugar
½ C. lemon juice
10 (2") cinnamon sticks
1 tbsp. allspice (whole)

Place allspice and cinnamon sticks in a piece of cheese cloth. Drop into cider in a pot.

Bring to a boil and simmer for 15 minutes.

— Sandy Allison

FIRST LADY'S HOT CHOCOLATE

6 tbsp. unsweetened cocoa
6 tbsp. sugar
Pinch of salt
2½ C. milk
2½ C. light cream
½ tsp. vanilla
Pinch of cinnamon powder (optional)
Whipped cream
Orange zest

Directions:

1. Mix cocoa, sugar and salt.
2. Add milk. Heat to dissolve.
3. Add light cream, vanilla and cinnamon. Heat to just under boiling.
4. Mix very well and pour into warm mugs.
5. Top with whipped cream, cocoa powder and fine orange zest.

Serves 6 to 8

— Lady Laura Bush

DAIQUIRI

2 oz. fresh lime juice
½ tsp. superfine sugar
2 oz. .light rum
3 ice cubes in a shaker

Shake and strain

— Rich Allison

COFFEE MOCHA PUNCH

2 qt. strong hot coffee
½ C. sugar
1 oz. unsweetened chocolate, melted
½ tsp. salt
½ tsp. vanilla
1 qt. vanilla ice cream
½ (1 liter) club soda chilled
2 C. half and half
1 C. whipped topping
1 C. chocolate syrup

Combine coffee, sugar, vanilla and salt in large container. Chill covered for several hours. Slice ice cream into cubes. Pour coffee mixture into punch bowl. Add ice cream, club soda and half and half. Mix gently.

Ladle into cups. Serve with whipped topping.

20 Servings – 1 Gallon

LONG ISLAND ICED TEA

½ oz. vodka
½ oz. light rum
½ oz. triple sec
½ oz. tequila
½ oz. gin
¼ C. orange juice

Fill glass with Pepsi or Coke and above.

In memory of
— Donna Burket

MAI TAI

2 oz. dark rum
½ oz. Triple Sec
1 oz. lemon juice
1 oz. simple syrup
½ oz. lime juice
½ oz. Orgeat Syrup (Almond flavoring)

Garnish with orange slice.

— Rich Allison

SUFFERING BASTARDS

Mix:

1 (15 oz.) bottle Lemon Perma Fresh Sour*
7 C. water
7 C. sugar water

(Sugar water is made by taking 5 C. water and 5 C. sugar and bring to a boil until mixture is crystal clear. Measure out 7 C. needed).

In a tall glass add:

1 shot brandy
1 shot light rum
1 shot dark rum

Fill glass half with ice and add above mix to top of glass. Garnish with oranges and cherries.

For 1 gallon:

14 oz. each of brandy, light and dark rum. Put in a gallon container and fill to top with lemon mixture. Serve over ice.

* Available at Calevas Foods - Washington, D.C.;
   Phone 202-842-2324

— Bim Burket
— Rich Allison

HOMEMADE KAHLUA

Mix a 2 oz. jar of instant coffee with 4 C. sugar.

Add 2 C. boiling water and let cool. Put 1 whole vanilla bean in ½ gallon jug.

Add cooled mixture, then 3 C. brandy and let stand for 30 days.

— Rich Allison

WINE SLUSH

1 bottle Lambrusco wine
1 (12 oz.) can frozen lemonade
1 (6 oz.) can frozen orange juice
1½ (6 oz. size) cans water

Blend all but wine in blender and freeze. Scoop into glass and pour wine over it.

DRINKS

SLUSH

1 lg. can frozen lemonade
1 lg. can orange juice
2 C. double strength tea (2 C. boiling water +
4 teabags)
7 C. water
1¾ C. sugar
2 C. Southern Comfort

Mix all together and freeze. Mix with Seven-up or orange juice.

SANGRIA

Mix:

¾ C. brandy
½ C. Cointreau
4 C. red wine
Juice of 3 lemons
Sugar to taste

Add:

2 thinly sliced oranges
1 thinly sliced lemon
¾ C. seeded sweet cherries
1 C. sliced fresh or canned peaches

— Bonnie Schultz

MARGARITA DRINK

1 fifth tequila
½ fifth triple sec
32 oz. Lapaz sours (from Mexico) or Dailey's
8 oz. Rose's lime juice

Put all above in a gallon container and fill to top with water. No ice.

When ready to serve, put in blender and froth them up.

Put ice in glass and pour mixture in glass and salt rim of glass.

— Rich Allison

WHISKEY SOUR

8 oz. orange juice
1 shot whiskey
1½ tsp. sugar
Ice

Add ice and place in blender.

— Rich Allison

PINA COLADA'S

1 can Coco Lopez coconut mix
1 can sliced pineapple (20 oz.)

Put both in blender with juice of pineapple. Makes about 36 ounces. Take ½ of mixture out of blender and leave 18 oz. in blender and add 1 C. rum.

Fill blender with ice and blend.

Makes about ¾ gallon total.

— Rich Allison

YELLOW BIRDS

2 (½ gal.) containers orange juice
2 (48 oz.) pineapple juice
1 (12 oz.) bottle Rose's lime juice
1 qt. Dailey's Cocktail mix
½ gal. white rum
fifth dark rum
fifth Appleton Punch (sub. Myer's Dark Rum)
fifth banana liquor
fifth Neopolitan or anise (licorice) liquor
fifth Kahlua
1 gallon water

Mix all together. Can be frozen and refrozen. Pour over ice and add 7-Up. Makes 4 gallons.

In memory of
— Donna Burket
— Louise Hidlebaugh

KID'S KORNER
AND FUN RECIPES

Cooking from the Farm
to the City

The Very Best
Recipes
of

Rich & Sandy Allison

and Their

Family and Friends

KID'S KORNER & FUN RECIPES

FUN RECIPES

PIZZA

English Muffins, cut in half
Pizza sauce
Mozzarella cheese
Pepperoni
Bake in toaster oven until bubbly.

ANTS ON A LOG

Celery sticks, washed and dried
Peanut butter
Raisins
Spread peanut butter on celery, top with raisins.

MOCK ANGEL FOOD CAKE

White bread, cut into cubes or sticks
Sweetened condensed milk
Coconut
Cinnamon sugar
Cut bread into cubes or sticks. Dip in milk and roll in coconut or cinnamon sugar.

APPLE SNACK

Cut an apple into sections
Roll the pieces in jello powder (your favorite flavor).

BIRDSEED OR GORP

Mix together several varieties of cereal, raisins, M&M's, peanuts, coconut, pretzel sticks, potato sticks, dried fruit, marshmallows and anything else you can think of. Be creative!!!

BANANA BOATS

Take one banana and peel a thin strip down the length of the inside curve. (Do Not Remove). Excavate a small ditch in the center of a banana; fill with chocolate chips, nuts, raisins, miniature marshmallows and coconut. Replace the strip, wrap in foil. Bake at 350° for 15 minutes.

WALKING SODAS

Using a small paring knife cut a slit through the middle of an orange. Place a peppermint stick through the opening. Sip the orange juice through the opening.

FUN RECIPES

GIRL SCOUT FUDGE

½ C. cocoa
½ C. peanut butter
4 C. powdered sugar
1 tsp. vanilla
Pinch of salt
2 sticks melted margarine

In a bowl mix cocoa, sugar and salt together. Add melted margarine and vanilla. Put into an un-greased pan to set or roll into small balls and place on a plate to set.

TOOTSIE ROLLS

2 tbsp. soft margarine
2 oz. liquid chocolate (Bakers)
1 tsp. vanilla
½ C. dry milk
3 C. powdered sugar
½ C. light karo syrup
Mix altogether well; roll, then cut and wrap.

ORANGE JULIUS

½ C. water
¼ C. sugar
½ tsp. vanilla
½ C. milk
⅓ C. frozen orange juice concentrate
10 ice cubes, crushed

EASY CANDY BAR DESSERT

1 graham cracker crumb crust recipe
16 lg. marshmallows
½ C. milk
5 Hershey almond or Reese's peanut butter bars
1 C. whipping cream

Press graham cracker mixture into a 9"x13" pan. Combine marshmallows, milk and candy bars in saucepan. Cook over low heat until melted; blend well. Cool. Whip cream in mixer bowl until soft peaks form. Fold in candy mixture. Spread in prepared pan. Freeze until firm.

Yield: 12 Servings.

KID'S KORNER & FUN RECIPES

KID'S FAVORITES

BEEF-N-BEAN BURGERS

1 lb. ground beef
16 oz. can pork-n-beans
½ C. ketchup
½ C. onion, chopped
1 tbsp. mustard
1 tsp. salt
1 can refrigerated biscuits

Preheat oven to 375°. Lightly grease 2 cookie sheets. Brown ground beef, drain. Stir in pork-n-beans, ketchup, onion, mustard and salt, then simmer. Pat out each biscuit to a 4" circle on the cookie sheets. Spoon about ⅓ C. meat-n-bean mixture over each. Sprinkle with shredded cheddar cheese.

Bake for 15 to 18 minutes, until crust is golden brown. Refrigerate any leftovers. Makes 10 servings.

CINNAMON TOAST SPREAD

1 stick butter or margarine, softened
4 tbsp. confectioner's sugar
2 tsp. ground cinnamon
2 dashes ground nutmeg
2 tsp. vanilla extract

Combine all ingredients in small bowl. Mix together with a fork. Spread on toasted bread, graham crackers, etc.

CRACKER JACK SNACKS

1 stick butter
1 C. brown sugar, packed
¼ C. light corn syrup
¼ tsp. baking soda
1 tsp. vanilla
6 C. fresh popcorn
2 C. toasted oat cereal*
2 C. crispy rice cereal*
1 C. nuts

In a heavy saucepan, melt first three ingredients. Bring to a full boil, stirring constantly. On medium heat, without stirring, cook to soft ball stage, 3 to 4 minutes. Remove from heat. Stir in baking soda and vanilla. Stir well. This will cause the mixture to foam. Pour immediately over a mixture of remaining and store in a covered container.

*I use Cheerios and Crispex cereals.

BLENDER BREEZE

1 C. apple juice
2 C. frozen strawberries
1 lg. sliced banana
1 C. vanilla yogurt

Combine above ingredients in blender. Blend until smooth.

— Tessa Knisely

SWEET TART LEMONADE

1 can frozen lemonade from concentrate
10 strawberries, mashed with a fork

Prepare frozen lemonade per directions. Add mashed berries to the pitcher. Stir well.

— Tessa Knisely

FINGER JELLO

2 sm. boxes Jello (any flavor)
1¼ C. boiling water

Mix well and let set for 10 minutes. Pour into a 4"x8" rectangle plastic container. Refrigerate until firm. Cut into squares.

— Brandon & Makayla Weyant

KID'S KORNER & FUN RECIPES

BERRY PARFAIT

Strawberry yogurt
Granola
Sliced strawberries
Whipped cream

Layer yogurt, granola and sliced strawberries. Top with whipped cream.

—Tessa Knisely

MAGNIFICENT MALT

Handful of malted milk balls
½ C. low fat milk
3 tbsp. malted milk powder
2 C. vanilla ice cream
1 C. strawberries

Put malted milk balls in plastic sandwich bag. Put bag in a towel, crush candy with rolling pin. Set aside.

Place remaining ingredients in blender. Blend well. Pour into glasses and sprinkle with crushed candy. Serve with a spoon.

—Tessa Knisely

CRUSH SLUSH

8 strawberries
6 ice cubes
½ C. lemon lime soda

Combine above in blender. Blend into a slush. Dip edge of glass in water and then in colored sugar. Pour drink into glass.

—Tessa Knisely

CRUNCHY YUMMY RAISIN TREATS

½ C. peanut butter
½ C. honey
¾ C. nonfat dry milk
½ C. crispy rice cereal*
½ C. raisins

Put all ingredients into a bowl. Mix well with a spoon. Roll into small balls. Put balls on waxed paper. Clean up. Chill for 1 hour and serve. Makes about 20 treats.

*I use Rice Krispies.

CUPCAKE CONES

Ice cream cones (flat bottom)
Frosting
Any cake mix

Mix cake mix by package directions. Fill ice cream cones ½ full.

Bake at 350° on cookie sheet standing upright for 25 minutes.

Cool. Frost and decorate. Great for birthday parties.

EASTER HUNT PIE

1 (6 oz.) graham cracker pie crust
1 (8 oz.) pkg. cream cheese, softened
1 (14 oz.) can Eagle Brand sweetened condensed milk
¾ C. cold water
1 (4 serving pkg.) instant vanilla flavor pudding and pie filling
1½ C. non-dairy whipped topping, thawed
16 miniature chocolate eggs or other holiday candies.

In large mixer bowl, beat cheese until fluffy; gradually beat in sweetened condensed milk until smooth. Add water and pudding; mix on low speed, beat until smooth. Gently stir in whipped topping. Spoon ½ of filling into pie crust. Place chocolate eggs evenly over filling. Top with remaining filling. Chill 3 hours. Garnish as desired. Refrigerate leftovers. Makes 8 servings.

The Very Best Recipes of Rich & Sandy Allison

EASY NACHOS

Tortilla corn chips
Salsa
Shredded Mexican cheese

Cover paper plate with chips, salsa and top with cheese. Microwave 45 seconds on high.

Enjoy!

HOLIDAY CONFETTI MIX

16 oz. pkg. M & M's
16 oz. pkg. M & M's with nuts
15 oz. pkg. raisins
12 oz. pkg. butterscotch morsels
12 oz. pkg. mixed nuts

Combine all ingredients and store in airtight containers.

PURPLE COW

Vanilla ice cream
1 can grape soft drink
Frosted glass

Put 3 or 4 scoops of ice cream in frosted glass. Add grape drink.

HOMEMADE FINGER PAINT
NOTE: THIS IS NOT A FOOD TO EAT!!!

½ C. cornstarch
¾ C. cold water
1 envelope gelatin
¼ C. cold water
2 C. hot water
½ C. detergent powder or soap flakes
Food coloring

Mix cornstarch and ¾ C. cold water in a medium size saucepan. Soak envelope of unflavored gelatin in ¼ C. cold water. Stir hot water into the starch mixture and cook over medium heat until it comes to a boil and appears smooth. Remove the starch concoction from heat and blend in softened gelatin. Add soap powder and stir until dissolved. For color, add food coloring or powdered dye. (For white, add white tempera paint powder). Store in container with tight fitting lid in cool place. Use with glazed shelf paper or butcher paper. Makes 3 C.

PINECONE BIRD FEEDER
NOTE: THIS IS NOT A FOOD TO EAT!!!

1 pinecone
Peanut butter
Birdseed
String

Take a pinecone and spread with peanut butter all over until it is covered. Put the birdseed in a plastic bag and add the peanut butter-covered pinecone. Shake until completely covered with birdseed. Tie a string to the end and hang outside for a treat for the birds.

CLEAN 'N EASY
MAGIC HOBBY CLAY
NOTE: THIS IS NOT A FOOD TO EAT!!!

1 C. corn starch
2 C. (1 lb.) baking soda
1½ C. cold water

Stir together cornstarch and baking soda in medium saucepan. Add water all at once and stir until smooth. Stir constantly over medium heat. Cook until mixture holds its shape like slightly dry mashed potatoes. Place it on a plate and cover with a damp cloth to cool. When cool enough to handle, knead thoroughly on lightly dusted cornstarch surface until smooth. Makes 2 pounds. (Clay may be stored in a cool place up to 2 weeks in a tightly covered container).

INDEX

APPETIZERS

Antipasta On A Shell, Italian, Georgetown Appetizer 25
Artichoke Dip, Baked 24
Artichoke Hearts 16
Bagels, Mini 32
Bean Dip 17
Beef Cheese Ball, Dried 26
Beef Dip, Dried 26
Beef Hors D'Oeuvres, Chipped 28
Bleu Cheese Cracker Spread 16
Bleu Cheese Dip or Salad Dressing 26
Bread Sandwich, Italian 34
Bread Spread, Garlic 19
Bread Sticks 20
Bread, Mexican Spoon 21
Brie, Baked With Carmelized Onions 22
Cheese Bell 32
Cheese Spread 28
Cheese-A-Butter 34
Chicken Dip, Buffalo 16
Chicken Pastries, Mini 20
Chicken Pizza, Grilled 25
Clam Dip 31
Cocktail Meatballs in Stroganoff Dill Sauce 27
Corn Dip, Mexican 23
Corned Beef Dip In A Round Rye Bowl 32
Crab Cheese Melt 19
Crab Dip 24
Crab Dip 30
Crabmeat-Mushroom Appetizer 29
Cracker Snack, Oyster 33
Dill Dip 26
Eggs, Deviled 30
Fruit Dip 28
Goop 17
Guacamole Dip 30
Ham Dip 26
Ham Puffs, Mini 27
Hot Dogs, Burgundy Wine 29
Jalapeno & Cheese Appetizer 26
Jalapeno Crab Dip 21
Meatballs, Cocktail 33
Mexican Dip Casserole 27
Mushroom Puffs 24
Mushroom Sandwich 23
Mushroom Spread 21
Mushrooms Stuffed With Sausage 28
Mushrooms, Crab Stuffed 19
Mushrooms, Crabmeat Stuffed 21
Mushrooms, Drunken 18
Nacho Dip 24
Nachos 33
Olive Oil, Bravo 23
Onion Blossom 22
Party Mix 29
Pepperoni Loaf 32
Pepperoni Rolls 20
Pickles, Fried 23
Pizza, Vegetable 31
Portabellas With Sausage & Boursin Cheese 25
Pretzels, Garlic 28
Salsa, Fire Roasted 18
Sauerkraut Balls 31

APPETIZERS

Sausage & Cheese Puffs, Hot 30
Shrimp Canapes 34
Spinach & Artichoke Dip 19
Spinach Dip 27

BREADS

Applesauce Nut Bread 198
Banana Nut Bread 195
Banana Nut Bread 198
Beer Bread 197
Cinnamon Rolls, Pinch Me 195
Corn Fritters 197
French Bread 194
Garlic Puffs, Yeast Raised 196
Honey Pecan Butter 196
Pumpkin Bread 198
Sour Dough Bread 197
Walnut Raisin & Carrot Loaf 198
White Bread 194
Zucchini Bread 195

CANNING

Apple Butter Boil 208
Apple Butter Made In The Oven 207
Bean Salad, Canned 212
Bread And Butter Pickles, Canned 207
Bread And Butter Pickles, Canned 207
Chow Chow, Canned 209
Christmas Relish, Canned 209
Corn Relish, Canned 203
Corn Salad, Canned 212
Corn, Drying 206
Cucumber Rings, Spiced, Canned 208
Dilly Beans, Canned 205
Garden Relish, Canned 211
Garden Relish, End Of, Canned 211
Garlic Jelly, Canned 210
Garlic Pepper Jelly, Canned 210
Grape Jelly, Canned 202
Green Peppers, Canned 210
Green/Yellow Beans, Canned 212
Hell's Butter, Canned 205
Home Canning, Step-By-Step Instructions 200
Horseradish, Fresh 212
Hot Banana Peppers in BBQ Sauce 210
Hot Pepper Butter, Canned 213
Hot Peppers With Sauerkraut, Canned 210
Jalapeno Pepper Jelly, Canned 203
Meat Cure For Table 213
Meat In A Barrel, Cure 213
Meatballs in BBQ Sauce 210
Mince Meat, Canned 208
Ox Heart Cherries, Canned 206
Peaches, Canned 202
Pears, Canned 203
Peppers, Pickled 211
Pickled Peppers, Stuffed, Canned 213
Pickled Red Beets, Canned 206
Pickles, 14 Day, Canned 204
Plums, Canned 206

INDEX

CANNING

Red Beet Jelly, Canned............................ 213
Red Beets Canned, Mom's 203
Salsa, Fire Roasted For Canning.................. 201
Scrapple, Old Fashioned.......................... 204
Soap, Homemade 214
Spaghetti Marinara Sauce, Spicy, Canned 202
Spaghetti Sauce.................................. 205
Spaghetti Sauce, Canned.......................... 201
Stewed Tomatoes, Canned 206
Strawberry Jam, Canned.......................... 202
Strawberry Pineapple Jam......................... 211
Tomatoes, Green Peppers, Onions, Canned 212
Watermelon Rind, Pickled, Canned 207
Zucchini Pickles, Canned 209

DESSERTS

7-Up Cake....................................... 149
A & P Spanish Bar Cake........................... 181
Angel Food Cake 162
Apple Butter Pies 125
Apple Cake 168
Apple Cobbler................................... 166
Apple Crisp..................................... 190
Apple Dapple Cake............................... 148
Apple Dumplings 147
Apple Fritters 169
Apple Nut Cake.................................. 161
Apple Nut Jar Bread 135
Apple Pie, Old World 157
Apple Strudel 141
Apples, Baked With Chocolate Pudding Sauce 166
Apples, Caramel & Chocolate 132
Applesauce Cake "No Oil," 146
Banana Cak...................................... 165
Banana Loaf 126
Bananas Foster 139
Bananas Foster, Southern Style 139
Berry, Peach, Apple Pie 147
Bird Nests 134
Biscotti, Italian 167
Black Bottom Pie, Famous 172
Black Walnut Cookies............................. 135
Brazilian Candy, Bia's 131
Bread Pudding, Cinnamon Raisin Nut with Vanilla Sauce... 183
Brown Sugar Chews.............................. 191
Brownie Cake 163
Brownie Midget Cupcake, Peanut Butter............ 153
Brownie Pizza, Peanutty.......................... 145
Brownies, Quick Cream Cheese 189
Buckeyes.. 165
Butter Cream Frosting............................ 142
Butter Nut Crunch Toffee 190
Butter Nut Twists 171
Butter Pecan Dessert............................. 143
Butter Shortbread 141
Caramel Corn 189
Caramel Icing 177
Carrot Cake & Frosting........................... 158
Carrot Cake..................................... 175
Cheesecake, New York Deli Style 152
Cheesecake, No Bake 156
Cheesecake, Pistachio............................ 150

DESSERTS

Cheesecakes, Mini 144
Cherries Jubilee.................................. 143
Cherry Fruit Cake 181
Cherry Nut Dessert 176
Cherry Pie 144
Cherry Pie, Coconut Crumb 153
Cherry Winks 137
Chess Cake 187
Chess Pie 168
Chess Pies, Jenny's 148
Choc-Au-Lait (White)............................ 174
Chocolate Cake, Perfect 185
Chocolate Chip Cookies 176
Chocolate Chip Cookies, Louise Hildebaugh........ 136
Chocolate Chip Cookies, Mint 161
Chocolate Chip Cookies, White 173
Chocolate Fudge Cake, Triple Layer 183
Chocolate Mousse Filling......................... 128
Chocolate Peanut Butter Pie 137
Chocolate Peanut Sweeties 190
Chocolate Pie 126
Chocolate Pudding Dessert........................ 170
Chocolate Surprise, Peanutty 190
Cinnamon Walnuts 138
Clouds.. 128
Coconut Balls 191
Coconut Cream Filling 129
Coffee Cake, Sour Cream 168
Cookie Killers................................... 180
Corn Flake Yummies.............................. 180
Cream Cheese Cookies, Grandma's 136
Cream Cheese Frosting............................ 158
Cream Cheese Icing 175
Cream Pie, Pudding 173
Cream Puffs..................................... 173
Cream Puff Dessert.............................. 138
Creamsicle Salad, Orange......................... 174
Creamsicles 182
Crème Brulee 124
Crème Frite, Fried Cream......................... 187
Dirt Pie 186
Dump Cake 139
Easter Bunny Cake 159
Easter Eggs 159
Éclair Cake, Chocolate 175
Eclairs, Homemade 129
Egg Custard Pie................................. 142
Enchiladas, Apple 130
Flan-Aruba Style................................ 145
Fluff.. 181
Fruit Bars 179
Fruit Cake 178
Fruit Dip 173
Fruit Salad...................................... 148
Fruit Salad...................................... 152
Fruit Tart 155
Fudge Sauce, Peanut Butter 180
Fudge, Million Dollar 176
Fudge, Peanut Butter............................. 175
Gingerbread..................................... 187
Glazed Icing, Confectioner's Sugar Water 186
Gob Cake 167
Gobs 127

INDEX

DESSERTS

Granger Pie	144
Heath Bar Cookies	177
Heath Bar Grahams	140
Heavenly Hash	189
Heavenly Pudding	166
Holiday Salad, Pink	130
Humming Bird Cake	178
Ice Cream Cake, Oreo	154
Ice Cream Topping	135
Ice Cream, Home Made	164
Icing, Margie Binotto	140
Icing, Susie's Favorite	142
Impossible Pie	172
Jello Cake	186
Key Lime Pie	166
Kitty Littter Cake	145
Lady Fingers	172
Lemon Bars	157
Lemon Curd Filling	129
Lemon Pudding Dessert	140
Macaroon Almond Cookies	163
Mace Cake	137
Marina Noodle Pineapple Dessert	174
Mexican Dessert	140
Mississippi Fudge Cake	167
Molasses Cookies, Double Ginger	160
Monkey Bread	144
Nut Cups	156
Nut Roll Ice Box Cookies	160
Nut Roll	150
Oatmeal Cake	180
Oatmeal Cinnamon Chip Cookies	131
Oatmeal Lace Cookies	147
Oatmeal Pie	151
Orange Slice Bars	174
Pastry, Vegetable Oil	126
Pawley's Island Pie	158
Peach Cobbler, Easy	188
Peach Cobbler, Fresh	142
Peach Flambe	188
Peaches & Cream Dessert	146
Peanut Blossoms	169
Peanut Butter Balls	139
Peanut Butter Balls	177
Peanut Butter Candy	160
Peanut Butter Cookies	162
Peanut Butter Crunch	143
Peanut Butter Icing	133
Peanut Butter Meltaway Cake	149
Peanut Butter Melt-Away Fudge	184
Peanut Butter Pie	157
Peanut Butter Pie, Frozen	155
Peanut Butter Pie, Frozen, Tom Jones	147
Peanut Butter Squares With Chocolate Topping	182
Peanut Delight	140
Pecan Grahams	187
Pecan Pie, Old Southern	156
Peppermint Chocolate Bark	151
Peppermint Creams	180
Pinacolada Coconut Cake	159
Pineapple Cookies	189
Pineapple Upside Down Cake	151

DESSERTS

Pineapple, Baked	191
Pinwheels, Date & Nut	171
Pizzelles	164
Popcorn Balls	184
Popcorn, Caramel	177
Popcorn, White Chocolate	174
Potato Candy	179
Potato Chip Cookies	173
Pound Cake, Vanilla Butter Nut	179
Pound Cake, W. Choc., Ice Cream and Frozen Fruit	190
Pudding Cake, Ice Box	184
Pudding, Bread	191
Pumpkin Bars	132
Pumpkin Bars, and Frosting	188
Pumpkin Cake	146
Pumpkin Log	169
Pumpkin Nut Jar Bread	134
Pumpkin Pie Cake	149
Pumpkin Pie	155
Raisin Filled Cookies	136
Raisin Squares	154
Raspberry Sauce	184
Rice Pudding	170
Ritz Ice Cream Dessert	127
Robert Redford Cake	154
Rum Cake & Topping	176
Russian Teacakes or Mexican Wedding Cakes	131
Sabayon Trifle, Strawberry & Grand Marnier	124
Sand Tarts, Drop	135
Snickerdoodle Coffee Cake	138
Snickerdoodles	153
Sock It To Me Cake	143
Sorbet (Citrus) Lime, Lemon Or Orange	192
Sorbet	192
Sour Cream Cookies	142
Spice Cake	158
Strawberries Dipped In Chocolate	192
Strawberry Cookies	161
Strawberry Pie, Glazed Fresh	127
Strawberry Pretzel Dessert	128
Sugar Cookies & Icing	186
Sugar Cookies, Soft	130
Tagalongs, Faux	131
Tapioca, Large Pearl	184
Tea Cakes	191
Tiramisu	125
Toads	148
Toll House Pie	170
Wacky Cake, Chocolate With White Chocolate Mousse	133
Wacky Cake, Peg's	133
Walnut Squares	137

DRINKS

Cider	216
Daiquiri	216
Hot Chocolate, First Lady's	216
Iced Tea, Long Island	217
Irish Cream	216
Kahlua, Homemade	217
Mai Tai	217
Margarita Drink	218

INDEX

DRINKS

Pina Colada's 218
Punch, Coffee Mocha 217
Rocket Fuel 216
Sangria 218
Slush 218
Suffering Bastards 217
Whiskey Sour 218
Wine Slush 217
Wine 216
Yellow Bird's 218

KIDS CORNER

Angel Food Cake, Mock 220
Ants On A Log 220
Apple Snack 220
Banana Boats 220
Beef-N-Bean Burgers 221
Berry Parfait 222
Bird Feeder, Pinecone 223
Birdseed or Gorp 220
Blender Breeze 221
Candy Bar Dessert, Easy 220
Cinnamon Toast Spread 221
Confetti Mix, Holiday 223
Cracker Jack Snacks 221
Cupcake Cones 222
Easter Hunt Pie 222
Finger Paints, Homemade 223
Fudge, Girl Scout 220
Hobby Clay, Clean & Easy 223
Jello, Finger 221
Lemonade, Sweet Tart 221
Malt, Magnificent 222
Nachos, Easy 223
Orange Julius 220
Pizza 220
Purple Cows 223
Raisin Treats, Crunchy, Yummy 222
Slush, Crush 222
Sodas, Walking 220
Tootsie Rolls 220

MEATS & VEGETABLES

Alfredo Sauce 114
Apples, Baked 122
Asparagus, Oriental 104
Baked Beans, Gus' 95
Baked Beans, Kass 84
Banana Peppers, Stuffed 111
Beans, Baked 101
Beans, Baked 117
Beef Brisket Sandwiches 87
Beef Rival Soup 112
Biscuits, Breakfast - Apples 82
Brasciole 103
Breakfast Casserole 95
Broccoli & Red Peppers 116
Broccoli Beef 102
Broccoli Casserole 104
Broccoli Casserole 89
Broccoli Cheddar Rolls 108
Broccoli-Chicken Casserole 100

MEATS & VEGETABLES

Buttermilk Pancakes 91
Cabbage Rolls 97
Cabbage, Red 120
Carmelized Onions 83
Carrots, Glazed 107
Cassoulett 88
Cheese Casserole, Breakfast 82
Cheese Sandwiches 92
Chicken & Tortellini In Cream Sauce 85
Chicken Cordon Bleu 84
Chicken Fried Steak 90
Chicken or Pork Schnitzel 117
Chicken Parmesan 103
Chicken Rice Casserole 100
Chicken Salad, Hot 87
Chicken Saltimbacca 96
Chicken Shepherd's Pie 119
Chicken Stuffing Casserole 100
Chicken, Claiborne 117
Chicken, Turkey or Veal Romano 106
Chilies Rellenos 92
Chilies, Baked, Cream Sauce 92
Chipped Beef on Toast, Creamed 96
Chipped Ham With Barbecue Sauce 122
Corn & Noodles Casserole 83
Corn Supreme, Scalloped 103
Corn, Baked 101
Corn, Dried 107
Country Boil With Chicken, Low 84
Eggplant Or Squash Parmigiana, Baked 109
Enchiladas, Sour Cream 81
Fladley 91
Flank Or Round Steak, Stuffed 110
French Toast 109
General Tso's Chicken 98
Gnocchi's 100
Green Bean-Mushroom Casserole 99
Green Beans, Key West 120
Green Beans, Mushrooms & Red Peppers . . . 115
Green Tomato Pie 105
Ham Bar-B-Que 90
Ham Loaf 109
Ham Loaf 86
Ham, Baked 121
Ham, Sauce 86
Hamburger & Vegetable Casserole 102
Hot Dressing, Lettuce/Endive 82
Irish Stew Pie, Guiness Stout 119
Jambalaya 99
Lasagna 80
Lasagna, Chicken Cheese 94
Lo Mein, Combination 93
Macaroni & Cheese 97
Macaroni-Chicken Casserole 102
Mashed Potatoes, Garlic 114
Meat & Cheese Roll, Italian 107
Meat Loaf 118
Meat Loaf 121
Meatball Recipe, Margie Binotto's 113
Meatballs-Turkey, & Mushroom Gravy Over Noodles 97
Monte Cristo Sandwich-Chesapeake 93
Mushrooms, Yellow Squash & Red Peppers 115

MEATS & VEGETABLES

Onion Pie 104
Onions & Peas, Small Boiling 116
Pancakes, Sour Dough 108
Pasta Sicilian Style, Vodka Pink 83
Pasta With Chicken 117
Pasta, Cajun Chicken 99
Pasta, Farfalle 92
Pasta, Pink 84
Pepper Steak 105
Pepperolio Pasta 91
Peppers, Stuffed 122
Pesto Sauce 91
Picadillo 116
Pierogi 120
Pizza Burger 89
Pizza Burgers 118
Pork Loin With Sauerkraut In Slow Cooker 111
Pork Loin, Roasted With Herb Spinach Stuffing 86
Pork Loin, Stuffed & Smoked 113
Pork Marinara 110
Pork Sandwiches, Smoked Pulled w/ Honey BBQ Sauce 2
Pork, Roasted, Chinese Cold 108
Pot Pie Dough 106
Pot Pie, Sweet 118
Potatoes Oregano 121
Potatoes, Friendship 112
Potatoes, Grilled 121
Potatoes, Jalapenos 94
Potatoes, Pam's 81
Quesadillas, Chicken 93
Ravioli 112
Rebelque-North Carolina Barbeque 101
Reuben Casserole 80
Rice & Broccoli Casserole 89
Rice Pilaf 99
Roast, Pot 122
Sausage & Wild Rice Casserole 89
Sausage, Summer 107
Shells, Stuffed, Taco 118
Shrimp Artichoke Pasta 85
Sloppy Joes 109
Spaetzle, Cousin Inge's 88
Spaghetti Sauce 97
Spaghetti Sauce, Sue Rotella's 87
Spaghetti-Pasta, Home-Made 111
Spinach, Broccoli & Cauliflower Souffle 120
Squash Casserole 104
Steak or Tuna Au Poivre 96
Steak, Pan Fried, Baked 111
Stuffed Shells - Stuffing & Chicken 95
Stuffing, Bread 110
Stuffing, Cajun 89
Sugar Peas & Potatoes In Cream Sauce 106
Sweet Potato Casserole 114
Tomatoes, Stewed Eastern Shore Style 95
Tortellini With Chicken & Asiago Cheese, Tri-Colored 98
Tournedos of Beef, Grilled 94
Turkey Tips 58
Vegetable Pie, Natalia's Russian 116
Vegetables, Grilled Italian 115
Vegetables, Grilled 115
Veggie Bake, Colorful 114

SALADS

Antipasto Salad With Romano Cheese Dressing 44
Bacon Dressing, Warm with Lettuce German Style 55
Balsamic Vinaigrette 51
Bean Salad 52
Bean Salad, Great Northern 48
Black Bean Fiesta Salad 49
Black Beans & Rice Salad 47
Broccoli Salad 49
Broccoli Salad 50
Broccoli Salad 54
Broccoli Salad 57
Broccoli Salad, Oriental 49
Broccoli Salad, Sweet & Sour 48
Cabbage Salad 54
Cabbage Slaw 51
Cabbage Slaw, Hot 51
Caesar Salad 45
Cauliflower Salad, Marinated 53
Cheese Tips 58
Chopped Salad with Garlic Vinaigrette Dressing 55
Coleslaw 45
Cranberry Salad 46
Cranberry Salad 54
Cucumber Salad, Creamy 52
French & Bleu Cheese Dressing 57
French Dressing 48
Fruit Salad 54
Grape Salad, Frozen 46
Italian Salad Dressing "Too" 55
Italian Salad For 15 People 48
Italian Salad, Garlic 50
Layer Salad 51
Lemon Dressing, Greek 52
Lettuce, Cold Cream 53
Linguini Salad 56
Macaroni Salad 56
Pasta Salad 47
Pea Salad 56
Potato Salad 46
Potato Salad 52
Potato Salad 56
Salad Dressing, Italian 50
Salad Dressing, No Refrigeration 57
Salad, Fatigati 46
Salad, St. Michael's Summer 47
Sauerkraut Salad 57
Seashell Salad, Pasta 48
Slaw, Texas Two-Step 45
Spinach Salad, Strawberry 50
Steak & Chicken Salads 49
Taco Salad 45
Tomato & Onion Salad 53
Vegetable Salad, All 44
Vinegar Dressing For Lettuce, Sweet/Sour Hot 53

SAUCES & DRESSINGS

Apple Sauce For Steak/Chicken 39
Barbecue Basting Sauce, All Purpose 39
Barbecue Dressing 40
Barbecue Sauce 40
Barbecue Sauce, Alabama 38
Barbecue Sauce, Bim's 39

SAUCES & DRESSINGS

Barbecue Sauce, Old Bill's 38
Barbeque Chicken Sauce, Galen Dively's 40
Barbeque Sauce For Ribs 37
Barbeque Sauce, Honey 36
Barbeque Sauce, Honey 42
Barbeque Sauce, Wild Bill's 42
Basting & Marinade Sauce 41
Basting Sauce, Chicken 37
Bourbon Sauce, Carmelized 40
Buffalo Wing Sauce, Traditional 42
Chicken Wing Sauces 42
Crab Dipping Sauce, Cousin Hermie's 36
Crab Seasoning, Les's 41
Dill Sauce 41
Hoezel Dressing 36
Honey Mustard Sauce, By Gus 42
Hot Dog Sauce, Texas 36
Marinade & Barbecue Sauce, Easy 38
Mustard Sauce, Joe's Stone Crab Inn 39
Pork Loin Glaze 41
Seasoning, Southwest 40
Steak, Flank, Southwest Marinade 41
Wing Sauce, Hot & Sweet, Shane's 42
Wing Sauce, Tim's 42

SEAFOOD

Country Boil, Low 72
Crab Cakes, Herman Harrison's Favorite 76
Crab Imperial 74
Crab Imperial 75
Crab Muffins 73
Crabcakes 72
Crabmeat Augratin 76
Crabmeat Hoezel 72
Crabs, Soft Shell 75
Crabs, Steamed 78
Fish, Grilled 78
Haddock, Pan Fried 78
Linguine With White Clam Sauce 74
Mussels, Steamed, Sauce for 2 lb., ... 75
Osters Rockefeller 75
Oyster Casserole, Minnie's 76
Oyster Stew 77
Oyster Stew, Asparagus 77
Oysters Bienville 76
Oysters Casino 76
Oysters With Bacon 77
Oysters, Baked 73
Oysters, Decanting 77
Oysters, Fried 77
Scallops, Sautéed 75
Seafood Casserole In Phyllo Dough 77
Seafood Pan Roast 73
Shrimp & Pasta With Pesto Aglio-Olio 74
Shrimp Batter 74
Shrimp Salad, Fresh 78
Shrimp, Steamed 72
Soft Shell Crabs, Cleaning 78

SOUPS

Black Bean Soup With Ham, Sausage & Bacon 67
Cheddar Soup, White With Roasted Garlic 68
Cheese Burger Soup 66
Cheese Soup 67
Chicken Corn Noodle Rival Soup-Tailgater's Soup 60
Chicken Or Beef Pastina Soup 64
Chili, Two Alarm 69
Chili, White Hot 64
Chili, White 68
Clam Chowder, Manhattan Style 64
Crab & Asparagus Chowder 65
Crab Chowder 62
French Onion Soup 62
Ham & Beans Cooked In An Iron Kettle 69
Lasagna Soup 69
Minestrone Soup, Rich's 63
Pasta Fagioli 62
Potato Cheese Soup 63
Tomato Cream Basil Soup 66
Tortilla Soup 66
Wedding Soup 61
Zucchini Soup, Cold 63

Cooking from the Farm to the City

Printed in China by Everbest Printing Co. Ltd through Four Colour Print Group, Louisville, KY

ISBN 978-0-9798-1830-1

52395

9 780979 818301

Some closing thoughts...

Growing up on the farm as kids, we thought we were poor. In retrospect, however, maybe it wasn't so bad.

While some kids had swimming pools, we had a trout stream in the front yard that stretched endlessly and had a swimming hole built in it.

Most of our friends had either a dog or cat for a pet. We had several dogs, a lot of cats, litters of puppies and kittens, calves, pigs, chickens, horses, etc for pets. More pets than any other kid.

Our friends may have had a nice house on a small plot of land, but we had a 100 year old farm house with lots of character and memories complete with buildings and field upon field of land with an endless view of mountains on both sides of us.

Some kids had nice playrooms. But we had the biggest — a barn complete with a basketball court and ropes to swing on and to jump into the hay.

Some kids had street lights for them to see, but we had the whole sky of stars which brightly lit up the sky in the dark countryside.

In grade school we were already trendy baby boomers wearing our blue jeans and flannel shirts, but yet we thought we were poor.

Our friends were eating lunch meat sandwiches on store bought bread while we were eating home cured ham on fresh home baked bread, and we thought we were the ones doing without.

While our friends went out to dinner for mediocre meals, we were having home cooked meals made with fresh vegetables, meats and fresh herbs.

When canned soup became the rage, we were eating home made soups which were made fresh daily.

We could never understand why kids went off to summer camp when we had it all year.

Our wildlife wasn't a night on the town. We had deer, turkey, pheasant, rabbits, deer, squirrel, etc. in the backyard along with peace and tranquility.

As hard working farmers, we were about 5% of the total US population who could take a seed, plant it, water it and watch it grow to maturity, harvest it, either eat it or preserve it or sell it to someone else who wasn't capable of doing that.

While the words organic and free-range didn't really become important until a few years ago, we were already doing both organic and free range.

Others may go off to a bed and breakfast with lots of charm, but we go back to the farm for comfort, quiet and peacefulness bundled with lots of great memories.

— Rich and Sandy Allison

ORDER FORM

Please send me _____ Cookbooks "Cooking from the Farm to the City" at $23.95 each = $ _____

Mail order to: Rich & Sandy Allison
                 165 Allison Drive
                 Claysburg, PA 16625
                 Phone: 814-239-2901

Shipping and Handling at $4.95 each = $ _____

6% Sales Tax . . . . = $ _____

TOTAL ENCLOSED. . . . . = $ _____

Total Per Book = $30.63

Mail Cookbook to:

Name: _____

Street/Box: _____

City/State/Zip: _____

Phone: _____

- -

ORDER FORM

Please send me _____ Cookbooks "Cooking from the Farm to the City" at $23.95 each = $ _____

Mail order to: Rich & Sandy Allison
                 165 Allison Drive
                 Claysburg, PA 16625
                 Phone: 814-239-2901

Shipping and Handling at $4.95 each = $ _____

6% Sales Tax . . . . = $ _____

TOTAL ENCLOSED. . . . . = $ _____

Total Per Book = $30.63

Mail Cookbook to:

Name: _____

Street/Box: _____

City/State/Zip: _____

Phone: _____